The Sources of Increased Efficiency

# The Sources of Increased Efficiency:
# A Study of Du Pont Rayon Plants

*Samuel Hollander*

The M. I. T. Press
*Massachusetts Institute of Technology*
*Cambridge, Massachusetts*

Library of Congress Catalog Card Number 65-15279
Printed in the United States of America
ISBN: 0-262-58235-X (Paperback)

*To my parents*

# Preface

This study is based on data relating to production costs of viscose-rayon manufacture at several plants of E. I. du Pont de Nemours and Company. The Textile Fibers Department of the Company kindly permitted me to use the annual cost sheets relevant to rayon operations at the Spruance (Richmond, Virginia) and Old Hickory (Tennessee) locations during the period 1929–1960. Considerable information relating to investment outlays was provided to supplement the cost data.

My initial contact with the Textile Fibers Department was through Dr. W. W. Heckert, Assistant General Director, Technical Divisions. Dr. Heckert arranged for the preparation of the statistical information, gave me most generously of his time, and offered valuable advice on the organization of the study at an early stage. I would like to express my sincere gratitude for Dr. Heckert's help, and for the generosity of the Department.

The technological basis for this study was derived to some extent from technical journals, but for the most part, I have relied on interviews with men personally involved in the development of the United States rayon industry. I would like to thank in particular Dr. William H. Bradshaw, formerly Research Director of Du Pont Rayon, Dr. G. Preston Hoff, and Dr. H. H. Parker, who were intimately connected with the development of "Cordura" and who gave firsthand accounts of the events of the 1930s; Dr. Charles Scott-Venable, Research Director at the American Viscose Corporation during part of the period under discussion, Dr. George Allen of the Research and Development Department of AVISCO, and Mr. J. L. Shields, Assistant Treasurer of AVISCO, who helped me obtain a broad understanding of the industry; and Dr. Church of Rayonier, Inc., who discussed with me developments by pulp manufacturers in general and the Rayonier company in particular during the period of my study. I am indebted to the late Dr. T. R. Milne, member during the 1930s of the "Cordura" research team of Du Pont's Rayon Technical Division and, for a number of years, Semi-Works Supervisor at the Buffalo location. Dr. Milne was later an officer of Chemtex, Inc. He provided much valuable information concerning the development of the United States rayon industry as a whole.

Thanks are due to Mr. Bill Ackerman and Mr. M. R. Bachlotte, at Spruance and Old Hickory, respectively, for their help in the processing of data. I appreciate also the advice of Mr. P. J. Pakurar and Mr. R. H. Stafford.

My greatest obligations are to Dr. S. W. Brainard, Manager, Du Pont Technical Service Section, Laboratory Service, and to Dr. E. M. Hicks, Jr., Technical Director, Du Pont "Orlon"-"Lycra" Technical Division. These men kindly tolerated numerous visits, phone calls, and letters; read and commented upon parts of the study; and provided the detailed information that permitted the successful completion of the project. Dr. Hicks' aid in the analysis and interpretation of the data has been invaluable.

Since *all* the cost data in this study were derived from the annual cost sheets prepared by the Spruance and Old Hickory plants, an explicit statement of "source" is usually omitted in the presentation of the data.

This monograph is, with some modification, my doctoral dissertation accepted by the Department of Economics, Princeton University, in 1963. My thesis advisors were Professors Fritz Machlup and Jesse W. Markham, to whom I am indebted for advice and encouragement. The funds for the thesis were from a Ford Foundation grant relating to a project directed by Professor Machlup on the economic aspects of patent protection, technological inventions, and their development.

The final preparation of the study for publication in book form has been carried out at the Institute for Economic Research, Queen's University, Kingston, Ontario, Canada. Funds for this purpose were provided by the Canada Council and the Institute. I am grateful to members of the Institute and above all to the Director, Professor M. C. Urquhart, for very helpful discussions and advice.

Samuel Hollander

*Toronto, Canada*
*July,* 1964

# Contents

The Sources of Increased Efficiency

*Chapter One*

# The Measurement and Causes of Productivity Change

At the level of the economy as a whole it is important to know how much of the rising trend in real national income is due to improvements in the use of resources, and how much to the increase in resources used. Similarly, an estimate of the extent to which the recorded increase in output per capita can be ascribed to the better use of resources, as distinct from a larger volume of resources per head, would be of value for a number of policy considerations.

Various macroeconomic studies of the causes of the secular increase in output per head over recent decades in the United States arrive at the conclusion that the contribution of "technical change" is of far greater significance than is the growth of resources per head, and that "technical change" accounts for a very high proportion (in some cases almost one-half) of the growth of real national income.[1] The term "technical change," however, is ambiguous and, as we shall see, is in effect a catchall including

[1] This result is in striking contrast with earlier conclusions that the increase in output in the United States over time was due largely to the greater volume of resources. The theoretical work relating to the Cobb-Douglas production function (in C. W. Cobb and P. H. Douglas, "A Theory of Production," *The American Economic Review*, Supplement, Vol. XVIII, March 1928, pp. 139–165), may be viewed as the formulation of a hypothesis to this effect, and the conclusion that a model based on the function fitted the indexes of output and input in all manufacturing industry in the United States for the period 1899–1922 (in P. H. Douglas, "Are there Laws of Production?" *The American Economic Review*, Vol. XXXVIII, March 1948, pp. 1–41) may be seen as the result of an attempt to test the hypothesis. For this view see Solomon Fabricant, "Study of the Size and Efficiency of the American Economy," in *Economic Consequences of the Size of Nations*, ed. E. A. G. Robinson, St. Martin's Press, Inc., New York, 1960, p. 39.

all influences on growth of output and output per head other than the increase in resources used: the effects of economies of scale, for example, changes in the efficiency of resource allocation, and all other determinants of economic growth not actually included in the measurement of resources in use are covered by the term. In most of the studies to be considered presently, very little is said about the contribution to growth of technical change narrowly defined as the introduction or the spread of cost-reducing changes in technique. The importance of technical change in the latter sense of the term remains, for the most part, an open question.

Moreover, the macroeconomic studies have cast doubt upon the often repeated contention that the growth of the capital stock, or net investment, is a *sine qua non* of the growth of output and of output per capita. At one time it was regarded almost as self-evident that the expansion over time of aggregate output per head was directly related to net investment. This belief finds some logical support in both the Classical and the Keynesian systems, but perhaps it receives its strongest underpinning from the recent literature on growth which often assumes a constant marginal capital-output ratio. A by-product of the attempts to attribute the growth of real national income and of output per head to alternative causes has been the conclusion that the contribution of net investment ranks low. Thus a second issue of great relevance is raised.

Whereas the macroeconomic investigations have been largely unable to separate the contribution to growth of technical change (narrowly defined) from the effects of a variety of other influences, a microeconomic investigation of particular plants should be able to arrive at some estimate of the extent to which productivity movements can be ascribed to "pure" technical change, by examination of the techniques in use and the changes therein over time. Moreover, the relationship between cost-reducing changes in technique and investment in plant and equipment can be considered by reference to the actual events occurring at the plants.

In this introductory chapter we shall consider the characteristics of a model where "technical change" is measured by the degree to which a Cobb-Douglas aggregate production function, applied to United States data, has shifted over time. We shall then evaluate the measurement of "technical change" by means of a method involving an index of "total factor productivity," familiarized by the National Bureau of Economic Research. Next we shall discuss attempts to separate the contribution of economies of scale from that of technical change, and more generally to account for interindustry and intertemporal movements in productivity, by means of statistical correlation methods. Finally, we shall outline the nature of the present investigation.

## TECHNICAL CHANGE AND THE AGGREGATE PRODUCTION FUNCTION

In this section the method used by Robert M. Solow[2] to estimate the contribution of "technical change" to the growth of output is summarized.

### The Method and the Assumptions

Solow defines "technical change" to cover "any kind of shift in the production function"; he does not, that is, ascribe the shift to any particular cause. By assuming that *technical change is "neutral,"* leaving the rate of substitution between inputs unchanged and simply increasing the output obtainable from a given factor combination, he is able to introduce technical change as a factor of proportionality $A(t)$ in the expression

$$Q = A(t) \cdot f(K, L) \tag{1}$$

where by a second assumption $f(K, L)$ is a *linear homogeneous production function* relating aggregate output $Q$ and inputs capital $K$ and labor $L$, and where $A$ is the index of the level of "technology" at various time periods $t$. On the basis of a third assumption to the effect that the returns to labor and capital are determined by their respective marginal physical productivities, or in other words, by assuming *competitive factor pricing*, Solow derives the expression

$$\bar{A} = \bar{Q} - a\bar{L} - b\bar{K} \tag{2a}$$

where $\bar{A}$, $\bar{Q}$, $\bar{L}$, and $\bar{K}$ refer to proportionate rates of change in the relevant variables per unit of time, and where the constants $a$ and $b$ represent the value of labor and capital respectively as a proportion of the value of output. In discrete terms the expression is simply

$$\frac{\Delta A}{A} = \frac{\Delta Q}{Q} - a\frac{\Delta L}{L} - b\frac{\Delta K}{K} \tag{2b}$$

Since the variables referred to are empirically obtainable, an index of $\Delta A/A$ can be derived. However, given the assumption that the production function is homogeneous of degree one, Expression 2a can be simplified to read

$$\bar{A} = \bar{Q}' - b\bar{R}' \tag{3a}$$

where $\bar{Q}'$ and $\bar{R}'$ refer respectively to the time rates of change in output and capital *per man-hour*. When discrete time intervals are used, Expression 3a becomes

$$\frac{\Delta A}{A} = \frac{\Delta(Q/L)}{Q/L} - b\frac{\Delta(K/L)}{K/L} \tag{3b}$$

[2] Robert M. Solow, "Technical Change and the Aggregate Production Function," *The Review of Economics and Statistics*, Vol. XXXIX, August 1957, pp. 312–320.

We then obtain an estimate each year for $\Delta A/A$ which measures that part of the annual percentage increase in gross national product per man-hour which can be attributed to all causes other than changes over time in capital per man-hour. In brief, the contribution of "technical change" each year is computed as the difference between the actual percentage changes in output per man-hour, and that part of these changes attributable to capital per man-hour, where the latter contribution is measured by the product of the share of property in total gross national product, and the percentage changes in capital per man-hour.[3]

The final steps in the procedure followed by Solow are the cumulation over the entire period under consideration of the annual percentage changes in output per man-hour due to "technical change," and the subsequent calculation of the part of the total increase in output per man-hour (as distinct from the percentage increases) during the relevant period which can be ascribed to "technical change."

*The Contribution of "Technical Change"*

Arbitrarily setting $A(1909)$ equal to unity, an entire series is derived by using the expression

$$A(t + 1) = A(t) \cdot [1 + \Delta A(t)/A(t)] \tag{4}$$

Solow employs data reflecting the private, nonagricultural sector of the United States economy during the period 1909–1949. $A(1949)$ is found to equal 1.809: the cumulative (annual) *percentage changes* in output per man-hour because of "technical change" amounts to 80.9 per cent. Using this calculation, Solow then argues that only one-eighth of the *total* increase in output per man-hour over the period is due to increased capital per man-hour, whereas the remaining seven-eighths, or 87.5 per cent, is due to "technical change."[4]

[3] A number of additional features of the method may be briefly mentioned. (*a*) The capital series is based on that developed in Raymond W. Goldsmith, *A Study of Saving in the United States*, Vol. III, Princeton University Press, 1956. Goldsmith's estimates are net of depreciation; on the other hand, the series representing "the share of property in income," or "*b*" in the preceding equations, includes depreciation as part of the return to capital. The output series is that for Private Non-farm Gross National Product. (*b*) Solow corrects the Goldsmith capital stock series by multiplying each year's figure by the proportion of the labor force employed during that year. In this manner a series approximating employed rather than existing capital is derived.

[4] Real gross national product per man-hour increases from $.623 (1909) to $1.275 (1949): $1.275 divided by the "full shift factor" for the forty-year period, 1.809, provides an estimate of "corrected G.N.P. per man-hour net of technical change," which amounts to $.705. In brief, only eight cents of the sixty-five cent increase in output per man-hour is because of an increase in capital intensity and the remainder is the result of increased productivity, i.e., of "technical change."

The calculation for the period 1909–1929 alone provides an estimate for the contribution of "technical change" to the observed increase in G.N.P. per man-hour of two-thirds; one-third is accounted for by increased capital per man-hour.

Other writers use Solow's method and arrive at estimates of a similar order of magnitude. For example, a study by Benton F. Massel of United States manufacturing over the period 1919–1955 ascribes 90 per cent of the recorded increase in output per man-hour to "technical advance."[5]

*Comments on the Method*

The procedure outlined in the preceding section for the measurement of the contribution of "technical change" to the growth of output per man-hour has various weaknesses, many of which have been recognized even by those making use of it:

*a.* In the first place, the term "residual" rather than "technical change" is a more accurate rendering of what is really implied by the model.[6] Every possible explication of a changing output per man-hour, other than that of an increase in capital per man-hour, is covered by the concept "technical change." Thus the effects upon output per man-hour of internal economies of scale, external economies, improvements in the quality of inputs (such as, for example, those owing to the improved education and health of labor), improvements in organization and in the allocation of resources, in addition to those of technical change in the *narrow* sense of the term (the introduction or the spread of cost-reducing techniques), are all covered. Our knowledge of the influences governing productivity movements is hardly increased by the observation that almost 90 per cent of the secular increase in productivity is due to this catchall, "technical change."

*b.* No specific relationship is drawn between the size of $A(t)$ and investment in plant and equipment. The statements to the effect that no more than, say, 10–15 per cent of the change in output per man-hour can be explained by additions to the capital stock or to net investment, refer to a specific kind of investment, namely investment in plant and equipment which does not change in "form, quality or composition,"[7]

---

[5] Benton F. Massel, "Capital Formation and Technological Change in United States Manufacturing," *The Review of Economics and Statistics*, Vol. XLII, May 1960, pp. 182–188.

An example of an estimate made for Norway using a method very close to Solow's is to be found in Odd Aukrust, "Investment and Economic Growth," *Productivity Measurement Review*, No. 16, Feb. 1959, pp. 35–53. Here the contribution of "better organization" is of a similar magnitude to that of Solow's "technical change" and of Massel's "technical advance."

[6] Cf. Evsey D. Domar, "On the Measurement of Technological Change," *The Economic Journal*, Vol. LXXI, Dec. 1961, pp. 709–729.

[7] Cf. Domar, *op. cit.*, p. 712. The effect on productivity of "simple expansion" is an interesting empirical question. Presumably the result would depend, in part, upon the rate of growth of population.

and once this is recognized, the conclusions drawn from the Solow-type models become less startling. For it is hardly to be expected that continued investment in plant and equipment of the identical types as existed previously would be largely responsible for the productivity movements. Indeed Solow himself points out that the conclusion should not be drawn from his analysis that

> the observed rate of technical progress would have persisted even if the rate of investment had been much smaller or had fallen to zero. Obviously much, perhaps nearly all, innovation must be embodied in new plant and equipment to be realized at all.[8]

It might be expected that technical change, *narrowly* defined, is possible only if some new input is introduced (in the form for example of new capital goods) although in some cases, organizational changes, "Taylorization," and the like may be important. Moreover, new capital goods may well be introduced as part of a replacement—rather than an expansion—program of capital expenditure, so that a strong relation may exist between *gross* investment and technical change narrowly defined.

Needless to say, if technical change actually requires investment in plant and equipment, it becomes difficult to argue that either technical change *by itself* or investment *by itself* can account for certain increases in productivity. Both together would be responsible.[9]

To summarize, the measurement of the input "capital" does not take account of changes over time in the "effectiveness" of plant and equipment; improvements in machinery and the like are included in the "residual." As a consequence of this procedure, the contribution of "capital" to the growth of output per man-hour is understated, and consequently that of the residual is exaggerated.

*c.* One of the most serious weaknesses of a Solow-type method applied to aggregative statistics is that the heavy weight given to the labor input and the correspondingly small weight allowed capital assures that the influence of increases in capital per head will be further minimized compared with that of the residual. For example, by working with a specific Cobb-Douglas production function: $Q = AL^a K^b$, with $a$ and $b$ (the shares of labor and capital respectively in the national product)

---

[8] Solow, "Technical Change and the Aggregate Production Function," *op. cit.*, p. 316.
[9] The well-known "technical-progress" function developed in Nicholas Kaldor, "A Model of Economic Growth," *Economic Journal*, Vol. LXVII, Dec. 1957, pp. 591–624, does not recognize a distinction between changing productivity owing to increased capital per man and to technical progress considered separately, on the grounds that it is impossible to distinguish between a "shift" in the production function and a movement along a given isoquant: the application of new knowledge usually involves a higher capital-labor ratio, and the use of a higher capital-labor ratio usually presupposes some "inventiveness."

given the values .75 and .25, as suggested by U.S. aggregative data, Domar[10] derives an estimate for the residual of about 80 per cent and shows it to be the direct result of the low weight given to capital. Under these assumptions, a doubling of the input "capital" would have relatively insignificant effects upon output per man-hour.[11]

In brief, a two-input function involves a bias against capital. A more fully defined function, expanded for example by the introduction of materials, would improve the technique.

*d.* It should be pointed out that the econometric procedure for calculating the series $A(t)$, at least with the degree of accuracy actually implied in the study, may be inadmissable since an error term which might in the present instance be very considerable is not included. In short, the absence of an error term in the equations renders the results of the analysis more difficult to interpret.[12]

*e.* Those using the macromodel tend to draw strong policy conclusions from their results. Specifically more attention, it is argued, should be directed in the quest for rapid economic growth toward those variables determining "the rate at which innovations are injected into the economic system," rather than toward the forces governing net investment.[13] Expenditures by firms on research and development, and policies relating to replacement of obsolescent equipment are singled out as examples of the relevant variables. It may well be true that these are the significant variables upon which increases in productivity largely depend, but the strength of the argument is seriously weakened by the narrowness of the conclusions which can be made by use of the model.

*Refinements in the Method:* (1) *Disaggregation*

We have seen that Massel's estimates of "technical advance," and of the change in capital per man-hour as contributions to the historical increase in output per man-hour, amount to 90 per cent and 10 per cent, respectively, in the case of the United States manufacturing sector over the period

[10] Domar, *op. cit.*, pp. 711–712.

[11] Other objections have been raised to the method of calculation: the procedure used to estimate the effect of technical change [see Eq. 4], differs from that used to calculate the change in output per man-hour and consequently capital per man-hour, which are based on the direct comparison of terminal years. See Edward F. Denison, *The Sources of Economic Growth in the United States and the Alternatives Before Us*, Supplementary Paper No. 13, Committee for Economic Development, New York, 1962, pp. 104–105.

[12] For a full discussion of this problem see Lawrence R. Klein, *An Introduction to Econometrics*, Prentice-Hall, Inc., Englewood Cliffs, N.J., 1962, pp. 105–108. The issue is even more serious in the analysis of individual plants; at the macrolevel the productivity changes are at least very large and the period under study very long, so that the various inaccuracies of measurement may be less serious.

[13] Cf. Massel, *op. cit.*, p. 188.

1919–1955.[14] The catchall "technical advance," however, includes improvements in the efficiency of resource allocation. Massel refines the calculations in further work on the subject. He shows that (for the period 1946–1957) the shift in the *aggregate* production function exceeds a weighted average of the shifts in *component* functions by a considerable margin.[15] The macrovariables, that is to say, are not the "exact counterparts of the microvariables," and to some extent the "advance in aggregate technical progress" results from the process of aggregating over sectors. The weighted sum of the improvement factors in individual sectors provides an estimate of *intraindustry* "technical advance," and the difference between this estimate and that obtained from the use of aggregative data provides the measure of *interindustry* improvement. The difference, which amounts to one-third of the change in aggregate "technology," is ascribed to the effect of improvements in the efficiency of resource allocation, mostly attributable to the shifting of capital to industries where its marginal productivity is higher.

The entire procedure, however, is based upon the application of the method outlined earlier of estimating the contribution of "technical change"; now the method is applied to individual industry groups too, and the assumptions that the shifts in the production functions are in all cases neutral, that constant returns to scale is a sufficiently accurate approximation, and that inputs are paid the values of their marginal products, are made in each case, as well as for the manufacturing sector as a whole. These assumptions, however, would appear to become increasingly unsatisfactory the smaller the section of the economy to which they are applied.

Moreover, the interpretation to be given to the interindustry component of aggregate "technical change" is very ambiguous. Formally, the

[14] Massel, *op. cit.*, pp. 182–188.

[15] Benton F. Massel, "A Disaggregated View of Technical Change," *The Journal of Political Economy*, Vol. LXIX, Dec. 1961, pp. 547–558. On the basis of the method described above, Massel derives an expression for the percentage rate of technical progress in the manufacturing sector as a whole:
$\bar{A} = c_1 + c_2 + c_3$, where $c_1 = \Sigma Q_i/Q \cdot \bar{A}_i$, or a weighted average of the rates of technical advance in the individual industry groups in the manufacturing sector (where $i$ refers to an individual industry group, and where the weights are provided by the ratio of output of the industry group to total output of the sector); where $c_2 = b\Sigma f_i^K/f^K \cdot \dot{w}_i^K$ and $c_3 = (1 - b)\Sigma f_i^L/f^L \cdot \dot{w}_i^L$. In the latter two expressions, $b$ refers to the share of capital in the product and $(1 - b)$ to that of labor; $f_i^K$ and $f_i^L$ refer to the marginal productivities of capital and labor respectively in the $i$-th industry group, and $f^K$ and $f^L$ to the respective marginal productivities in the sector as a whole; and, finally, $\dot{w}_i^K$ and $\dot{w}_i^L$ represent the derivatives with respect to time of $K_i/K$ and $L_i/L$, respectively.

In brief, $c_1$ represents the intraindustry component of aggregate technical change, whereas $c_2$ and $c_3$ represent interindustry technical change due to the fact that either capital or labor may shift from industries where their marginal productivities are low to where they are high.

component is an estimate of the increase in (manufactured) output that would have occurred had there been no change in the "productivity" of any individual industry group (that is, if intraindustry "technical change" had been absent), but if the percentage distribution of inputs between sectors had altered. However, the earnings of labor, for example, may differ between industries as a result of differences in the *quality* of labor. The functional relationship between output and inputs, described by the Expression 2a (which constitutes the core of the method), assumes that the inputs "labor" and "capital" are homogeneous: inputs are in no way corrected or adjusted for quality differences. If, however, quality differences are the only reason for earnings differentials between sectors, and if all inputs were adjusted for quality differences, then in fact no part of the growth of output could be ascribed to the movement of resources between industries. In point of fact, no such correction is made, so that "interindustry technical change" may simply reflect the increase in aggregate output due to the acquisition by labor, for example, of higher skills.[16]

*Refinements in the Method:* (2) *"Embodied" Technical Change*

In a further paper by Solow, an attempt is made to calculate the amount of fixed investment necessary to support alternative rates of growth of potential output in the United States, in the near future. An answer is provided by Solow, who estimates an aggregate production function which is above all distinguished from previous estimations by the assumption that all "technological progress" must be embodied in *newly produced* capital goods, before output can be influenced.[17] Thus, new

[16] Procedures to obtain estimates for the increase in national product that would have occurred had there been no change in the productivity of any sector, and only a percentage change in the distribution of resources between industries, are criticized in these terms by Edward F. Denison, *The Sources of Economic Growth in the United States and the Alternatives Before Us*, Ch. 20, "Shifts in Industrial Structure as a Source of Measured Growth." The ambiguity is recognized by Massel himself.

[17] Robert M. Solow, "Technical Progress, Capital Formation and Economic Growth," *The American Economic Review*, Proceedings, Vol. LII, May 1962, pp. 76–86. It is assumed that capital goods produced in any year are $100\lambda$ per cent more productive than those produced the year before; that if gross investment $I(v)$ is made in year $v$, the amount surviving in a later year will be $B(t - v)$, and that labor, and machines of various vintages are arranged in such a way as to yield maximum output. In any year $t$, the "equivalent stock of capital" $J(t)$ is found as the sum of the survivors of each vintage, weighted by the relevant productivity-improvement factor. Thus the equivalent stock of capital in year $t$ is expressed as

$$J(t) = \sum_{v = -\infty}^{t} (1 + \lambda)^v \cdot B(t - v)I(v)$$

A further refinement is the introduction of an unemployment rate $u(t)$ into the production function, in order to relate actual (rather than potential) output to a series of

technology can be introduced into the production process only through gross investment in plant and equipment, each unit of capital equipment carrying with it a certain "factor of improvement" over older vintages. In brief, in the second model Solow considers technical change as requiring embodiment in new kinds of capital goods only; existing capital goods can in no way be influenced by improved technology. By contrast, in the earlier model developed by Solow both new capital goods and those goods already in existence participated in technical change without distinction.

Another feature of the model is the fact that not only "new technology" but also potential economies of scale, improvements in organization and in schooling, and other elements of progress, cannot be exploited except through the use of newly designed plant and equipment.

On these assumptions, labor productivity and the growth of output generally are found to depend on the pace at which old capital is *replaced* by capital of newer vintage, and on the amount of new capital *added* to the stock.[18] However, it is quite clear that since many of the variables, assumed in the earlier model to be buried in the residual, now play their roles only *via* the input "capital," expenditures on investment in plant and equipment, both for replacement purposes and in order to add to the capital stock, come back into their own as a vital determinant of economic growth.

[18] Technical change in Solow's initial model (I) is sometimes referred to as "disembodied" to distinguish it from the "embodied" technical change of the second model (II). However, this terminology may be misleading, for it implies that technical change requiring investment is assumed *not to occur* in Model I as distinct from Model II. Now it is possible that technical change in Model I is of the "organizational kind" which does not require investment, but the method does not *exclude* technical change which requires investment. For A(t) *may* depend, partly, upon simple additions to capital per man-hour; technical change in Model I is "disembodied" only in the sense that even though investment may be required, high-productivity equipment is not differentiated from low-productivity equipment in any way. In Model II, equipment of different productivities are distinguished and, in particular, it is assumed that new capital goods are superior to old.

The theoretical implications of a model incorporating "embodied" technical change are explored further by Kenneth J. Arrow, "The Economic Implications of Learning by Doing," *The Review of Economic Studies*, Vol. XXIX, June 1962, pp. 153–173. It is assumed that technical change is entirely embodied in new capital goods and that, once built, no alterations can be made to improve their efficiency. Progress is generated in the capital-goods industry only.

full-employment man-hours. In brief, potential output in any year $t$ is related to the equivalent stock of capital $J(t)$ and a series of full-employment man-hours by the expression: $P(t) = F[J(t), N(t)]$, and the production function containing actual output becomes

$$A(t) = f[u(t)] \cdot P(t) = f(u) \cdot F(J, N)$$

The precise form given to the production function is $A = a10^{b+cu+du^2} \cdot J^\alpha N^{1-\alpha}$; the function is given a Cobb-Douglas form for simplification. All possible causes of changing productivity now are embodied within "$J$."

A number of important questions are raised. In the first place, what is the empirical relevance of the assumption that it is impossible to influence the productivity of existing equipment? Is it inaccurate, empirically, to assume that gross investment in plant and equipment in no way affects the productivity of old capital goods and only bears upon new capital goods?

Second, the contribution to increased productivity of the introduction and extension of cost-reducing techniques is still not distinguished from those of other variables influencing productivity. What is the contribution of technical change in this narrow sense?

## TOTAL FACTOR PRODUCTIVITY

Another method for the determination of the residual (that part of the increase in output or output per head which can be ascribed to an increase in the "productivity" of factors rather than to an increase in resources used) involves the estimation of "total factor productivity."[19]

### The Method and the Assumptions

As a first step in the calculation of total factor productivity, indexes of labor and of capital (both inputs measured in real terms) are combined into an index of "total resources," where the weights used are the base-period earnings of the respective inputs. On the basis of a variety of assumptions, to which we shall refer presently, the index is used to show how national product would have grown had there occurred no changes in the "efficiency" of resources over time. The ratio of index numbers of output to the index numbers of input is then taken as "a measure of the changes in the efficiency with which factor services are utilized in the processes of production, i.e., of their productivity."[20]

[19] Examples of the method and its use are to be found in Jacob Schmookler, "The Changing Efficiency of the American Economy, 1869-1938," *The Review of Economics and Statistics*, Vol. XXXIV, Aug. 1952, pp. 214-231; Moses Abramovitz, "Resource and Output Trends in the United States Since 1870," *The American Economic Review*, Proc., Vol. XLVI, May 1956, pp. 5-23; John W. Kendrick, "Productivity Trends: Capital and Labor," *The Review of Economics and Statistics*, Vol. XXXVIII, Aug. 1956, pp. 248-257; and Kendrick, *Productivity Trends in the United States*, NBER, Princeton University Press, Princeton, 1961. A recent contribution, to be considered below, is that of Edward F. Denison, *The Sources of Economic Growth in the United States and the Alternatives Before Us, loc. cit.* The method has also been used for a comparative analysis of productivity in a number of countries; see Evsey D. Domar, *et al.*, "Economic Growth and Productivity in the United States, Canada, United Kingdom, Germany and Japan in the Post-War Period," *Review of Economics and Statistics*, Vol. XLVI, Feb. 1964, pp. 33-40.

[20] Kendrick, *Productivity Trends in the United States*, p. 31.

On the assumption of *competitive factor pricing*, the base-period
earnings are taken to measure the marginal productivities in the base
period of the relevant inputs. Weighting the inputs by their respective
earnings in the base period, we freeze the contribution of each unit of
input to output at its implied base-period level of efficiency, and obtain
an index of total input; this index is then taken to show how output
would have changed, if all changes in the efficiency of inputs were excluded
while only the quantities of the inputs increased. But this also demands
the assumption that the implied aggregate production function portrays
*constant returns to scale* and that there are *no changes in the quality of
inputs* over time. Moreover, it is implied that *technical change is neutral*;
otherwise the relative marginal productivities will vary as a result of
technical change. In brief, all possible determinants of the efficiency of the
inputs such as, for example, changes in the quality of inputs, and technical
change narrowly defined, are assumed to have no influence upon the
measure of the index of inputs; this index reflects changes in the quantity
of inputs of constant (base-period) efficiency.[21] It can therefore (assuming
constant returns to scale) be used to show how output would have grown
with changes in the quantity of inputs alone.

The ratio of output to input provides an index of "total productivity,"
or a measure of the change in output per unit of combined input. But all
influences playing upon efficiency are included: the index "shows changes
in the amount produced by a unit of input as a result of increasing
scientific, technological, and managerial knowledge, changes in the
efficiency of the economy, economies and diseconomies of scale, and all
other influences not measured in the input indexes."[22]

[21] But see the discussion below, p. 17.
The capital series in Kendrick's work is not corrected for underutilization. The labor
series, however, refers to employed labor. Kendrick justifies these procedures on the
grounds that employed labor is "available for use" although it is "not always fully
used"; when employed, labor constitutes a direct cost. Private capital, however, is
"wholly available during its lifetime, even if in periods of reduced activity some units
are not utilized. It represents a cost . . . " (*Productivity Trends*, pp. 31–32).
The capital series is net of depreciation, as is that used in Solow I (*ibid.*, p. 35).
Although Kendrick provides a variety of estimates, some employing Net and others
Gross Product, he prefers the *net* measure (*ibid.*, p. 64).
The use of depreciated real stocks, argues Kendrick, does not violate the principle of
"measuring stocks of resources employed in terms of units representing equal capacity
to contribute to output over time, assuming base-period technical conditions throughout," for "in the base period itself newly produced units of a given type presumably had
a larger capacity to contribute to output and net revenue than older units." It is assumed
"that the rate of technological advance and, thus, of obsolescence has been roughly the
same throughout the entire period in that the life-spans (reflecting both physical and
economic factors) used to calculate depreciation are generally taken to be the same over
time for given types of capital goods" (*ibid.*, pp. 35–36).
[22] Denison, *op. cit.*, p. 145.

*The Contribution of Increased "Productivity"*[23]

The average annual (compound) rate of growth of real net national product, over the period 1889–1953, amounts to approximately 3.6 per cent. Kendrick, using the general method outlined above, calculates that over the same period total factor productivity increased at an average annual rate of 1.6 per cent, accounting therefore for almost one-half of the increase in output. The remainder is explained by an increase of resources—labor and tangible capital—which is estimated at 2.0 per cent annually. Until 1919, however, the contribution of increased "productivity" amounted only to one-third of the increase in output, whereas during the later period productivity growth and the expansion of inputs contributed equally to the growth of output.

Over the entire period ouput per capita grew at an average annual rate of 2.1 per cent. The gain of 1.6 per cent in the average annual rate of productivity growth accounts for three-quarters of the increase in output per capita. The remainder is attributable to the expansion of input per capita (0.54 per cent a year). Of the 0.54 per cent annual average increase in total input per capita, the (weighted) input "capital" accounts for 0.36 per cent and (weighted) "labor" accounts for only 0.18 per cent. The increase of "capital" per capita is therefore responsible for approximately 16 per cent of the total increase in output per capita; by contrast, "productivity" improvement explains 75 per cent and the remainder is due to the change in "labor" per capita.

*Comments on the Method*

The explicit and the implicit assumptions underlying the calculation of the contribution to economic growth of increased "productivity" are precisely those which were encountered earlier in our description of the model used by R. M. Solow, wherein "technical change" is measured by the upward "shift" over time of an aggregate production function. It is to be expected, therefore, that the resultant variable "total factor productivity" portrays similar characteristics to those of Solow's "technical change." Both terms refer to all forces contributing to economic growth other than the increase in resources used. Individual causes of the growth

---

[23] All the calculations in this section are from the volume by Kendrick, *op. cit.*, pp. 79 ff. The high estimates for the contribution to growth of improved "productivity" appear in the other references given earlier (except that to Denison's work). For example, comparing the decades 1869–1878 and 1944–1953, Abramovitz, *op. cit.*, shows that a combined index of labor input per capita and the supply of capital per capita rises only 14 per cent over the period whereas net national product quadruples, leading him to the conclusion that the productivity of "a representative group of resources" must have increased by 250 per cent, to explain the phenomenon; on the basis of his calculation, almost the entire increase in net national product per capita is therefore caused by increased productivity.

of output or output per capita are again inextricably mixed together in a "catchall"; above all, the contribution of technical change, narrowly defined, is not isolated from the effect of economies of scale and numerous other variables.[24]

The relatively small contribution of capital per capita to the growth of output per capita is once more, at least in part, the result of the manner in which "capital" is measured; the effects of quality changes are largely excluded from the capital index and capital is accorded a relatively low weight. Whether the implication that technical change does not require embodiment in new type plant and equipment is preferable to alternative assumptions is a question which is again brought to the fore. Moreover, as in Solow's model, materials are excluded so that a bias is introduced against the input "capital."

However there are some interesting differences between Solow's "technical change" and Kendrick's "total factor productivity." The contribution of "total factor productivity" tends to be somewhat less striking than that of "technical change." This seems to derive partly from the fact that Kendrick's capital index is not corrected for underutilization so that the input "capital" plays a more important role, and partly from the fact that both Kendrick's "labor" and "capital" inputs reflect— although to a limited extent and in a special sense—"improvement in quality" over time. For relative earnings, by which the labor in different industries and capital in different industries are weighted, may be taken to approximate relative marginal productivities, and historically there has occurred a tendency for a faster rate of growth of the higher-paying than the lower-paying industries. Thus Kendrick's weighting system excludes "improved quality" due to the changing composition of the labor force from the residual.[25]

[24] As we shall shortly point out, this charge is, formally at least, unjustified in the case of Denison's work since the author attempts to break down the "catchall."

[25] Kendrick, *op. cit.*, p. 64.

The weights are applied on an industry basis. The *only* element of improved quality reflected in the input series is that due to the relative expansion of higher-paying industries. The series do not reflect higher quality owing to improvements throughout the labor force, for example, and new entrants into any particular industry-group are treated on a par with those originally in the group. These remarks apply to the capital input too. In brief, particular groups of workers and particular items of capital have *fixed weights* over time and increased efficiencies within the groups are not reflected.

Kendrick provides an estimate of the difference between the residual when inputs are weighted by base-period earnings and when unweighted inputs are used, man-hours and unweighted capital being combined by shares of national income. For example, for the period 1889–1957, real gross product per man-hour increased at an annual average rate of 2.4 per cent, compared with a 2.0 per cent annual average increase in output per unit of *weighted* labor; similarly, output per unit of the combined unweighted inputs increased at an annual average rate of 2.0 per cent compared with 1.7 per cent in the case of "the preferred total factor productivity measure" (pp. 64–65).

In concluding this section, it may be noted that a distortion tends to enter the calculations by the use of a fixed base year from which subsequent "changes in technique" are measured. It would be preferable to estimate "technical change" in each year by reference to the productivity of resources in the preceding year. This procedure might tend to reduce somewhat the estimate of the residual. The problem is partly overcome, however, by the use of a chain index with occasionally changing weights.[26]

*Refinements in the Method: A Breakdown of the Residual*

In his recent addition to the literature on the sources of economic growth, E. F. Denison[27] gives a relatively low rank to the contribution of what has been referred to above as the "residual," or in his terminology, the contribution of changes of "output per unit of input." Constructing an index of total factor productivity, he estimates that over the period 1929–1957, 32.0 per cent of the total growth of real national income is the result of increased output per unit of input, whereas the growth of (combined) inputs is responsible for the remaining 68.0 per cent.[28] Of the increase in real national product *per person employed*, 42.0 per cent is attributed to the increase in total inputs per person employed, and 58.0 per cent to the increase in output per unit of input. The growth of the capital input alone per employed person contributes only 9.0 per cent.

As Denison himself points out, however, the relatively large contribution of input expansion, and the correspondingly low contribution of "productivity" change (compared for example with the results obtained by Kendrick), are the result in large part of a novel procedure for the classification of inputs: "The difference lies in my classification in labor input of improvements in the quality of an hour's work, whereas the

---

[26] See Kendrick, *op. cit.*, p. 55.

The NBER method involves arithmetic weighting (in contrast with Solow's method, which involves the weighting of the logarithims of the inputs). The choice of base year is important and will influence the rate of change in productivity derived from year to year over a long period. With long time series continually changing weights are somewhat impractical, however, and the NBER has therefore resorted to occasionally changing weights.

[27] Denison, *op. cit.*, Ch. 23, "The Sources of Past and Future Growth."

[28] If the precise assumptions and classifications used by Kendrick were applied, the contributions of increased productivity and of the growth of inputs for the same period (1929–1957) would amount to 62.0 per cent and 38.0 per cent respectively. Denison's estimate of 32.0 per cent as the contribution of increased productivity is therefore relatively very low. For a comparison of the work of Kendrick and Denison, see a review article by Moses Abramovitz, "Economic Growth in the United States," *The American Economic Review*, Vol. LII, Sept. 1962, pp. 762–782.

A review article by Evsey D. Domar, "On Total Productivity and All That," *Journal of Political Economy*, Vol. LXX, Dec. 1962, pp. 597–608, is also very helpful.

alternative merges them with technological advance and other sources into output per unit of input."[29]

The major contribution of Denison, however, is the attempt to allocate the residual among the various influences encompassed therein. Indeed, in referring to the contribution of output per unit of input as a "residual" we have prejudged the issue: Denison in fact allocates to *economies of scale* of various kinds the responsibility for 11.0 per cent of the growth of output over the period. The true residual accounts for only 20.0 per cent. This contribution is termed by Denison growth due to the "advance of knowledge."

Unfortunately, the estimate for the contribution of scale economies to growth is arbitrary. The argument runs as follows: decreasing returns to scale cannot exist in the economy as a whole; experience suggests that increasing returns are more likely than constant returns. It is then assumed that, over the period 1929–1957, scale economies "increased the contribution of all other sources of economic growth by 10 per cent" so that economies of scale associated with national markets are assumed to be responsible for one-eleventh of total economic growth.[30] Similarly, the contributions of other forces are based upon general assumptions. If we bear in mind this arbitrary allocation, we must conclude that we are justified in calling the entire growth of output per unit of input a "residual." We are not substantially closer to an estimate of the contribution by technical change, narrowly defined as the introduction or the adoption of cost-reducing changes in technique.[31]

## MEASUREMENT OF THE RELATIONSHIP BETWEEN SIZE AND EFFICIENCY

A number of attempts have been made to account for differences in productivity (measured in a variety of ways) between industries over time. However, there is no generally proven statistical method which permits

[29] Denison, *op. cit.*, pp. 149–150.

Denison's aggregate man-hours are adjusted, for example, for increased experience and better use of women in the labor force, changes in the age-sex distribution, the greater efficiency per man-hour due to the shorter work week and the rise in education. In contrast to Kendrick, he does not weight man-hours in different industries by average earnings at some base period, and therefore does not incorporate, in his measure of inputs, shifts in the industrial composition of the labor force over time from low-paying to high-paying industries.

It may be added that Denison's capital series is undepreciated rather than net in contrast to those of Solow I and Kendrick.

[30] Denison, *op. cit.*, Ch. 16, "Economies of Scale and Increased Specialization," in particular p. 175.

[31] It may also be added that the residuals in all cases pick up the errors in all other estimates.

the calculation of the contribution of "scale" to productivity, when it cannot be assumed that technical change (in the sense of the introduction or the spread of cost-reducing techniques) is absent.[32]

The major problem encountered has been summarized by Solow, who writes that "the strong intercorrelation between the time trend for technical progress and the effect of scale" creates a situation where "a multiple regression finds it difficult to impute more-than-proportional increases in output as between increases in scale and the mere passage of time."[33]

Essentially, increased output may permit changes in technique which have been known but have only become profitable at the new rate of production, or increased output may stimulate the development of new techniques. Furthermore, as an industry grows it may enjoy a number of *external* economies, as other sectors provide specialized services.

But there is a further difficulty: autonomous technical change (that is, technical change not induced by increased output) may reduce costs and output may increase in response to an increase in the quantity demanded at the lower prices made possible. A statistical correlation between efficiency and scale cannot usually state which is the dependent and which the independent variable. If, as is probable, both "induced" and "autonomous" technical changes are occurring, the problem is magnified.[34]

[32] Partly as a reaction against the Solow-type and the NBER-type methods with their highly restrictive assumptions relating to constant returns, competitive equilibrium, and the like, there have appeared a number of econometric studies of the production function which, among other features, derive *estimates* of the coefficients to be used as weights, and do not restrict the analysis to constant returns. See Zvi Griliches, "The Sources of Measured Productivity Growth: United States Agriculture, 1940–1960," *Journal of Political Economy*, Vol. LXXI, Aug. 1963, pp. 331–346; and Murray Brown and Joel Popkin, "A Measure of Technological Change and Returns to Scale," *Review of Economics and Statistics*, Vol. XLIV, Nov. 1962, pp. 402–411. These studies—which in some instances attribute a considerable portion of the expansion of output to economies of scale—are, however, still at the exploratory stage. See also A. A. Walters, "A Note on Economies of Scale," *Review of Economics and Statistics*, Vol. XLV, Nov. 1963, pp. 425–427.

[33] Robert M. Solow, "Investment and Economic Growth: Some Comments," *Productivity Measurement Review*, Nov. 1959, No. 19, p. 64.

[34] A recent example of the attempt to measure the significance of scale is to be found in a study by Nestor E. Terleckyj in *Sources of Productivity Growth. A Pilot Study Based on the Experience of American Manufacturing Industries*, 1899–1953, unpublished Ph.D. dissertation, Columbia University, 1959. A statistically significant degree of correlation is found between relative changes in output and in total factor productivity for twenty manufacturing groups; for every 3 per cent difference in the growth rates among industries, productivity advance differed by 1 per cent. Moreover, the author's net regression coefficients indicate that rates of productivity differ by approximately 0.5 per cent for each tenfold difference in research activity. For a full discussion of this study, see Kendrick, *Productivity Trends in the United States*, pp. 179 ff., where the conclusion is reached that "it is clear that the output-productivity relation does not provide an unambiguous measure of scale effects" (p. 186).

The general problem of the measurement of the effects on productivity of scale is discussed fully in *Cost Behavior and Price Policy*, National Bureau of Economic Research, New York, 1943, Ch. X, "Costs and the Size of Plants and Firms."

In an attempt to account for labor-productivity changes in various United Kingdom industries over time, W. E. G. Salter[35] arrives at the conclusion that he is unable to distinguish productivity movements due to scale economies and those due to technical change in the narrow sense. Salter uses statistics on the interindustry behavior of labor cost, capital cost, and materials cost per unit of output, and also prices, and earnings per operative, to explain the pattern of productivity change over the years 1924–1950 in various U.K. industries. He tests his technique by an application of the same approach to U.S. data, from which he derives similar results.

One hypothesis, tested by Salter, is that the interindustry productivity movements observed in his material can be explained by the substitution of capital for labor. Relative input prices and changes in relative input prices are assumed to be the same for all industries; the elasticity of substitution between inputs, however, may differ. Those industries with the greatest elasticity of substitution will experience the greatest increases in labor productivity and will require the greatest amounts of additional capital, upon a relative rise in wage rates and the subsequent substitution of capital for labor. Capital costs per unit of output would rise relatively the most in those industries with the highest elasticities and the largest increases in labor productivity. In point of fact, Salter finds that industries with the largest increases in output per head have the *smallest* increases in gross margin costs per unit of output, and he therefore rejects this hypothesis. Moreover, the data disclose that precisely those industries that have the greatest increases in output per head also have the greatest differential price reductions. One would not expect this to be the case if the cause of the higher labor productivity were simply the substitution of capital for labor; in the latter situation, one costly input is replaced by another, and there occurs no net saving of costs.

Increases in labor efficiency, that is, in the quality of labor as an explanation of the interindustry behavior, are rejected, on the grounds that no association is apparent between movements in labor productivity and earnings such as would be expected from this hypothesis.

Salter therefore turns to the possibility of absolute factor saving rather than the saving of one particular input (labor) as an explanation of his statistical material. Uneven rates of technical advance cannot be rejected as an hypothesis explaining the differential movements in productivity. However, the data are not inconsistent with some degree of factor substitution *combined* with technical advance. Indeed, he argues, we expect technical advance in the capital-goods industries to lead to a relative

[35] W. E. G. Salter, *Productivity and Technical Change*, Cambridge University Press, Cambridge, 1960.

decline in the price of capital goods. Thus, superimposed upon the savings of both labor and capital produced by technical advance, there occurs an even greater labor-saving tendency and a somewhat lesser capital saving due to factor substitution: "new techniques . . . would save more labor than other factors because labor was becoming dearer relatively to other factors."[36]

Furthermore, the data could be explained by scale economies, either internal or external to the firms in each industry examined. However, no way is suggested to distinguish productivity changes due to scale from those due to technical change. Indeed, Salter rejects the contention that a separation should be sought: "while a completely self-contained explanation of the results along the above lines (in terms of differential scale economies) is possible, it is much more plausible to think of technical progress and economies of scale as complementary to each other."[37] He suggests that industries are stimulated to expand by technical progress and are thereby enabled to take advantage of latent scale economies.

Although Salter is able to go a little further than Solow, his conclusions remain highly conjectural. Above all, the conclusion that the material is explicable by a mixture of scale economies and technical change does not take us too far.

### THE PRESENT INVESTIGATION: A MICROECONOMIC STUDY OF PRODUCTIVITY MOVEMENTS

Many of the problems which beset an aggregative study of the extent to which movements in productivity can be ascribed to particular causes, and above all to technical change, narrowly defined as cost-reducing changes in technique, can be avoided in a closely documented microstudy. The general problem remains the same. At the level of the economy as a whole it is important to know how much of the rising trend in real national income is due to improvements in the use of resources and how much to other causes, such as an increase in the quantity of resources in use. Similarly, at the microeconomic level we are interested in explaining the company's efficiency in producing its product. In particular, to what extent can changes in the productivity of the firm's inputs be ascribed to "technical change" in the narrow sense?[38] An answer can be provided by close examination of the unit costs of production of particular plants (corrected for input price variation) and the relation of movements

---

[36] *Ibid.*, p. 140.
[37] *Ibid.*, p. 142.
[38] The use made in the present study of the term "technical change" will be considered in Chapter 2.

therein to changes in technique. A central question which is asked in the present study therefore is: Are cost reductions observed at particular plants the result of changes in the technique of production?

The relationship between scale and technical change will also be considered. It will be possible to state whether technical change in each instance had been alone responsible for the variation in costs per unit or whether both scale and technical change have to be taken into account. The particular relationships which may exist between the two variables can also be specified.

Another problem which will interest us is the relation between the various changes in technique and investment in plant and equipment. Whereas some writers have questioned the significance of net investment in accounting for economic growth, most agree that gross investment is probably important. We shall attempt to determine whether or not particular technical changes were dependent upon preceding expenditures on plant and equipment, and whether the outlays were part of a program of replacement or of expansion.

In our review of certain macroeconomic studies of productivity increase over time, we have encountered the conclusion by some authors that more attention should be centered upon those variables determining the rate of introduction of new technology into the economic system: expenditures by firms on research are singled out as a relevant variable. In this study we shall attempt to throw some light on the problem, by considering whether the specific technical changes which we are able to isolate depend upon technology developed by the formal research activities c
in question, and whether or not the technologies are patent
be that most of the reductions in costs are dependent upon small improvements in technique rather than upon large changes based on laboratory research work, pilot plants, and patented technology.

Our main concern will be with changes in unit cost rather than with improvements in the quality of the product, since only the former variations can be quantitatively defined.

*Chapter Two*

# The Definition of "Technical Change"

By the term "technical change" we shall refer throughout this study to changes in the technique of production of given commodities by specific plants, designed to reduce unit production costs. These changes in technique may be of a "technological" nature, they may represent the introduction of different or improved inputs from those hitherto used at the plant, or they may be "managerial" and consist in improved organization of work, "Taylorization" and the like. It is intended, however, that the term should apply only to such changes which are brought about by a deliberate decision to reduce costs, although it is not necessary that the decision be taken by "high-ranking" management.

"Technical changes" include methods used for the first time by the plant, or modifications in methods, regardless of the source of the underlying technology, and whether from the point of view of the entire industry, the whole nation, or the whole world the methods are imitative or not.[1]

It is convenient to distinguish our use of the term "technical change" from the meaning given to this and related terms elsewhere in the literature in order to establish the precise scope of the present study.

---

[1] We do not intend to define precisely at this point the "first" use of a particular technique by a plant. It may be noted, however, that the McGraw-Hill surveys of business' plans for new plants and equipment use a three-year criterion of novelty in the definition of a "new" product: for example, "new" products planned in 1956 for 1960 are products "not produced in 1956, or products sufficiently changed to be reasonably considered as new products." See annual surveys prepared by the McGraw-Hill Department of Economics, *Business Plans for New Plants and Equipment*.

TECHNICAL CHANGE, IMPROVEMENTS IN QUALITY OF
FACTORS, AND "ECONOMIES OF SCALE"

We have seen in the previous chapter that in certain macroeconomic studies of productivity, the term "technical change" is used in effect as a catchall which includes improvements in the quality of inputs such as those due, in the case of labor, to improved health and education, and both internal and external economies of scale.

Although our use of the term includes the introduction of different kinds of inputs, the definition is framed to exclude changes which are not part of a deliberate effort to reduce costs. With the passage of time, labor of a higher general level of education and health will be available to all plants, and plant managers are not in a position to choose between such labor and the labor available at some earler time period. Quality changes of this kind, even if productivity should be increased as a result, are excluded from our definition.[2]

"Economies of scale" are excluded from "technical change" if by this expression we mean the reduction of unit costs following plant expansion and the spreading over a larger volume of output of certain fixed items of total cost, and where no changes other than the duplication of plant (and the concomitant expansion of certain inputs) are involved.[3] Instances may be found where efficient methods and machines are only practical at higher levels of output: such instances of unit cost reduction are generally classified in the literature as scale economies;[4] however, strictly speaking, since the introduction of the relevant method or machine is dependent upon a deliberate decision to reduce costs of production, such cases should be included, in the present context at least, within our category of "technical change." Cases of this kind will, however, be referred to as "technical changes *dependent upon scale of operation or volume.*" Deliberate changes in technique may be required in order to permit a larger volume of output to be forthcoming from a given establishment; if, as a consequence of increased production, costs per unit fall (relatively fixed items of total cost being spread over a greater volume), then the economies will be regarded as the result—albeit an indirect result—of "technical change."

---

[2] In practice, unfortunately, there is no satisfactory way of measuring the effect on productivity at the plants to be considered of "better education and health." A rough measure of the effects of more intensive training of labor *at the plants* can, however, be obtained.

[3] Cost reductions due to duplication of plant will be said to result from "the plant-expansion effect."

[4] See, for example, Fritz Machlup, *The Economics of Sellers' Competition*, The Johns Hopkins Press, Baltimore, 1952, pp. 323 ff. The best known instance of such phenomena is, of course, the specialization by workers in Adam Smith's pin factory.

TECHNICAL CHANGE AND THE SOURCES OF
TECHNOLOGY

Our definition of "technical change" includes the introduction of new techniques (from the point of view of the plant in question), regardless of the originality of the underlying technology. We avoid the implication that cost-reducing changes in technique are dependent upon the occurrence of recent inventive activity.

### Technical Change and Invention

Even if we were to limit the use of the term "technical change" to changes in technique which are *truly novel* and which are introduced literally for the first time, it would be preferable to avoid the suggestion that recent inventive activity is a necessary prerequisite. In some studies, however, the implication is present that cost-reducing "innovations" are in fact contingent on new technology. Thus, for example, in his attempt to account for interindustry productivity differentials over time, N. E. Terleckyj[5] makes use of indirect measures of innovational activity, such as the number of patents issued to industries, research and development outlays by industry relative to sales, and research and development personnel relative to all employees of each industry. The introduction of *new methods* is identified, for purposes of measurement at least, with attempts to develop *new technology.*[6]

The identification of new methods with new technology carries with it the implication that the establishment, industry, or sector of the economy

---

[5] Terleckyj, *Sources of Productivity Growth, op. cit.*

[6] Much of the business-cycle literature by the "Over-investment School" apparently assumes that inventive activity is a necessary condition for innovation. Both Wicksell and Spiethoff, for example, argue that the upturn in business activity is due to the adoption of novel techniques of production which in turn are based on new technology, that is, on technology which has recently (during the preceding downswing) become available. Invention occurs discontinuously, and is particularly stimulated by the period of depression, and research activity (in the broadest sense) determines the cyclical path of innovation. See for example Arthur Spiethoff, "Business Cycles," *International Economic Papers*, No. 3, 1953, pp. 75–171. (This paper is a shorter version of "Krisen," *Handwörterbuch der Staatswissenschaften*, 4th and later editions, Jena, 1923); and Knut Wicksell, "Notes on Trade Cycles and Crises," in *Lectures on Political Economy*, The Macmillan Company, London, 1935, Vol. II, pp. 209–214.
The assumption that innovation (the introduction of truly novel techniques) depends upon additions to the stock of knowledge appears also in some definitions of innovation which run in terms of a change in the production function. For the production function of economic theory is normally regarded as describing the frontier of technological knowledge; only best technology is included. Moreover, the firm is assumed to be working at the frontier. In order to innovate, therefore, the firm must somehow alter the form of the function, and this is possible only by extending the body of technology.

under consideration will apply the new technology as soon as it is developed. This, however, is an unjustified presumption which assumes away the necessity of explaining why lags exist in practice between the development of technology and its application. Some attention will be given to this question in this study.

### The Variety of Sources of Technology

That the introduction of new techniques by a sector of the economy is dependent upon technology developed *formally* by that *particular* sector is also implicit in the indirect measures of innovational activity referred to above. It should be recognized, however, that the ideas underlying changes in technique (even when the changes are truly original and not simply original from the point of view of the establishment introducing them), derive from a variety of sources including "unorganized" activities. In particular, ideas may originate as a consequence of problems met with on the floor of the plant by operating personnel or plant managers;[7] it is conceivable that such ideas constitute the wellspring of a considerable part of cost-reducing technical change.

Moreover, in the case of individual companies, technology may be acquired from other companies in the same industry, and in the case of an industry the source of its changes in technique may originate with developments occurring in other industries; in particular, suppliers of equipment and of raw materials may be responsible for widening the body of new knowledge available to the industry in question. Customers of a firm may be similarly instrumental in altering the body of knowledge available to that firm. We must also bear in mind the growing importance of research foundations, governmental research, and research by universities, the results of which are broadly available.[8]

Because of the variety of sources of knowledge, it is desirable to divorce the term "technical change" from any conceptual association with formal research activities by the establishment in question. One of the problems to be faced in this study is, in fact, *whether* the technical changes encountered depended upon formal research activity by the relevant company and whether such technology was patented or not.

---

[7] Cf. Martin Segal, "Introduction of Technological Changes in Industrial Plants," *Explorations in Entrepreneurial History*, Vol. VI, Oct. 1953, pp. 41–61.

[8] A further disadvantage of using indirect measures of technical change is the fact that much inventive activity is directed toward the development of new products or the improvement of old ones rather than toward new techniques which will permit a higher productivity. Moreover, it is implied that the attempts to obtain new knowledge are all successful and that the volume of commercially utilizable inventions deriving from "given amounts" of formal research activity does not vary between industries and over-time.

## "Technical Change" and Schumpeterian "Innovation"

Joseph A. Schumpeter's famour definition of "innovation"[9] is formally both broader and narrower than our own definition of "technical change," for it includes a variety of events which are excluded from our concept but unconditionally excludes imitation. However, a conciliation of the two concepts cannot be accomplished merely by extending our definition on the one hand, and insisting upon genuine novelty on the other, for "innovation" in the Schumpeterian system is concerned with *major* changes rather than with relatively small improvements, however original, in the efficiency of producing given commodities. Moreover, Schumpeterian innovations are characterized by a certain degree of riskiness, whereas the improvements with which we shall be concerned under our own definition of "technical change" *may* be carried out with complete certainty concerning the effect on costs. The two concepts are not, therefore, closely related.

[9] Cf. Joseph A. Schumpeter, *Business Cycles*, McGraw-Hill Book Co., Inc., New York, 1939, Vol. I, p. 84.

# Chapter Three

# On the Determination of Unit Costs of Production in Viscose-Rayon Yarn Manufacture

The Textile Department of E. I. du Pont de Nemours and Company has made available, for the present study, cost data relating to four viscose-rayon manufacturing plants at Richmond, Virginia (to be referred to as Spruance Plants I, II, II-A, and III) and to rayon operations at Old Hickory, Tennessee.

A brief summary of the period of operation of each plant may be in order. During 1924, Old Hickory Plant I was under construction; operations commenced in January 1925. A second newly built plant, Old Hickory II-A, began production in December. Shortly after, the third of the Old Hickory plants, II-B, was constructed and was in operation by September 1928. All three plants produced textile filament yarn by the viscose process. Production came to an end at Plant II-B in 1957 and at II-A in the following year, when all production at the location was consolidated in the remaining plant. Cost data are available for the period 1928–1960.

Rayon textile yarn by the viscose process was produced at Spruance Plants I and II, and rayon tire-cord yarn by the viscose process at Spruance Plants II-A and III. Construction of Spruance I was completed in 1929 and operations were begun in June. Operations at the newly built Plant II began in May 1935. The first tire-cord yarn ever produced at a plant constructed especially for this product was forthcoming at Spruance III in September 1936. During 1943, part of Spruance II was converted from textile to tire-cord production; operations at the converted section, Spruance II-A, began in 1944. Production was terminated at Spruance I in 1953, at Spruance II in 1954, and at Spruance III in 1957. Cost data have been made available for the entire periods of operation at these plants, and up till 1956 in the case of Spruance II-A.

In this chapter, the most significant variables entering into an explanation of the differential behavior, over time and between plants, of unit costs of viscose-rayon yarn manufacture will be considered. It is convenient to introduce the analysis of cost determination with a brief review of the stages involved in the viscose process. The notion of the "capacity" of a rayon plant, the various categories of labor employed in rayon manufacture, and the nature of the unit of output, or the meaning of a unit of rayon yarn, will also be considered.

### THE VISCOSE PROCESS

There are three major operations involved in viscose-rayon yarn manufacture:[1] the preparation of the viscose solution, "spinning" of the solution to form filaments, and the subsequent treatments given to the rayon filaments after "spinning."[2]

#### The Preparation of the Viscose Solution

The stages involved in the preparation of the viscose solution, to which we now turn, were common to all the early plants and have remained substantially unchanged over time:

*Steeping:* In the first stage, sheets of commercially pure cellulose are soaked in caustic soda. The excess solution is then extracted by pressing, leaving sheets of "alkali cellulose."

*Shredding:* The sheets of alkali cellulose are then ground into "crumbs."

*Aging:* The crumbs are passed into aging tanks, where controlled reactions help provide the ultimate solution with the required viscosity.

*Xanthation:* Carbon bisulphide is then added to the aged alkali cellulose crumbs forming "cellulose xanthate."

*Mixing:* The cellulose xanthate is mixed with dilute caustic soda. It is at this stage that the viscose solution results.

---

[1] The plants that will be considered in this section will be the first United States rayon plant—that of the American Viscose Corporation—which began operations in 1911 at Marcus Hook, Pennsylvania; Du Pont's first rayon plant at Buffalo, New York, where operations began in 1921; and Du Pont's first plant at Old Hickory, Tennessee, where production began in 1925.

[2] For more detailed accounts of the processes of production—viscose and others— see for example Mois H. Avram, *The Rayon Industry,* D. Van Nostrand Company, New York, 1927; R. E. Wheeler, *The Manufacture of Artificial Silk, with Special Reference to the Viscose Process,* D. Van Nostrand Company, New York, 1931; *The Rayon Industry,* United States Tariff Commission, Washington, April 1944, pp. 44–51; Joseph Leeming, *Rayon. The First Man-made Fiber,* Chemical Publishing Co., Inc., New York, 1950.

*Blending, Ripening, Filtering, Deaeration:* Several batches of the solution are blended together to assure uniformity of quality during subsequent operations;[3] further aging or ripening of the solution then takes place, followed by the removal of impurities by filtration, and the evacuation of air from the solution.

*Pumping:* Finally the viscose solution is passed through to the "spinning room."

### Spinning

"Spinning," in the present context, should not be confused with the traditional, or textile, use of the term. Spinning, as used here, has the specialized meaning which will now be described. The viscose solution is extruded through tiny orifices, in thimblelike objects known as nozzles or spinnerettes. Each nozzle is immersed in a "spinning bath" containing sulphuric acid, sodium sulphate, zinc sulphate, corn sugar or glucose, and warm water. The liquid streams of viscose solution (alkaline) are converted back into filaments of solid *cellulose* upon contact with the acid bath. These are rayon filaments. There emerges one filament from each hole in each nozzle. The several filaments from each nozzle are then drawn together into a thread of rayon yarn.

There are two alternative methods of accomplishing the collection of each group of filaments as it leaves the bath. In the "bucket" method, each group is drawn up over a revolving wheel (the "godet" or feed wheel) and is then guided downwards through a funnel into a rotating cylindrical box, whose motion causes the filaments to be twisted together, forming thereby a thread of yarn. The thread is laid against the side of the bucket by the centrifugal force, and a cylinder or "cake" of rayon yarn is formed in this manner. In the alternative or "bobbin" method, the filaments from each nozzle are drawn up in parallel form over a revolving bobbin and no twist is applied at this stage. As a result, a separate stage of twisting is called for at some subsequent operation.

### Postspinning Operations

Following *bucket spinning*, various methods were used in the early plants in the preparation of the yarn for sale. In the first American Viscose Corporation plant, the "acid-reeling" technique was practiced: the main stages involved were the reeling of the rayon yarn, still saturated in acid, from the cakes to skeins; the skeins were then washed, bleached, and purified; drying followed, and, finally, after inspection, the skeins were

---

[3] The stage of blending was necessary in the early plants but has since been abandoned as a result of improved pulp and other changes.

prepared for sale. It may be added that the yarn might be wound to "cones" should the customer so desire this form of delivery; coning would involve an additional stage.

The first *bucket* plant operated by the Du Pont Company (beginning production at Old Hickory in 1925) washed the cakes free of acid and dried them *before* the reeling operation. The main sequence involved at this plant was: cake washing and draining, drying, reeling to skeins; washing, desulphuring, and bleaching of the skeins; drying, inspection, and preparation for sale. Coning might also be carried out. There were, therefore, additional stages in the Du Pont process as compared with the early American Viscose Corporation process (cake washing and draining, and cake drying), resulting directly from the fact that the cakes of rayon were washed free of acid *before* the reeling stage.[4]

Following *bobbin spinning*, as for example in the first of the Du Pont plants at Buffalo where operations began in 1921, two further steps are required: the transfer of the filaments from the skeins to spools, and the twisting of the filaments into threads, since the filaments leave the bath in parallel form and are collected on bobbins without twist.

It may be mentioned at this point that each stage in the postspinning operation as well as each of the earlier stages requires both additional labor and equipment.

## THE NOTION OF CAPACITY

The capacity of a rayon plant is commonly defined by the industry in terms of the number of spinnerettes or nozzles installed in the spinning room. This is because to a large degree the nozzles act as a "bottleneck"—as limiting factors—in the sense that, if all nozzles are in operation, a larger output can be produced only after more nozzles are installed.

For this index to be considered as an unambiguous measure of capacity output, certain qualifications must be made. In the first place, the *speed of spinning* must be assumed constant. Even assuming that all the nozzles are in use, it will still be possible to increase output from the given plant if the "spinning speed"—measured in inches per minute—is increased. This variable will be considered in detail later in the chapter.

Second, the *denier* must be assumed unchanged for the number of nozzles to act as a satisfactory index of capacity output. The notion of the denier of a rayon yarn will be examined in some detail shortly, but, essentially, the denier is a measure of the weight of a given length of yarn: a given length of a high denier yarn is heavier than the same length of a

---

[4] Skeining of yarn while it was saturated in acid was dangerous for operators and was avoided at Du Pont plants.

lower denier yarn. The spinning speed determines the *length* of rayon yarn per period which can be produced by a given spinning machine; assuming a constant spinning speed it is possible to raise the output, *in terms of weight* (pounds), by raising the denier.[5] As a result, unless the denier is assumed unchanged, or unless certain corrections are made to allow for the change in denier, capacity output is not uniquely related to the number of installed nozzles.

Third, it may be noted that if a given number of nozzles could be operated at one, two, or three shifts, then the index would be an unsatisfactory measure of capacity output. In rayon production, however, because of the chemical nature of the operations involved, the expense of interrupting production for part of the day is so great that plants are run continuously, with no possibility of adding extra shifts.

Finally, the possibility of "alternative-active" spinning may be mentioned. A plant may be fitted out with, for example, 10,000 *positions* for nozzles, whereas only 5,000 nozzles may actually be *installed*. In this case installed nozzles as an index of capacity would be less relevant—for the medium-long run—than nozzle positions available.

With these qualifications in mind, and in particular the assumption that both spinning speed and denier are constant, the number of nozzles is a satisfactory index of capacity output. The implication is that an increase in the number of installed nozzles involves a proportionate increase in the volume of potential output, and an increase in the number of existing nozzles in operation increases actual output in proportion.

Although as a general rule it is satisfactory to assume that the (maximum) volume of output is uniquely determined by the nozzle capacity, the denier, and the recorded spinning speed, attempts are continually being made to permit an expansion of output by means of small improvements such as simplifications in the process which reduce waste. Moreover, it may be possible to raise the spinning speed by *small* steps in certain circumstances which may be unrecorded in currently available data. Although for the present we adhere to a strict interpretation of "capacity output," these latter possibilities will be taken into account in later chapters.

THE LABOR FORCE

The skill required in rayon production by laborers is relatively high. The most skilled men are those employed in the chemical department

---

[5] It will be made clear at a later stage that for an increase in denier to permit a larger volume of output to be forthcoming, it is necessary for sufficient viscose-making equipment and equipment for the treatment of the acid bath to be available.

preparing the viscose solution, maintenance craftsmen, powerhouse engineers, and generator-switchboard operators. Workers of "intermediate" skill include the spinners (who regulate the passage of the solution through the nozzles and the winding of the filament when formed on the bobbins or buckets), the doffers (who remove the collecting device from the spinning machines), the operators of washers, wringers, and dryers (who treat the filaments), product inspectors, routine laboratory testers, reelers (who transfer the yarn to skeins), throwers (involved in the twisting of filaments), winders (who prepare the ultimate package for shipment), and craftsmen's helpers in the maintenance department. The least-skilled workers are truckers, cleaners, and general laborers.

In the study from which these categories were drawn, made in 1944, it was further reported that workers were concentrated in relatively few occupations.[6] Thus in May 1944, in the United States rayon and acetate industry, four-fifths of all workers were employed in 18 out of 58 representative occupations. Of these, 25 per cent were throwers (twisters), 15 per cent were spinners, doffers, or topmen, and 10 per cent worked in the chemical department. However, the occupational structure between plants differs depending upon the technique of production used. For example, in a bucket plant, reelers and throwers are not employed.[7]

By the term "operating labor" which will be used in this study of individual plants is meant labor involved in the direct handling of the product at some stage or other; it includes all workers in the chemical building, in the spinning room, and those involved in the postspinning operations. This group is to be distinguished from the maintenance men, certain salaried workers, and "service" labor of various kinds.

The majority of the operating laborers would be considered as variable labor with respect to changes in output. The chemical department in particular, however, employs crews on various operations (such as steeping press workers, operators of shredders, aging machines, xanthation machines, and the like) and the same crew can deal with a relatively wide range of output variation before additional men must be employed. This is also true for certain of the finishing operators such as operators of dryers and of purification-solution equipment.

Of the other members of the labor force—whether wage or salary earners—the majority fall into that category which does not change directly with variations in output: this group includes a large portion of

[6] Willis C. Quant, "Wages in the Rayon Industry, May 1944," *Monthly Labor Review*, United States Bureau of Labor Statistics, Vol. LIX; 6, Dec. 1944, pp. 1141–1157.

[7] It may be added here that men predominate in the chemical building, the spinning room, the coagulating-bath preparation area, and the washing and bleaching area. Women are employed in the textile area on spooling, reeling, twisting, and winding, which are light occupations.

the maintenance men; research workers; chemical, experimental, and testing workers; mechanical engineers; men involved in selling and purchasing; the guard; the doctor; powerhouse labor; restaurant labor; and some supervisory personnel.

A preliminary measure of the labor which does not vary with output is provided by the "overhead" items in the plants to be examined, after some deductions have been made for non-labor items (approximately 10 per cent of overhead costs), and an allowance made for the "fixed portion" of operating labor (estimated at approximately 20 per cent.)

Although it is true that the larger part of operating labor varies directly with changes in output, a distinction should be drawn between the short run and the long run. For example, upon a reduction in the utilization of capacity from 10,000 to 8,000 nozzles, sufficient operating labor may be retained to deal with 9,000 nozzles. Should it appear probable that the output reduction will not be short-lived, only those men required for 8,000 nozzles will be retained. As a result, under seemingly identical conditions, different unit costs of production may be recorded depending upon the expectations concerning the length of time during which the particular level of production is likely to last.[8]

### THE UNIT OF RAYON OUTPUT

The Du Pont Company uses a *pound* of rayon as the unit of output. On the other hand, the rayon industry trade journal *Rayon Organon* argues that actual output should be corrected to allow for the fact that different denier yarns are involved.[9] As mentioned earlier, the denier is a measure of the weight of a given length or vice versa. One pound of 150-denier rayon (which is often used as a standard or representative category for viscose-rayon yarn) is 59,528 yards in length; one pound of 75-denier rayon, being finer, is double that length. The journal reduces all rayon produced to pounds of standard (150)-denier rayon by marking down actual pounds of yarn of above-standard denier and marking up actual pounds of below-standard denier: in this way cognizance is taken of the fact that the higher-denier rayons are shorter per pound, and the

[8] A definition of the short and the long run of economic theory, in terms of the length of time for which the changed output is expected to prevail, may be found in Fritz Machlup, *The Economics of Sellers' Competition*, *op. cit.*, p. 40. Here it is argued that "a better understanding of the concepts ["short period" and "long period"] might be achieved by associating the degree of planned plant adjustment with the length of time for which the changed production volume is expected to be maintained. If an increased demand is expected to prevail for a short period only, it will not pay to invest in plant expansion, and "short-run cost" will determine output . . . "

[9] Cf. "Rayon Labor Productivity," *Rayon Organon*, Vol. XVII: 9, Sept. 1946, pp. 140 ff.

lower-denier yarns longer. In brief, the correction for denier is simply an allowance for the *length* of a pound of rayon. The Bureau of Labor Statistics, however, leaves output uncorrected. The following calculations provide examples of the conversion of actual to standard pounds:

| Denier | Quantity in Actual Pounds | Conversion Factor* | Quantity in Standard Pounds |
|--------|---------------------------|--------------------|-----------------------------|
| 75     | 100                       | 2.00               | 200                         |
| 100    | 100                       | 1.50               | 150                         |
| 150    | 100                       | 1.00               | 100                         |
| 200    | 100                       | 0.75               | 75                          |
| 300    | 100                       | 0.50               | 50                          |

* The conversion factor is standard denier/actual denier. Thus 100 pounds of 75-denier yarn becomes 100 × 150/75 = 200 pounds of corrected standard yarn.

For some purposes the correction of all pounds to standard pounds is useful. For example, in estimating "capacity output" a different result is obtained depending upon the denier which is assumed, so that correction may clarify matters. However, for purposes of estimating productivity, which is our main concern, it would appear to be less justified. As we shall indicate later in this chapter, the use of materials in the viscose solution and acid bath varies in proportion to the change in *pounds* of yarn regardless of denier. Furthermore, certain, though not all, of the operating-labor elements also increase proportionately with pounds of output. To deflate the output of above-standard denier would result in the recording of higher operating-labor and material costs *per unit* of (corrected) output than is warranted. A deterioration in the efficiency of certain inputs would be shown where no such deterioration occurred in fact.

Furthermore, large increases in denier (from 250 to 1000 for instance) should, strictly, be viewed as instances of technical change—dependent upon novel technology in some cases—designed to permit unit-cost reductions by means of the spreading of relatively fixed overhead costs over a large volume. These cost changes are obscured when high-denier output is deflated.[10]

For purposes of productivity analysis it appears to be more revealing to consider output *in terms of actual pounds* and to estimate unit costs of

[10] The estimates of the Bureau of Labor Statistics (which do not involve a corrected output series) show an increase in output per man-hour in the rayon industry between 1943 and 1945 of approximately 15 per cent. The Textile Economics Bureau, however (which does correct the output series) records a decline till 1944 and constancy in output per man-hour thereafter. During this period the proportion of higher-denier tire-cord rayon rose (*ibid.*, pp. 142–143.) Productivity (output per man-hour) is greater in the production of high-denier rayon than in that of low-denier rayon. By correcting the output for denier, this improvement in productivity is hidden.

production therewith; the denier can then be considered as an *explicit* variable with which to explain all or part of the changes in unit costs over time.

THE DETERMINATION OF COSTS PER POUND OF RAYON

The variables which are likely to exert an influence on the unit costs of production, and which will be considered now, are the proportion of capacity being operated, the size of the plant itself, the denier of rayon yarn, the spinning speed, the size of the packages of product handled at various stages during the production of yarn, the "properties" of the yarn, the technique of production, and, finally, the prices and the nature of inputs, including the capital equipment.

### The Rate of Plant Utilization

In the plants to be examined in this study, the item "total manufacturing cost" comprises "materials cost," "operating labor and direct items," "overhead" (which includes several maintenance items, power, superintendence, laboratory and other "plant burden"), and finally "general burden" (which covers those costs allocated to the plant, in part at least from outside, as for example from the central administrative offices, depreciation, insurance, taxes of various kinds, and research in the Company's laboratories). Our main interest will be centered on "factory cost," which includes all the preceding items with the exception of "general burden." Our study therefore relates to *all* labor and materials costs but will not attempt to analyze depreciation costs because of the difficulties of interpretation of this and related items.[11]

The proportion of overheads to total or net factory costs at the plants to be considered in this study fluctuates between 20 and 30 per cent. (If we consider the proportion of overhead, plus general burden, to total manufacturing costs, the result is a somewhat higher ratio of from 30 to 45 per cent.) The overhead items can be taken as a tolerably good index of that part of total factory costs that does not vary directly with changes in production. We have already mentioned that about 90 per cent of the overhead items involves labor; the remaining 10 per cent covers materials of various kinds. However, we have seen that even the operating-labor category includes men—approximately 20 per cent of the total—who should not be considered as belonging to a "variable" category, so that

---

[11] "Depreciation" and "amortization" are the important items excluded. However, spot checks show that our coverage extends to *at least* 80 per cent of all costs and in many years considerably more.

our estimate of the "fixed" element of net factory costs should be raised somewhat.

Curve *B* in Fig. 3.1, which is taken from Jesse W. Markham's study of the rayon industry,[12] portrays unit costs relative to the proportion of installed capacity operated. The curve is expressed in index form, that is, for percentages applying to the largest plant operated by the company

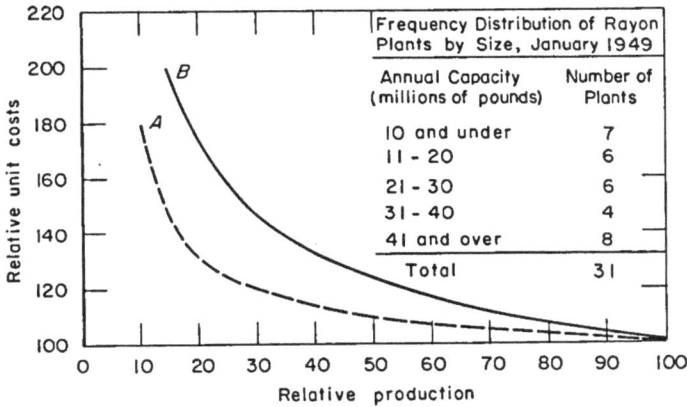

Fig. 3.1. Variation in Unit Cost (*A*) with Size of Plant and (*B*) with Per Cent of Installed Capacity Operated.

*Source:* Jesse W. Markham, *Competition in the Rayon Industry*, p. 150.

providing the information. The assumption is made that input prices remain constant; the plant is assumed unchanged but allowance is made "for the most economical adjustments of the variable factors." Markham points out that the period of adjustment has to be moderately long before the firm will release any direct labor, and even longer before any of the inputs falling into the overhead category will be released: hence, the curve representing the relation between unit costs and the proportion of

[12] Jesse W. Markham, *Competition in the Rayon Industry*, Harvard University Press, Cambridge, 1952, p. 150. Much of the discussion in this and the following section is drawn from Markham, pp. 148–157.

The curves represent *total* unit costs, whereas our concern is with *total* unit costs *minus* that part due to general burden. The changes in unit costs portrayed in Fig. 3.1 cannot therefore be used to provide a *precise* indication of the effect of variation in per cent of capacity operated (*B*) or in capacity itself (*A*) upon unit factory costs, but will serve as a reasonable approximation.

capacity operated will in the longer run be shallower and rise less steeply upon a reduction in output than it does in the short run.[13]

The shape of the curve is such that it rises at an increasing rate as output is cut back; furthermore, unit costs begin to rise immediately upon a reduction in output from 100 per cent utilization of installed "capacity" (defined presumably with reference to the number of nozzles or some similar criterion). The large proportion of fixed to total costs would explain the first phenomenon. The fact that a plant on the assumption of constant technique of production cannot vary the spinning speed to any significant extent[14] means that (assuming a constant denier) management will not consider producing beyond "capacity" defined in terms of installed nozzles, so that "capacity," in the present context, can be treated also as that output level beyond which it is not possible to produce, rather than as the minimum point on a U-shaped average-cost curve. This "relative inflexibility of operation" also helps explain the two features of the cost curve mentioned above.

### The Size of Plant

Curve *A* of Fig. 3.1 represents the relation between plant size (in terms of the proportion of the capacity of the largest plant operated by a multiplant company) and the lowest point on the total unit cost of each of the plants operated, relative to that of the largest. As the particular company providing the information operated only large and medium-sized plants, the estimate for smaller plants had to be made from past experience.

The behavior of this curve can also be explained, in part, by the fact that fixed costs represent a large proportion of total costs; some overheads remain constant and others do not increase in proportion to the increase in plant size. Furthermore, the indivisibility of certain plant installations is relevant: even the smaller plants need expensive facilities which increase

---

[13] It should be borne in mind that "continuity of operation" is of special importance for the production of rayon. Sudden reductions in output may result in exceptionally high unit costs as a result of excessive waste. For example, the viscose solution, once prepared, must be converted into yarn within a definite number of hours. During any interruption of the spinning operation, the viscose solution is allowed to flow to waste, for the alternative of holding back the flow is too expensive unless a complete shutdown is contemplated. In the latter case filter presses and pipe lines must be washed out. Thus, depending upon the period for which the reduction of output (in this example) is expected to last, there are a number of alternative reactions. Reductions in output which are expected to be short-lived, or unexpected reductions, are likely to be accompanied by very high unit costs; if the period of slackness is expected to be of long duration, unit costs may be reduced somewhat from these high levels. (The same problem may arise whenever a denier change occurs, or some minor maintenance operation is required on a spinning machine.)

[14] The curves are drawn on the assumption of constant technique; to change the spinning speed significantly, the technique must be changed.

only slightly upon an increase in scale. These installations include the boiler plant, the power-generating plant, the water-supply system, the spinning-bath recovery system, the fume stack, repair shops, offices, and other facilities. In addition, Markham refers to "the more effective utilization" of power plants, filter plants, recovery systems, laboratories, staff personnel, and other facilities that do not vary with plant size. Finally, the fact is brought out that there exists the possibility of introducing or expanding various auxiliary plant installations at high output levels, thereby permitting economies.

In brief, both the variation of unit costs with changes in the proportion of capacity operated and with changes in size of plant are heavily influenced by the abnormally large investment required by a rayon-manufacturing plant, and generally by the heavy burden of "fixed costs."

### The Denier

Denier is a direct measure of the coarseness of a yarn, higher denier reflecting heavier or coarser yarns. As defined by the trade journal of the rayon industry, the denier of a yarn "is its weight in grams for a length of 9,000 meters, e.g., 9,000 meters of 100 denier yarn weigh 100 grams. In terms of pounds and yards, one pound of 100 denier yarn is 44,645 yards long, one pound of 200 denier yarn is 22,322 yards or half as long, etc."[15] Yarn of a given *length* and *denier*, therefore, weighs half as much as yarn of the *same length* but twice the denier: yarn of a given *weight* and *denier* will be twice as long as yarn of the *same weight* but twice the denier.

The volume of production in terms of *pounds* of rayon can be increased, under certain circumstances, by raising the denier of the yarn despite an *unchanged nozzle capacity* and an *unchanged spinning speed*. To expand the volume of output given these conditions, it is necessary that more viscose solution be prepared; this, in turn, demands either the construction of increased capacity in the chemical building, or the more intensive utilization of given capacity (if initially sufficient equipment had been installed to allow for a range of variation in denier). Similarly, equipment for the treatment of the spinning-bath chemicals must either be available or especially installed. Unless the necessary equipment for the preparation of the viscose solution and the treatment of the acid-bath chemicals is at hand, output cannot be expanded under the assumed conditions of constant nozzle capacity and spinning speed.

---

[15]*Textile Organon*, Vol. XXIX: 1, Jan. 1958, p. 10.
This relationship is opposite to the commonly known *cotton* numbering system, where "count" decreases as the coarseness of the yarn increases.

Frequently, an increase in package size, made possible by the installation of larger buckets or bobbins, accompanies a major increase in denier. These changes will be treated in a separate section shortly. Moreover, heavy-denier yarns are less fragile and, in general, allow higher yields as a result. (For example, the spinnerette orifices tend to "plug" less frequently in the high-denier yarns.)

Assuming that it is possible to expand output by means of increased denier, certain economies will result by so doing. Fixed overhead items may be spread over a larger volume so that unit overhead costs fall. Unit costs of the fixed categories included in operating labor and maintenance labor will also be reduced. Although more men may be required in the spinning room upon an increase in volume due to higher denier, there is no need for a proportionate expansion.

As far as the unit costs of the various materials—pulp and chemicals, in particular—are concerned there will be no reduction with increases in denier and pounds produced, since these inputs must be increased in proportion to the denier increase.

Should the production of a higher-denier yarn be accompanied by the introduction of larger package size, then economies of operating labor will result from the fact that the yarn is handled in larger units by an unchanged labor force at various stages. Furthermore, insofar as waste is reduced and yields raised there exists an additional characteristic of high-denier yarn which tends to reduce operating-labor costs per unit of output.

Finally, it may be noted that power costs per unit of output tend to fall upon an increase in denier, since less water and heat are required at the purification stages.

A plant is normally designed to produce a variety of deniers within a limited range. The average denier will vary within this range upon a change in the pattern of demand. Variations in costs per unit resulting from the changes in denier within this range are "forced" upon the plant. In certain circumstances, however, customers may be indifferent to high- or low-denier yarns. The plant may then deliberately introduce "technical changes" which permit substantial increases in denier beyond the range initially envisaged.[16] In this way the cost reductions outlined in this chapter can be enjoyed.

[16] A number of changes are required in order to raise the denier. (a) The spinning bath must be modified to assure a satisfactory reaction by the viscose solution. (b) The viscosity of the spinning solution must be modified. (c) Changes in the number and size of the orifices in the nozzles, changes in gear wheels, and the adjustment of the speed of viscose delivery may be necessary. (d) Small changes in package formation are also necessary. (e) It is often essential to increase the bucket or bobbin size and to alter the bucket or bobbin motor to handle the larger units.

### The Spinning Speed

It is not possible to consider alterations in spinning speed as simply a mechanical matter; rather, the spinning speed is intimately linked with, and dependent upon, the degree of control of the process of production and the chemical reactions. Technical change in part takes the shape of the introduction of mechanisms, containers, and chemicals which permit increased spinning speeds.

As mentioned earlier, a given plant is constructed as a rule, to spin at a given spinning speed; that is, without relatively important adjustments in the equipment, and in a variety of features of the spinning bath it is scarcely possible to vary the output by increasing the spinning speed. However, if all the necessary conversions are carried out then certain economies may result. Assuming, as in the case of increased denier, that the necessary facilities are available in the chemical building and for the treatment of the acid bath, then the volume of output from a given number of spinning machines can be increased. As a result unit costs of the various fixed items of labor will fall.[17]

### The Size of Packaging Units

The size of the units in which the rayon yarn is treated at the various stages of production is significant for cost determination. The weight of the cake in bucket spinning, the length of the skein when skeining is involved, the size of the bobbins in bobbin spinning, and the size of the ultimate package are typical examples of such units. As the sizes of these collecting and packing devices increase, there is likely to be a corresponding decline in the operating labor required per unit of output for several reasons: in the first place, one man can handle a wide range of sizes at the various stages of production; furthermore, the yarn undergoes less handling, so that there are fewer breaks to mend and ends to string up. Material costs per unit are not likely to be affected unless the improvement in quality permits a reduction in the wastage involved.[18]

### The "Properties" of Rayon Yarn

There are various objective criteria comprising the "properties" of a rayon yarn. The most important of these criteria in the case of textile

[17] To increase the spinning speed, a number of changes must be made. (a) The spinning bath must be modified to assure adequate reaction. (b) Alterations in the "traverse mechanisms," which regulate the cake formation, are required. (c) The bucket or bobbin speeds (measured in revolutions per minute) must be increased. (d) Changes in the purification stages are necessary.

[18] Increasing the size of cakes, buckets, and bobbins involves changing the spinning-machine motors, stabilizers, traverse mechanisms, bobbin structures and chucks (devices for holding the bobbin at various stages), and the spinning bath itself. Moreover, adjustments at the purification stage are required.

rayon are the tenacity (at least until some minimum standard has been attained), the elongation, and the fineness and number of the filaments comprising the thread. *Tenacity*, or the tensile strength of yarn, is a measure of the capacity to resist breakage: if 120-denier rayon tears upon the exertion of a load weighing 180 grams, the tenacity is recorded as 1.5 grams per denier. Tensile strength is measured for yarn both in a wet and in a dry state. *Elongation* is a measure of the maximum elongation (in per cent) which a thread reaches the moment it breaks. The *size* (measured in deniers) of the individual filaments comprising a thread of yarn and the *number of filaments* in each thread are important determinants of the softness and other features of textile rayon. Assuming a standard thread of 150-denier rayon to contain 15 filaments, then each filament will be of 10-denier size; should the number of filaments for this same standard thread be increased to 150, for example, then each filament will be of 1-denier size. Strength, softness, pliability, covering power, and other features of a yarn are all increased by the trend towards finer filaments and multifilament threads. In addition to these properties, the *lack of sheen*, the *dyeability*, *textural effects*, and the like enter into the consumer's estimate of a yarn.

Some of the properties of rayon yarn are of direct relevance to costs of production. For example, the early rayon yarns were of very low tenacity and tended to break easily during the spinning and textile operations; the breaks had to be mended in time-consuming operations. The amount of waste and the proportion of inferior grade yarns would also be high, so that unit costs generally would be affected. Beyond a certain degree of tenacity, however, further increases tend to raise unit costs. The finer-filament and the multi-filament yarns are more costly to produce; greater control throughout the process is called for, so that spinning speeds are reduced, and again the relative proportion of inferior grades is high. Thus, in some cases, improved properties permit production at lower costs, and in others costs rise as improved rayon is produced.

The relation between the properties of a yarn and the cost of production may be *indirect*: the increase in output permitted by the increased marketability of improved yarn permits in some instances the spreading of heavy overhead costs and other relatively fixed items over a larger volume. Several of the properties enumerated above are of significance both from the viewpoint of the consumer and from that of the producer: improved tenacity, from very low levels, is desired by both. Other properties, such as the dyeability, the lack of sheen, and various novel effects, are of interest to the consumer in particular. Costs will not be reduced for example, by the introduction of an improved delustrant other than in the *indirect* manner suggested. It should also be borne in mind that an improved delustrant may be more expensive than the displaced delustrant.

In Fig. 3.2, the changes are shown that have occurred over time in the tenacity and the elongation of Du Pont's 150-denier textile rayon

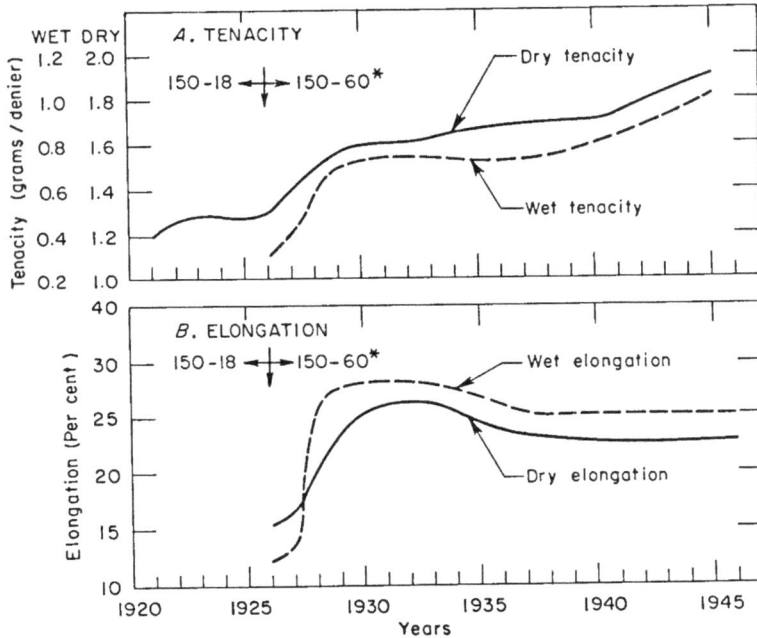

Fig. 3.2. Changes in Physical Properties of Du Pont 150-Denier Yarn, 1921–1946.
* 150-denier, 18-filament yarn until 1926; 150-denier, 60-filament yarn thereafter.

*Source: Du Pont Monograph*, Ch. 1, "Viscose Yarns," p. 130.

yarn.[19] Prior to 1926, the rayon yarn is assumed to be of 18-filament count, and after that date, a 60-filament count yarn is regarded as representative. (The drop in the index of elongation after 1932 is the result of a deliberate attempt to overcome certain problems arising in the textile treatment of the yarn as a result of high elongation.) In both diagrams, important improvements are seen to occur in the late 1920s.

*The Technique of Production*

The problem of the technique of production will not be discussed in any great detail in this section. This subject will be left for a subsequent

[19] These curves are taken from a monograph published by the Du Pont Corporation, Ch. 1, p. 130, referred to in this study as *Du Pont Monograph*.

chapter; the broad outlines, however, of the changes that have occurred and their likely effects on unit production costs will be considered.

The main difference between alternative methods of viscose-rayon production lies in the method of spinning and collecting the yarn. The bucket method has several distinct advantages over the bobbin method. In the first place, the necessary twisting of the filaments into the single thread of yarn occurs automatically as the filaments are collected by the bucket device; a separate stage of twisting is therefore avoided. As a result, there are economies of operating labor, particularly of throwers (twisters). Furthermore, bucket-spun rayon, particularly during the early years of the industry, was less subject to mechanical degradation. The bobbin technique, in the 1920s and early 1930s, however, had the advantage in the lower-denier yarns, where the bucket tended to treat the filaments too roughly. As a result, unit production costs of the finer-denier yarns were—as will be seen—above those of the higher-denier yarns, but would have been greater still if the bucket process had been used.

Efforts were made, particularly during the 1920s, to improve the physical properties of the rayon yarn. Our main concern in this study will be with process rather than product improvements, but since the heavy proportion of fixed to total costs increases the significance of *volume* of production, consideration must be made of improvements in properties too. What is considered by rayon manufacturers as a most significant development was the introduction in the late 1920s and early 1930s of improved methods of "stretch spinning," whereby tension is applied to the yarn at some stage during the spinning operation. The result of the new methods was strengthening of the yarn, and the improvement of the yarn both with respect to dyeability and elongation. Improvements relating to the quality of yarn include the introduction of delustered rayon by various methods in the late 1920s, and the growth of various novelty yarns.

As was seen earlier in this chapter, the original plant of the American Viscose Corporation at Marcus Hook, Pennsylvania, used a process which was relatively more efficient than that used by the first Du Pont plant at Old Hickory. In the mid 1920s, however, the Du Pont Company developed and installed the so-called "cake-to-cone" method for knitting yarn, and in the early 1930s a similar process was developed for weaving yarn. All the postspinning operations are carried out without reeling the yarn from the cake to skeins in the cake-to-cone process. As a result of this development important cost reductions were made possible, and greater tenacity, improved mechanical quality, and greater dyeing uniformity were allowed. This change was generally adopted by the industry as a whole. Other general developments in the attempt to reduce costs include the trend to larger packages and to higher spinning speeds, improvements in the quality and yield of chemical cellulose (the major ingredient) and in the bath constituents, improved recovery mechanisms permitting economies in the use of materials, and the trend toward *continuous*, rather than batch, methods of production.

A highly important development in the domestic rayon industry, the introduction of *tire-cord* rayon, will later be considered in detail. At this point it will suffice to point out that tire-cord rayon can be produced at lower unit costs compared with the traditional textile yarns. Tire-cord yarn can be conceived of as the ultimate result of the trend towards improved tenacity which has already been referred to.

### The Prices and the Quality of Inputs

Unit costs of production are, of course, directly affected by the movement of the prices of the inputs used. In this study, however, we shall be concerned with unit costs corrected for price changes in order to center attention upon productivity movements over time. Indexes of Average Hourly Wage Rates used for correction of labor items are given in Appendix C, Table C.6. An effort will be made, however, to leave uncorrected that part of a change in the price of an input which is caused by the fact that the supplier of the particular input has improved its quality. If, for example, the whole of an increase in the price of a particular input is corrected for, at a time when some part of the higher price results from the fact that the input is somehow "improved," it might appear that the rayon producer is more efficient than is really the case. Yet it is not always possible to make an estimate of the causes of an increase in the price of an input, and in fact this is quite impossible in the case of labor.

### SUMMARY

In this section the conclusions deriving from the present chapter will be briefly summarized. It may prove convenient to review the principal examples of "economies of large-scale production" that are relevent in rayon production and which have already been commented upon.[20]

---

[20] Professor Fritz Machlup in *The Economics of Sellers' Competition, op. cit.*, pp. 323 ff., presents nine possible reasons to explain why unit costs may be higher at small-scale output levels. The discussion here will be centered around these reasons. Since in this study changes in input prices are corrected for, no mention is made in the summary of the fact that higher prices must be paid for some materials if purchased in smaller quantities although this factor is present in the purchase of some inputs used in rayon manufacture. Examples of the situation where smaller machines cost more relatively, resulting in higher capacity costs per unit, can be found, but are not relevant to this study.

Of great importance in this respect is the large proportion, in total costs, of those costs that are relatively fixed with respect to output variation. In particular, overhead costs amount to between 20 and 30 per cent of net factory costs.[21] This feature is of significance both for the pattern of unit costs over time in a single plant and for interplant comparisons of costs. In the first place, larger output permits the spreading of fixed costs over more units; and, insofar as the overhead items in many instances do not increase in proportion to plant size, the large plants can enjoy economies not open to small plants. In addition, certain crews at various stages of the production process must be employed even if insufficiently used at small outputs. Increasing output permits unit costs of these employees to be lowered. Certain major plant facilities must be installed even in small plants, and the size of these installations does not increase proportionately with increases in the size of plants. Economies resulting from these features will be said to be due to "the plant-expansion effect."

Efficient methods and machines are possible at higher levels of output so that economies of labor are made possible: this aspect of economies of scale can be seen, for example, in the trend toward the rendering of certain stages of the production process by continuous method, in the use of high-speed buckets and bobbins and of recovery mechanisms, and also in the fact that certain auxiliary plant installations are economical only at high-output plants. Such changes will be referred to as "technical changes dependent upon volume." Specialization of labor was made possible in the early years of the industry as output expanded from very low levels: initially it was common practice for one man to be occupied with several operations, for example, in the chemical building, where one man might operate machines at different stages of the preparation of the solution. With increases in output, the specialization of operators became practical. However, this particular instance is unlikely to be of great importance after 1925, the period with which we will be mainly concerned.

Thus far, we have referred to a number of instances where larger volume has permitted "changes in technique." However, the converse relationship—technical changes designed to permit a higher volume—has also played a part in the development of the industry. Because of the high proportion of overhead cost, and generally the potential importance of scale economies, a large part of the effort made by research departments has been toward the more intensive utilization of given plant and equipment. Thus, the attempts to increase the spinning speed and the denier (in some instances) have been directed toward this end. Similarly, efforts

---

[21] The ratio of overhead and general burden to total manufacturing costs is, it will be recalled, even higher.

directed toward improved properties of rayon yarn have been, in part at least, influenced by the desire for high output.[22] We refer to developments of these kinds as "indirect technical changes."

The effect of the properties of the yarn and of improvements in quality upon costs is, we have argued, also *direct*: certain features such as tenacity are important, at least until the attainment of some minimum standard, for efficient production. Other improvements, however, may necessitate production at higher cost.

In brief, technical changes permitting improvements both in the properties of the yarn itself and in the technique of production have been directed toward the expansion of output in order to permit various economies to be enjoyed. In addition, certain "product improvements" have been of direct relevance to unit costs.

The increase in efficiency resulting from increased volume depends upon *the manner in which output is increased*. The economies which can be enjoyed by expanding output by means of an increase in denier, for example, will not be identical to those enjoyed by other means of output expansion. This latter factor is of particular relevance in the development of the high-denier, high-tenacity tire-cord yarn. It was because of the fact that very high deniers were possible that the heavy overhead costs could be spread over a sufficient output in terms of *pounds* that this fiber could compete with other fibers hitherto used in the manufacture of tire cord.

Thus, not only has technological change taken the form of an attempt to permit economies owing to higher volume to come into their own, but this trend has often involved changing the nature of the product.

Not all the improvements in process have played upon production costs by way of volume of output. Improvements in the effectiveness of the inputs used have played an important role in the trend toward lower material costs; these developments originate often at the raw material and equipment suppliers. Improved recovery techniques employed in order to economize in the use of materials have played an important role. The major improvements in techniques will be considered in detail in a subsequent chapter.

---

[22] Du Pont, for example, introduced many novel yarns during the depression years of the early 1930s in order to maintain output.

*Chapter Four*

# Intraplant Analysis of Unit Costs

Several well-known studies of the cost functions of companies and plants are to be found in the literature. The essential purpose of these studies is to derive empirical counterparts to the short-run, static cost function used in economic theory. For this reason the analyses are limited, for the most part, to materials covering relatively short periods of time, to ensure that technical change and changes in the "fixed equipment" of the establishment under observation will be at a minimum.[1]

In contrast, the purpose of the present analysis is to examine the effect upon unit costs of production of those variables excluded from the earlier investigations. In particular, our interest is centered on the effect of technical change upon the productive efficiency of the plant.

### THE ORGANIZATION AND THE NATURE OF THE UNIT COST DATA

We shall attempt in the case of each of the plants to be considered to account for the major changes in unit costs, that is, in costs per pound of

---

[1] Cf., for example, the analysis made by the United States Steel Corporation, under the supervision of Theodore Yntema, and submitted to the Temporary National Economic Committee, to be found in *Hearings Before the T.N.E.C.*, January 23, 24, and 25, 1940, 76th Congress, 3rd Session, Part 26, pp. 14,032–14,082; Joel Dean, "Statistical Determination of Costs, With Special Reference to Marginal Costs," reprinted in *The Journal of Business*, Vol. IX, Part 2, October 1936; and Joel Dean, "The Relation of Cost to Output for a Leather Belt Shop," National Bureau of Economic Research, *Technical Paper* 2, Chicago, 1941.

rayon.[2] Unit costs might be expected to vary with changes in the size of plant and the rate of plant utilization, even in the absence of technical change. We have seen that unit costs will also be influenced by changes in the denier of the yarn, the spinning speed, the size of various collecting and packaging containers, the nature of the inputs (including the capital equipment) used in the process, and technical changes of other kinds.[3] Random events will also play a part in the determination of the level of unit costs at any time. It would be desirable to distinguish, as far as possible, those changes in unit costs, and above all those reductions which are caused by technical change, from those which can be ascribed to the effect of variations in the volume of output (caused in turn by changes in "capacity" and the percentage of capacity utilized), and to random events.[4]

### Direct-Factory Costs and Overhead Costs

The organization of the cost data under consideration is, broadly speaking, along lines which correspond to the distinction between inputs which are "variable" and those which are "fixed" with respect to changes in the volume of production resulting from changes in capacity or the rate of utilization of capacity. Inputs falling within the category "direct-factory costs" are, with certain exceptions, variable inputs, whereas those falling in the category "overhead costs" are largely fixed. The most important single input in direct-factory costs is operating labor; this item includes direct superintendence (foremen and the like). It has been estimated that from 10 to 20 per cent of operating labor should be considered as "fixed" to allow for the supervisory personnel and for certain crews which remain unchanged in size and number despite wide variations in volume.[5] The essential materials required in the production of rayon fall within direct-factory costs and are variable inputs. Maintenance expenditures (on labor and materials) applied directly to the machinery and

[2] Throughout this chapter, we consider a "major" change in unit costs to be any change exceeding 2 per cent.

[3] See Chapter 3, "On the Determination of Unit Costs of Production in Viscose-Rayon Yarn Manufacture," pp. 36 ff. It was there argued that at least the large changes in denier and spinning speed, and changes in the size of the various collecting and packaging units, should strictly be viewed as instances of "technical change."

[4] Throughout this study, "capacity" is normally defined in terms of the number of nozzle positions, or the number of spinning machines multiplied by the number of nozzle positions per machine. In this section, however, we use the term "capacity" to refer to the number of spinning machines. For the most part there is a one-to-one relation, for usually nozzle positions are increased by installing additional spinning machines. As we shall see, however, to some extent it may be possible to add nozzle positions to existing machines; this possibility is limited.

[5] The nature of the labor input in rayon-manufacturing plants is discussed in greater detail in Chapter 3, pp. 32–34.

equipment, rather than to buildings and plant-overhead facilities, are also included in direct-factory costs; these items should be regarded as fixed.

By considering the essential materials and operating labor in isolation, we will be able to examine the influence of technical change upon groups of inputs, assured that the influence of changes in capacity and the rate of utilization of capacity will be at a minimum. Direct-maintenance costs and overheads will be considered separately.

### The Nature of Standard Costs

Actual unit costs are influenced by a large number of random events which tend to obscure the effects of technical change. Estimates are prepared by the plants to be examined of the "ideal" unit costs which, given existing levels of technology, can be achieved at the volume of output actually produced at any time. These calculations—referred to as "standard" calculations—are prepared monthly, and are altered upon the introduction of changes in technique which are designed to reduce unit costs, or which have the incidental effect of altering unit costs. We shall make use of standard rather than actual costs wherever possible, since the influence of technical change upon efficiency can be more clearly observed. Standard calculations are prepared for the direct-factory items only.[6]

The methods used in the calculation of standard unit costs, during the period with which we shall be concerned, should be borne in mind. In the case of operating labor a number of procedures are followed:

*Fixed Allowance per Month.* For that part of operating labor which we have termed "fixed," an allowance is made (in current dollars) each month. This allowance is retained regardless of the variations in volume which may occur during the period.

*Fixed Allowance per Spinning-Machine Day.* In the case of a large part of the labor operating in the spinning room, an estimate is made (in current dollars) of the labor required for each spinning-machine day. The allowance is then multiplied by the number of spinning-machine days actually in operation during the relevant month. The implication of this procedure is that for every level of technology there is a fixed complement of labor (of certain categories) to each spinning-machine day, no matter how many spinning-machine days are actually operated.

---

[6] Many reductions in *actual* unit costs presumably reflect a "groping" toward the *existing* "production function" rather than a change in the production function. Since standard calculations are made monthly, there will be little delay in allowing for the effect of changes in technique designed to reduce unit costs. Standard unit costs reflect rapidly the shifts in the production function rather than a tendency to grope towards the production function.

A reduction in the utilization of capacity from 100 to 50 per cent, for example, is achieved by halving the number of spinning-machine days operated, and, consequently, the allowance for the fixed labor complement will also be halved.

*Direct Estimate of Unit Costs.* For some elements of operating labor, an estimate is made directly of the minimum unit costs; the implication is that at any level of output, unit costs will be the same. The total allowance is derived by multiplying the estimated unit costs by actual output.

Estimates for other operating-labor items are calculated in similar fashion to the second and third categories just outlined. The total allowances are summed and divided by actual output to obtain standard unit costs.

In brief, variations in output due to changes in capacity, or the proportion of capacity operated, are assumed to be accompanied by proportional changes in the allowances made for operating labor, with the exception of that part which is based upon a fixed allowance per month. As mentioned earlier, this "fixed" element amounts to no more than 20 per cent of total operating labor. Standard operating-labor costs *per unit of output* will therefore be little affected, for the most part, by changes in volume due to plant expansion or changes in the rate of plant utilization. However, we shall not neglect the fact that a strictly "indivisible" portion of operating labor is recognized in the preparation of standard calculations, so that the potential influence of volume on unit operating-labor costs cannot be entirely neglected.

Standard estimates in the case of materials are based upon a calculation of the minimum requirements per pound of rayon. Standard calculations for maintenance items cannot be made with the same degree of accuracy as those for materials and operating labor. The standard allowances are based upon past experience at the plant with adjustments for some of the inefficiencies due to random events actually experienced. Decisions may be made at certain times to accelerate or postpone the maintenance expenditures, and such decisions may be reflected in the standard calculation. As a rule the maintenance standards are based upon a fixed allowance per working day, regardless of the poundage produced.

The discussion thus far has been limited to the influence upon standard unit costs of variations in volume which are the consequence of variations in plant utilization or in the size of plant. But volume may change with a variation in denier and in spinning speed. In the latter instances a higher volume is obtained from the same number of spinning machines. That part of the allowance for operating labor which is based upon a fixed complement per spinning-machine day will remain unchanged upon an increase in pounds produced by means of a higher denier or a higher spinning speed. The proportion of operating labor which must be considered "fixed" rises.[7] The denier and the spinning speed are taken into account in estimating standard allowances. It is necessary, therefore, to bear in mind at all times the fact that unit costs may differ upon a given change in pounds produced, depending upon the manner in which the change is brought about.

The size of various collecting and packaging containers is also taken into consideration in preparing the standard estimates.

The unit costs with which we shall be concerned have been corrected for changes in input prices in order that productivity movements should be accurately reflected.[8] In the case of each plant, we shall attempt to account first for the changes in standard unit costs and second for the changes in unit overhead costs.

### MAJOR AND MINOR TECHNICAL CHANGES

In the following sections, we shall attempt to classify the various technical changes introduced over time as "major" and "minor." The criteria used in establishing the categories *do not relate to the effect on unit costs of the technical changes, or to the investment expenditures*, if any, required to introduce the techniques into the plants. A technical change will be regarded as "major" if its development was considered "difficult" to accomplish by men "skilled in the pertinent arts" *prior* to the successful development. A "minor" technical change will be one which was considered simple to accomplish.[9]

---

[7] The conditions which must be satisfied for an increase in denier or spinning speed to increase volume are discussed in Chapter 3. In the case of textile-yarn plants approximately 25 per cent of total operating-labor costs should be considered as fixed upon an increase in volume by means of denier, spinning speed or added nozzles per machine; in the case of tire-cord plants up to 40 per cent may be fixed.

[8] Standard calculations are made monthly and usually are in current dollars. Even if *expected* input prices are taken into account there is little danger of serious distortion arising from the fact that our further correction after the event would involve a "double" correction for input-price changes. The input-price change from month to month is unlikely to be great. The procedures followed in our correction of unit cost data are discussed in Appendix A.

[9] S. C. Gilfillan has argued that patents should be granted to those technological developments which are judged "difficult," "just prior to the inventor's achievement of his most solvent idea," and which would not have been accomplished without the expected reward of a patent. See S. C. Gilfillan, "The Root of Patents, or Squaring Patents by Their Roots," *Journal of the Patent Office Society*, Vol. XXXI, Aug. 1949, pp. 611–623. Our interest here, however, is not with the required conditions for patentability of a technological change.

The distinction between major and minor will be dependent upon the judgment of individuals recalling, *after the event*, their own opinion and that of other research workers at some earlier date. The time, effort, and expense involved in developing the necessary technology are, presumably, taken into account in establishing whether a technical change is to be considered major or minor.

A major technical change may, in fact, have a small effect on unit costs and may be inexpensive to introduce into the plant, whereas a minor technical change may have extensive effects on unit costs and be expensive to introduce. Moreover, it is not necessary that the major technical changes be based on patented or indeed on patentable technology. The extent to which investment in plant and equipment was required is discussed in Chapter 6, and whether or not each change was patented is considered in Chapter 7.

In most cases it will be possible to describe precisely the major changes which have been introduced over time. In some instances, minor changes can also be isolated and described. Often, however, whereas we might be able to state that minor changes were responsible for certain unit-cost reductions, it will not be possible to state with certainty which particular changes occurred. It is, therefore, convenient to illustrate typical instances of minor technical changes.

Examples of small technical changes introduced over time are the development of yarn finishes which eliminated the need for applying oil to the coning machines and, therefore, avoided a step in the process; the introduction of fork trucks and conveyers for handling cases and bales; the introduction of Teflon-coated barattes which permitted the dumping of the "xanthate charge" without the use of considerable labor; and the substitution of knit sleeves for woven cake wraps, which permitted more efficient production.

Increased spinning speed and denier, increased cake size, and the addition of nozzle positions to existing spinning machines will in some circumstances be considered major technical changes and in others minor, depending upon the degree of variation involved: an increase in cake size, for example, from 1.5 to 4.5 pounds involves considerable technological difficulties, whereas an increase to 2.0 pounds might be considered a minor technical change.

It should be borne in mind that minor improvements are in fact occurring *continuously*, so that even in those instances where a major technical change occurs, it is probable that minor changes are also taking place, even if they are not specified in the available records. Thus, any final estimate of the relative significance of minor changes is likely to be an understatement.

## Analysis of Unit Costs at Old Hickory

### A. STANDARD UNIT COSTS

From the beginning of operations at Old Hickory in 1925, rayon textile yarn has been produced by bucket rather than by bobbin spinning machines.[10]

*Original Processes*

In 1925–1926, 128 spinning machines, each with 100 nozzle positions, were installed at Old Hickory. The spinning speed was 46 yards per minute and the average denier was approximately 150. The filaments were twisted together by the insertion of three or four turns per inch as the yarn was packaged on the spinning machines. Weaving yarn was produced by a process characterized by the following features: cakes of yarn, of 6-inch diameter and weighing approximately one-quarter pound, were removed or "doffed" from the spinning machines, given a preliminary water-drip wash, dried rapidly, and reeled to skeins of one-quarter pound weight; the skeins were then passed to the wash and bleach area to be purified (desulphured, bleached, and finished) and dried in skein form; finally, after inspection, the yarn was either packed and shipped in skeins, or was wound to cones and then shipped.

In 1927–1928, a new process was introduced for the production of knitting yarn (the so-called "Type 1" process). The cakes of knitting yarn were spun and given a preliminary wash as in the original weaving process, but were then desulphured (with hot sodium carbonate solution), washed again, and dried in cake form before winding to cones (with $6\frac{1}{2}$ per cent winding oil). The yarn was not bleached and the cones were two or three pounds in weight. Unit costs were lower than in the case of yarn produced by the weaving process because reeling to skeins and the subsequent purification and drying of the yarn in skein form were avoided: the treatment of the yarn while still in cakes involved considerably less labor. The process could not be applied to weaving-yarn production since the shrinkage differential between the yarn collected on the inside, compared with the yarn collected on the outside of the cake, was too great. The dyeing spread was also too great for weaving purposes.

In 1928, rayon capacity was expanded by 52 spinning machines, each with 100 nozzle positions. The spinning speed in the expanded section was 100 yards per minute. Both knitting yarns, by the new process, and weaving yarns were produced.

---

[10] See Chapter 3, pp. 30–31 on the distinction between rayon production by bobbin and by bucket process.

*Variations in Standard Unit Costs:* (1) *Operating Labor*

Standard unit costs in the case of operating labor declined from 23.70 cents in 1929 to 4.58 cents in 1958 (Table 4.1). Standard calculations are not available after 1958, but actual unit costs—which in the case of operating labor are invariably *above* standard unit costs—fell to 3.81 cents in 1960. Using this latter figure as an estimate of the upper limit of the true standard unit cost in 1960, the average annual reduction between 1929 and 1960 amounted to 5.7 per cent.[11]

We now turn to the consideration of the changes in unit operating labor costs in particular years.

*1930–1931:* Unit costs declined by 29.1 per cent in 1930 (Table 4.2). In the same year the percentage of capacity operated *fell*[12] and, as a result, the volume of output declined from 15,695,000 to 11,810,000 pounds, despite a slight increase in average denier. Changes in volume cannot, therefore, account for the striking reduction in unit costs in 1930.

A variety of events occurred which contribute to an explanation of the cost reduction. In the first place the cakes were increased from one-quarter to one-half pound in weight, a change made possible by increasing the buckets from six to seven inches in diameter; the size of the skeins was also increased. In addition, the quality of the yarn was substantially improved by the introduction of stretching mechanisms in the spinning bath, which increased the tenacity of the filaments and, therefore, permitted production with fewer breakages. Moreover, operators were better trained in the early years of the 1930s than had been the case previously. Finally, there took place extensive improvements in the methods used for process and quality control. The processes had hitherto been characterized by a high proportion of wasted production as a result of crude methods of process and quality control. The sharp reduction in unit costs occurring in 1930 and the further small decline in 1931, amounting in total to 7.50 cents, can be viewed as the consequence of the cumulative effect of a number of small improvements (both organizational and technological) rather than the effect of any single, major technical change.

*1932–1936:* Unit operating-labor costs fell by 8.8 per cent in 1934 (following an increase of 6.4 per cent in the previous year), by 20.9 per cent in 1935, and by a further 13.2 per cent in 1936.

The volume of production rose over the same period from 13,149,000

---

[11] All average annual rates are cumulative, not simple, averages.

[12] In Appendix C (Table C.1) are shown actual output, denier, and the proportion of capacity operated. These data are referred to throughout this chapter.

*Table 4.1    Standard Costs per Pound of Rayon, Corrected for Input-Price Changes, Old Hickory, 1929–1960 (in cents)*

| Year | Operating Labor | Viscose Solution | Acid Bath | Total Materials | Direct-Factory Costs Excl. Maintenance | Direct Maintenance | Total Direct-Factory Costs |
|------|------|------|------|------|------|------|------|
| (1) | (2) | (3) | (4) | (5) | (6) | (7) | (8) |
| 1929 | 23.70 | 9.87 | 1.87 | 11.74 | 35.44 | 5.86 | 41.30 |
| 1930 | 16.80 | 8.66 | 2.09 | 10.75 | 27.55 | 5.52 | 33.07 |
| 1931 | 16.20 | 8.36 | 2.01 | 10.37 | 26.57 | 4.61 | 31.18 |
| 1932 | 16.20 | 7.64 | 1.97 | 9.61 | 25.81 | 4.85 | 30.66 |
| 1933 | 17.24 | 7.82 | 2.02 | 9.84 | 27.08 | 5.17 | 32.25 |
| 1934 | 15.74 | 7.34 | 2.03 | 9.37 | 25.11 | 3.53 | 28.64 |
| 1935 | 12.46 | 7.60 | 2.04 | 9.64 | 22.10 | 3.22 | 25.32 |
| 1936 | 10.83 | 7.37 | 1.79 | 9.16 | 19.99 | 3.13 | 23.12 |
| 1937 | 8.60 | 7.26 | 1.83 | 9.09 | 17.69 | 2.43 | 20.12 |
| 1938 | 7.41 | 7.60 | 1.65 | 9.25 | 16.67 | 2.12 | 18.79 |
| 1939 | 7.00 | 7.32 | 1.37 | 8.69 | 15.69 | 1.95 | 17.64 |
| 1940 | 5.91 | 7.07 | 1.26 | 8.33 | 14.24 | 1.91 | 16.15 |
| 1941 | 5.59 | 7.09 | 1.27 | 8.36 | 13.95 | 1.51 | 15.46 |
| 1942 | 5.94 | 7.07 | 1.28 | 8.35 | 14.29 | 1.61 | 15.90 |
| 1943 | 5.92 | 7.05 | 1.05 | 8.10 | 14.02 | 1.34 | 15.36 |
| 1944 | 5.82 | 7.29 | 1.02 | 8.31 | 14.13 | 1.28 | 15.41 |
| 1945 | 5.59 | 7.15 | 1.04 | 8.19 | 13.78 | 1.39 | 15.17 |
| 1946 | 5.89 | 7.09 | 1.01 | 8.10 | 13.99 | 1.39 | 15.38 |
| 1947 | 5.67 | 7.20 | 1.00 | 8.20 | 13.87 | 1.05 | 14.92 |
| 1948 | 5.52 | 7.22 | .98 | 8.20 | 13.72 | .93 | 14.65 |
| 1949 | 5.44 | 7.18 | .98 | 8.16 | 13.60 | 1.01 | 14.61 |
| 1950 | 5.34 | 7.08 | .95 | 8.03 | 13.37 | .92 | 14.29 |
| 1951 | 5.15 | 6.91 | .96 | 7.87 | 13.02 | .96 | 13.98 |
| 1952 | 5.04 | 7.07 | .95 | 8.02 | 13.06 | 1.08 | 14.14 |
| 1953 | 4.95 | 7.04 | .95 | 7.99 | 12.94 | 1.14 | 14.08 |
| 1954 | 4.97 | 7.25 | .98 | 8.23 | 13.20 | 1.37 | 14.57 |
| 1955 | 4.89 | 7.03 | .98 | 8.01 | 12.90 | 1.53 | 14.43 |
| 1956 | 5.62 | 7.42 | **1.04** | 8.46 | 14.08 | 1.67 | 15.75 |
| 1957 | 5.45 | 7.63 | **1.02** | 8.65 | 14.10 | 1.70 | 15.80 |
| 1958 | 4.58 | na† | **na** | na | na | na | na |
| 1959 | 4.43* | na | **na** | na | na | na | na |
| 1960 | 3.81* | na | **na** | na | na | na | na |

\* Actual costs.
† *na*: not available.

Table 4.2 Percentage Changes in Standard Costs (Corrected), per Pound of Rayon, Old Hickory, 1929–1960

| Year | Operating Labor | Viscose Solution | Acid Bath | Total Materials | Direct-Factory Costs Excl. Maintenance | Direct Maintenance | Total Direct-Factory Costs |
|------|------|------|------|------|------|------|------|
| (1) | (2) | (3) | (4) | (5) | (6) | (7) | (8) |
| 1930 | −29.1 | −12.3 | +11.8 | −8.5 | −22.3 | − 5.8 | −19.9 |
| 1931 | − 3.6 | − 3.5 | − 3.8 | −3.5 | − 3.6 | −16.5 | − 5.7 |
| 1932 | 0 | − 8.6 | − 2.0 | −7.3 | − 2.9 | + 5.2 | − 1.7 |
| 1933 | + 6.4 | + 2.4 | + 2.5 | +2.4 | + 4.9 | + 6.6 | + 5.2 |
| 1934 | − 8.8 | − 6.1 | + 0.5 | −4.8 | − 7.3 | −31.7 | −11.2 |
| 1935 | −20.9 | + 3.4 | + 0.5 | +2.9 | −12.0 | − 8.8 | −11.6 |
| 1936 | −13.2 | − 3.0 | −12.3 | −5.0 | − 9.5 | − 2.8 | − 8.7 |
| 1937 | −20.6 | − 1.5 | + 2.2 | −0.8 | −11.5 | −22.4 | −13.0 |
| 1938 | −13.8 | + 4.7 | − 9.8 | +1.8 | − 5.8 | −12.8 | − 6.6 |
| 1939 | − 5.6 | 3.7 | −17.0 | −6.1 | − 5.9 | − 8.0 | − 6.1 |
| 1940 | −15.6 | − 3.4 | − 8.0 | −4.1 | − 9.3 | − 2.1 | − 8.5 |
| 1941 | − 5.5 | + 0.3 | + 0.8 | +0.4 | − 2.0 | −20.9 | − 4.3 |
| 1942 | + 6.2 | − 0.3 | + 0.8 | −0.1 | + 2.4 | + 6.6 | + 2.8 |
| 1943 | − 0.3 | − 0.3 | −18.0 | −3.0 | − 1.9 | −16.8 | − 3.4 |
| 1944 | − 1.6 | + 3.4 | − 2.9 | +2.6 | + 0.8 | − 4.5 | + 0.3 |
| 1945 | − 4.0 | − 1.9 | + 1.9 | −1.4 | − 2.5 | + 8.6 | − 1.7 |
| 1946 | + 5.4 | − 0.8 | − 2.9 | −1.1 | + 1.4 | 0 | + 1.4 |
| 1947 | − 3.8 | + 1.6 | − 1.0 | +1.2 | − 0.9 | −24.5 | − 3.1 |
| 1948 | − 2.6 | + 0.3 | − 2.0 | 0 | − 1.1 | −11.4 | − 1.8 |
| 1949 | − 1.4 | − 0.6 | 0 | −0.5 | − 0.9 | + 8.6 | − 0.3 |
| 1950 | − 1.8 | − 1.4 | − 3.1 | −1.6 | − 1.7 | − 8.9 | − 2.2 |
| 1951 | − 3.5 | − 2.4 | + 1.1 | −2.0 | − 2.6 | + 4.3 | − 2.2 |
| 1952 | − 2.1 | + 2.3 | − 1.1 | +1.9 | + 0.3 | +12.5 | + 1.1 |
| 1953 | − 1.7 | − 0.4 | 0 | −0.4 | − 0.9 | + 5.6 | − 0.4 |
| 1954 | + 0.3 | 3.0 | + 3.1 | +3.0 | + 2.0 | +20.2 | + 3.5 |
| 1955 | − 1.6 | 3.0 | 0 | −2.7 | − 2.2 | +11.7 | − 1.0 |
| 1956 | +14.9 | + 5.5 | + 6.1 | +5.6 | + 9.1 | + 9.2 | + 9.1 |
| 1957 | − 3.0 | + 2.8 | − 1.9 | +2.2 | + 0.1 | + 1.8 | + 0.3 |
| 1958 | −16.1 | na* | na | na | na | na | na |
| 1959 | − 3.3 | na | na | na | na | na | na |
| 1960 | −14.0 | na | na | na | na | na | na |

* na: not available.

pounds in 1932 to 25,464,000 pounds in 1936. This expansion resulted from an increase in the spinning speed on a number of machines from 46 to 100 yards per minute in 1933 and 1934 (an increase made possible in part by the replacement of the original belt-driven motor system by electric-spindle motor drives), the installation of 51 additional spinning machines raising the capacity from 18,000 to 23,100 nozzle positions in 1934, and the addition of extra nozzle positions on some of the machines during 1935 and 1936 raising the capacity to 23,778 nozzle positions.[13] The denier remained relatively constant during these years.

In 1932, a new process was introduced at Old Hickory for the production of weaving yarn. Small quantities of yarn were produced by this process—the so-called "Type 5" or "cake-to-cone" process—in the period 1932–1934; the replacement program was accomplished largely in 1935 and 1936. We have seen in the preceding section that knitting yarns had been produced as early as 1928 by a process involving cake purification and cake drying rather than skein purification and skein drying. The process introduced in 1932 permitted the treatment in cake form of *weaving* yarn. The cakes were doffed from the spinning machines, completely purified in cake form,[14] dried (while wrapped in rubber sleeves), and either skeined or coned for final shipment. Labor savings resulted from the fact that both the supplementary stage of washing prior to skeining—introduced to prevent operators from handling acid cakes—and the stage of reeling to skeins were abandoned, and also from the replacement of the costly procedures of skein purification and skein drying by treatment in cake form.[15]

We shall discuss the nature of the underlying technology in Chapter 7. At this point it should be noted that a major feature of the new process involved "compensation spinning," that is, variation of the spinning speed during the formation of the cake in order to limit the shrinkage differential between yarn on the inside of the cake and yarn on the outside, and also to limit the dyeing spread. This particular feature necessitated the reorganization of the stage of doffing. Hitherto, one side of each spinning machine was operated by a single worker who, starting at one end of the machine, would work his way from bucket to bucket, stopping the accumulation of the yarn on each in turn by hand brake, dumping the cakes from the buckets, replacing the buckets on the machine, and setting in motion the collection of new cakes; each cake was "doffed" or removed from the

---

[13] No more spinning machines were installed at Old Hickory (rayon plants), although periodically one or two nozzle positions were added to some machines.

[14] Unlike knitting yarn, the weaving yarn was bleached during purification.

[15] See Table 4.3 for the proportion of output dispatched by processes avoiding skeining.

machine at a different time and the formation of new cakes in the buckets occurred at different times on each spinning machine.[16] With the introduction of compensation spinning, it became necessary to organize the doffing of cakes in such a way that all the cakes were removed at the same time. This was achieved by the introduction of "gang doffing" in 1932; five men working on each side of the machine under the direction of a foreman were able to break the filament ends at the same time and doff the cakes at the same time. It has been estimated that whereas one worker could accomplish the doffing of one side of a machine in 45 minutes, a crew of five could accomplish the task in a total of 30 labor minutes. Moreover, waste was reduced by the change.[17] Gang doffing could have been applied prior to the new weaving-yarn process; however, the new process made the reorganization essential. Gang doffing was applied to machines producing knitting yarn too.

On the basis of a number of assumptions, to which we have already referred, concerning the proportion of total operating-labor costs which should be considered as "fixed" upon variations in volume (due in turn to changes in the rate of plant utilization, in the number of spinning machines, in the number of nozzles per machine, in denier, and in spinning speed), it is possible to arrive at estimates of the percentages of the net reduction of 5.37 cents which can be attributed to the various changes occurring during the period.[18] Increased volume accounted for approximately 2.57 cents or 48 per cent of the net reduction: more specifically, the addition of 51 spinning machines caused a decline of .72 cent, or 13 per cent of the net reduction; the addition of nozzles to each machine led to a decline of .12 cent, or 2 per cent; the increased spinning speed was responsible for 1.31 cents, or 24 per cent; and finally, an increase in the rate of capacity utilization of approximately 15 per cent, from a low level in 1932, accounted for a further reduction of .42 cent, or 8 per cent. The remaining 2.80 cents,

[16] More specifically, one man would stop the power to the motors in *groups* of four or five so that the cakes were doffed consecutively *within* each group, and the formation of new cakes commenced at different times from group to group on each spinning machine, as well as from machine to machine.

Unit operating-labor costs rose somewhat in 1933. This increase can be attributed to a variety of inefficiencies—recognized in the standard cost calculation—which accompanied the period of conversion from single-man doffing to gang doffing.

[17] The development depended partly upon the introduction of electrical means to stop groups of buckets quickly. The use of tools to dump the cakes out of the buckets also contributed to the possibility of reorganizing the stage. Apart from labor savings deriving from the rapid accomplishment of the required operations, wasted output declined; hitherto threads had built up on the feed wheels during the slow doffing operation and were removed as waste.

[18] Throughout the chapter the percentages of net cost reductions due to particular "causes" are intended to be rough approximations which provide a satisfactory order of magnitude.

or 52 per cent, was the result of the cake-to-cone process, and the related change in organization of the doffing stage.[19]

It may be noted that although volume increased throughout the period, total operating-labor costs *declined* in 1935–1936 from $3,494,000 (1934) to $2,758,000. The cake-to-cone process was in fact largely installed during these years. The new process is considered as a major direct technical change. The increases in spinning speed and in the number of nozzle positions per machine are regarded as minor indirect technical changes.

*1937:* Unit operating-labor costs declined by a further 20.6 per cent in 1937. The reduction resulted from a sharp increase in volume from 25,464,000 to 30,617,000 pounds and a slight *decline* in total operating-labor costs from $2,758,000 to $2,633,000. The expansion of output was largely the result of the introduction of 106 spinning machines of a new type—known as "Type 10" machines—which had 4 per cent more spinning nozzles and were capable of higher spinning speeds than the machines

---

[19] The "fixed" element in total operating-labor costs, it will be recalled, is approximately 20 per cent for changes in output due to larger "scale" (additional spinning machines) or to increases in the rate of capacity utilization, and approximately 25 per cent for changes in volume due to increased denier, spinning speed, or added nozzle positions per machine.

Total operating-labor costs amounted to $2,130,000 in 1932. Capacity increased by 28.3 per cent as a result of added spinning machines; assuming that 20 per cent of the total is fixed and that the remainder varies in proportion to output, then total costs would have increased to $2,612,000 if the only change to occur had been the expansion of plant, and output would have increased by the full 28.3 per cent from 13,149,000 to 16,870,000 pounds. Unit costs would have fallen to 15.48 cents, so that .72 cent (16.20 cents—as in 1932—*minus* 15.48 cents) can be ascribed to the expansion of plant.

The other calculations have been made in analogous fashion. The rate of plant utilization increased by 15 per cent during the period: if this had been the only change to occur, total costs would have amounted to $2,386,000, output to 15,121,000 pounds and unit costs would have been 15.78 cents, .42 cent below the level in 1932.

Added nozzles per machine increased capacity by 2.9 per cent; had this been the sole event, total costs would have amounted to $2,176,000, output to 13,530,000 pounds, and unit costs would have fallen to 16.08 cents, that is by .12 cent.

Output increased by 93.6 per cent between 1932 and 1936; increased nozzles by added machines and added nozzles per machine, and an increased rate of capacity utilization account for 46.2 of the percentage points; the remaining 47.4 percentage points were due to increased spinning speed. Assuming an increase in volume by 47.4 per cent as a result of increased spinning speed, total costs would have risen to $2,894,000, output to 19.4 million pounds, and unit costs would have fallen by 1.31 cents to 14.89 cents.

We have thus accounted for a total of 2.57 cents out of a net reduction amounting to 5.37 cents. The remaining 2.80 cents can be ascribed to the major technical change and the related reorganization of doffing.

It is convenient to consider the reduction by .42 cent which resulted from increased capacity utilization as part of the unit-cost reductions of the period 1929–1932. For in 1929, 100 per cent of capacity was in use, and unit costs would have fallen more than they in fact did in these early years, if the rate of utilization had remained high. The reductions of 1929–1932 will, therefore, be taken as amounting to 7.92 cents rather than 7.50 cents.

which they replaced: the bucket speed was increased and a lower degree of twist was acceptable on the yarn produced from these machines.[20] The Type 10 machines were able to produce yarn both for knitting purposes (by the Type 1 process) and for weaving purposes (by the Type 5 process); 45 per cent of the existing spinning machines were replaced during the conversion. Unit costs would tend to fall as the result of the spreading of a large proportion of "fixed" operating-labor costs over a greater volume and also because of various direct effects of the equipment. The technical change is not classified as "major."

However, we have noted that total costs declined in the case of operating labor. This phenomenon can be explained by the final abandonment in 1937 of the original weaving-yarn process—the skein-purification process— which still accounted for 4.6 per cent of total production in 1936 (Table 4.3, Col. 3).

Of the net reduction in 1937 of 2.23 cents, the replacement program was responsible for approximately .46 cent or 20 per cent by means of expanded volume, and for a further 1.28 cents, or 57 per cent, "directly." The final abandonment of the original weaving process accounted for the remaining decline of .49 cent. Unit operating-labor costs, therefore, declined by a total of 3.29 cents between 1932 and 1937 as a result of the introduction of the new weaving process.[21]

*1938–1940:* Unit operating-labor costs continued their decline in the period 1938–1940; the annual reductions during the three years amounted to 13.8, 5.6, and 15.6 per cent respectively. The reduction in 1938 occurred in spite of the fact that the rate of plant utilization fell from 82.3 to 69.3 per cent, and the volume of output from 30,617,000 to 24,504,000 pounds. Output increased again in 1939 to 31,216,000 pounds (exceeding slightly the level attained in 1937), and in 1940 to 32,379,000 pounds. Total operating-labor costs declined in greater proportion than the reduction in volume in 1938, from $2,633,000 to $1,816,000; in 1939 total costs amounted to $2,185,000 and in 1940 total costs were only $1,913,000. We cannot account for the reduction in unit cost of 1938 in terms of volume; moreover, it appears unlikely that the reductions in 1939 and

[20] Generally twist should be considered as a dependent variable: given a spinning speed of 2,000 inches per minute and a bucket speed of 8,000 revolutions per minute, twist will be 4 turns per inch.

[21] The decline in total costs with output constant represents a reduction in unit costs of .49 cent, from 10.83 to 10.34 cents. This reduction is a rough measure of the effect of the final abandonment of the original weaving process. Output increased by 20.2 per cent because of the equipment-replacement program. Assuming 25 per cent "fixed" operating labor, total costs would have increased from $2,758,000 to $3,176,000 in 1937 and unit costs would have declined to 10.37 cents, that is by .46 cent. In fact costs declined from 10.83 to 8.60 cents; the remaining reduction of 1.28 cents resulted from the *direct* effect on costs per unit of the new equipment.

*Table 4.3   Form of Dispatch of Rayon from Old Hickory: Proportion of Output, 1932–1960*

| Year | Skeins* | Cones from Skeins | (2) + (3) | Cones from Cakes† | Cakes‡ |
|------|---------|-------------------|-----------|-------------------|--------|
| (1)  | (2)     | (3)               | (4)       | (5)               | (6)    |
| 1932 | 44.8    | 14.3              | 59.1      | 37.8              |        |
| 1933 | 45.6    | 25.4              | 71.0      | 27.6              |        |
| 1934 | 45.6    | 19.8              | 65.4      | 33.2              | 0.1    |
| 1935 | 34.8    | 15.1              | 49.9      | 45.8              | 2.0    |
|      |         |                   |           |                   |        |
| 1936 | 29.7    | 4.6               | 34.3      | 60.3              | 3.1    |
| 1937 | 27.0    |                   | 27.0      | 68.8              | 3.1    |
| 1938 | 21.6    |                   | 21.6      | 75.9              | 2.5    |
| 1939 | 14.7    |                   | 14.7      | 83.8              | 1.5    |
| 1940 | 9.0     |                   | 9.0       | 89.5              | 1.5    |
|      |         |                   |           |                   |        |
| 1941 | 9.8     |                   | 9.8       | 88.3              | 1.9    |
| 1942 | 14.8    |                   | 14.8      | 85.1              | 0      |
| 1943 | 13.7    |                   | 13.7      | 85.0              | 1.3    |
| 1944 | 13.7    |                   | 13.7      | 84.6              | 1.7    |
| 1945 | 10.4    |                   | 10.4      | 83.0              | 6.0    |
|      |         |                   |           |                   |        |
| 1946 | 8.6     |                   | 8.6       | 81.0              | 10.4   |
| 1947 | 6.8     |                   | 6.8       | 83.3              | 9.9    |
| 1948 | 6.5     |                   | 6.5       | 84.2              | 9.3    |
| 1949 | 5.6     |                   | 5.6       | 85.0              | 9.4    |
| 1950 | 5.1     |                   | 5.1       | 86.0              | 8.9    |
|      |         |                   |           |                   |        |
| 1951 | 4.8     |                   | 4.8       | 89.5              | 5.7    |
| 1952 | 6.0     |                   | 6.0       | 86.6              | 7.4    |
| 1953 | 7.8     |                   | 7.8       | 74.6              | 17.6   |
| 1954 | 5.1     |                   | 5.1       | 74.9              | 20.0   |
| 1955 | 4.1     |                   | 4.1       | 70.2              | 25.7   |
|      |         |                   |           |                   |        |
| 1956 | 4.2     |                   | 4.2       | 68.8              | 27.0   |
| 1957 | 2.9     |                   | 2.9       | 52.5              | 39.6   |
| 1958 |         |                   |           | 63.8              | 36.2   |
| 1959 |         |                   |           | 69.3              | 30.7   |
| 1960 |         |                   |           | 65.5              | 34.5   |

* It is possible that some portion of yarn dispatched as skeins is in fact produced by the "cake-to-cone" process and then transferred to skeins.
† 1943–1949, this heading should read "Cones, Spools, Caps, etc.," and after 1950, "Cones, Tubes, etc."
‡ "Cakes and Beams" after 1950.

*Source:* Du Pont Cost Sheets.

1940 can be explained by larger volume, since total costs fell considerably below the 1937 level in these years, whereas output increased by a very small percentage margin compared with 1937. Specifically, in 1940 total operating-labor costs were 27.4 per cent below total costs in 1937, whereas output was 5.7 per cent higher.

There are a number of features common to the entire period 1938–1940 which help explain the cost reductions. Although cake-purification processes had been installed throughout almost the entire location by 1936, a relatively large percentage of the yarn was still reeled to skeins rather than transferred to cones *for final shipment*. The proportion of output dispatched as cones produced from purified cakes rose from 68.8 per cent in 1937 to 89.5 per cent in 1940 (Table 4.3, Col. 5). The proportion reeled to skeins declined from 27.0 to 9.0 per cent during this period (Col. 2). Although the processes for the alternative forms of dispatch are identical except for the final stages, unit costs are a little lower in the case of dispatch in cone form. Part of the unit cost reduction during the period 1938–1940 can, therefore, be ascribed to the growing proportion of yarn dispatched as cones. The speed of this development depended entirely upon the requirements of the converters and not upon the rayon producer.

During the period 1938–1940 there occurred considerable progress in the reduction of waste as a consequence of a variety of small improvements. A number of improvements were introduced in the shipping area in particular. Labor efficiency increased in the late 1930s as a result of better training.

In the final years of the 1930s, all remaining small-size cakes were replaced by cakes one pound in weight. This exerted an important effect on unit costs. At the same time a number of changes were introduced in the nature of the equipment used in the preparation of the viscose solution. Automatically controlled *shredding* churns reducing the time cycle from three hours to one hour and permitting the treatment of 600-pound batches of alkali cellulose were introduced; completely "water-jacketed" barattes of 900-gallon capacity which permitted operations at a reduced time cycle were introduced at the *xanthation* stage; and equipment at the *mixing* stage, capable of treating large batches of cellulose xanthate at a time cycle of three hours (compared with six or even eight hours in the case of the original French equipment), were installed. In the case of the new type of mixers, the viscose solution was discharged by compressed air or vacuum. The large-size shredders and barattes, in particular, would be of importance in the reduction of labor costs.[22]

[22] The stages prior to the spinning operation are described in Chapter 3, p. 29.

We cannot therefore account for the reductions occurring in 1938, 1939, and 1940, amounting to 2.69 cents, in terms of any major technical change. A variety of minor improvements were occurring at the same time which cumulatively exerted an important influence upon the efficiency of production.

In addition to the technical changes introduced in the late 1930s, unit costs declined because of more rigorous cost control by management during the depression year 1938; attempts were made to eliminate all excess labor. The effects of the effort remained even after 1938. Nevertheless, the larger part of the unit operating-labor cost reductions was due to the cumulative effect of the technical changes referred to above.

*1941:* A reduction in unit operating-labor costs of 5.5 per cent in 1941 can be explained partly in terms of a temporary increase in the average denier from 148.3 to 160.0. (In the following year, the average denier fell to 138.2 and unit costs rose once more.) Moreover, in 1941 the bleaching step at the purification stage of the processes was abandoned because of wartime restrictions on the chemicals; the whiteness of the yarn fell somewhat as a result too.

During the war and immediate postwar period, unit operating-labor costs remained substantially unchanged. In 1948, units costs were 5.52 cents, whereas in 1941 they had been 5.59 cents. Unit costs were relatively stable in spite of an increase in volume from 34,977,000 pounds in 1941 to 46,056,000 pounds in 1948, which in turn was due largely to an increase in denier during the 1940s; the average denier rose from 149.4 in 1943 to 185.0 in 1948. The effect of increased denier on unit costs was, in the period under observation, partly outweighed by a number of exceptional events: in particular, "lower-quality" labor was employed, and many supervisors were transferred to essential wartime work so that textile-yarn production suffered. The net reduction of .39 cent during the period can be ascribed to *routine* increases in denier.

*1949–1953:* Unit operating-labor costs declined by small percentage amounts in 1949 and the early 1950s. The annual reductions in the period 1949 to 1953 were 1.4, 1.8, 3.5, 2.1, and 1.7 per cent, respectively.

The volume of production increased from 46,056,000 pounds in 1948 to 52,022,000 pounds in 1951. This expansion was, in part, the consequence of an increase in denier from 185.0 to 204.1. Moreover, the spinning speed on one-half of the spinning machines was increased in the years 1949 and 1950 from 100 to 140 yards per minute by the introduction of "tube spinning." Whereas the increase in denier is considered as purely a routine matter, "tube spinning" was a *major* indirect technical change.[23]

[23] The source of this, and the other technical changes mentioned in this chapter, will be discussed in greater detail in Chapter 7.

(In the same period one or two nozzle positions were added to each of the Type 10 spinning machines, as part of a broader bottleneck-reducing program.) As a result of the changes in denier and spinning speed, output increased substantially (until 1951) from an unchanged total number of spinning machines and their operating-labor complement, so that unit costs declined. Of a net reduction amounting to .37 cent, approximately .13 cent resulted from the higher denier, and .24 cent from the higher spinning speed permitted by tube spinning.[24]

In 1952 and 1953, unit operating-labor costs continued to fall despite a sharp reduction in the percentage of capacity operated in these years: the rate of capacity utilization fell from 98.4 to 77.8 per cent in 1952 and rose very slightly to 80.3 per cent in 1953. The volume of production declined from 52,022,000 to 47,860,000 pounds in 1952, although in the same year the average denier increased to 248.8 (from 204.1). In 1953, output fell somewhat upon a reduction in average denier which outweighed the small increase in percentage of capacity utilized.

A number of circumstances help account for the reduction in unit costs of 1952 and 1953. First, it should be noted that the element of wasted output is somewhat reduced in the production of high-denier—and therefore, coarser—textile yarns. Second, and of great importance, the size of the spinning package or cake was increased from 1.0 to approximately 1.8 pounds in the case of the heavier-denier production at Old Hickory: yarn of at least 300-denier accounted for 50 per cent of total production. Third, increasing quantities of yarn were sold to the crepe trade. The requirements for the cake drying of rayon for crepes are less rigorous than for the dispatch of regular knitting and weaving yarns. It has been estimated that simplified drying would permit a saving of one or two cents per pound.

The reduction in wasted output, the increase in the size of the spinning package and the increase in crepe production help account for the cost reductions after 1951. In 1953, the percentage of rayon dispatched in cake form increased substantially, from 7.4 to 17.6 per cent (Table 4.3, Col. 6). The avoidance of winding to cones after purification permitted a reduction in unit operating-labor costs. As a consequence of a change in the requirements of customers, it was possible to cut short the sequence of stages. It has been estimated that shipment as cakes would save approximately 5 cents per pound.

[24] The added nozzle positions would not have exerted any marked effect. Assuming that the increase in denier by 10.3 per cent had been the sole event, total operating-labor costs would have increased from $2,542,000 (1948) to $2,738,000 (1951) and output to 50,800,000 pounds; unit costs would have fallen from 5.52 cents to 5.39 cents. In fact unit costs declined to 5.15 cents and the further reduction of .24 cent can be explained by tube spinning.

In 1950, a change in the technique of production was introduced, although the intention was not to reduce unit costs at Old Hickory. A number of pounds were transferred to beams rather than to cones; the dispatch of yarn on beams permitted the converters to enjoy cost reductions: in particular, the converters had hitherto undertaken the stage of transferring yarn from cones to beams, and this stage could now be avoided.

*1956:* Unit operating-labor costs rose in 1956 by 14.9 per cent. This increase was largely because of a reduction in the rate of capacity utilization from 85.4 to 69.4 per cent, and a reduction in the average denier from 240.6 to 223.3 (with an attendant decrease in the average package size); volume fell from 46,715,000 to 33,822,000 pounds.[25]

*1957–1958:* Unit operating-labor costs declined in 1957 by 3.0 per cent and in 1958 by 16.1 per cent. Output continued to decline, but total operating-labor costs declined by a greater percentage amount. In these years a number of plants were closed and remaining production was consolidated at Plant I. A number of "fixed" crews could therefore be disbanded. The reduction of 1958, however, was also the consequence of significant technical changes introduced in the late 1950s.

*1958–1960:* We have seen that unit operating-labor costs fell by 16.1 per cent in 1958. After 1958 standard estimates are not available. An idea can be obtained of the behavior of the standard unit costs in 1959 and 1960 by consideration of the actual unit costs which are available. The true standard unit costs fell by *at least* 3.3 per cent in 1959, and by approximately 14 per cent in 1960.[26] Output during the period 1958–1960 declined from 28,706,000 to 19,962,000 pounds. The reductions in unit costs can be explained by a number of technical changes: mechanized-purification devices which were introduced in these years permitted a large reduction in unit labor requirements; continuous-steeping and continuous-shredding equipment replaced the original batch-operated equipment and labor costs fell further as a result; and in addition, larger barattes were introduced at the xanthation stage, a change which had some effect on unit costs. Dielectric drying—drying by electric means—was also

[25] After 1955 the category "operating labor" was broadened to include superintendence up to the "area supervisor" level; prior to 1955, only the salaries of direct foremen had been included in operating-labor costs.

[26] In all the years studied, actual unit costs, in the case of operating labor, have exceeded standard unit costs. We can assume, therefore, that this was the order in 1959 and 1960. Actual costs were 4.43 cents in 1959 and standard costs may have been lower; the reduction in standard unit costs this year was, therefore, at least 3.3 per cent. On the assumption that the percentage differential between the "true" standard unit cost and actual unit cost was the same in 1960 as in 1959, we use the percentage reduction—14.0 per cent—in actual unit costs in 1960 as our estimate of the reduction in standard unit costs.

introduced, but this change was not designed to reduce labor costs. It may be noted that the quality of the yarn was substantially increased by mechanized purification and dielectric drying.

*Summary, 1929–1960:* Of the reduction by 19.89 cents in unit operating-labor costs between 1929 and 1960, 12.09 cents (61 per cent) can be explained by minor direct technical change, 1.89 cents (9 per cent) by minor indirect technical change, 4.43 cents (22 per cent) by major direct technical change, and .24 cent (1 per cent) by a major indirect technical change. Plant expansion, that is, increased volume owing to the addition of spinning machines and complementary inputs, accounted for only .72 cent (4 per cent) of the net reduction. Reductions because of routine increases in denier amounted to .52 cent (3 per cent).[27]

Output tended to decline after 1951. If 1951 is chosen as the terminal date, then the net reduction in unit operating-labor costs will be 18.55 cents. Of this net reduction, minor direct technical change accounted for 11.89 cents (64 per cent), minor indirect technical change for 1.89 cents (10 per cent), major direct technical change for 3.29 cents (18 per cent), major indirect technical change for .24 cent (1 per cent), "plant expansion" for .72 cent (4 per cent), and routine increases in denier for .52 cent (3 per cent).

*Variations in Standard Unit Costs:* (2) *Viscose Solution*

The average annual rate of decline in the case of unit material costs as a whole, from 11.74 cents in 1929 to 8.65 cents in 1957 (Table 4.1), amounted to 1.1 per cent. In the present section we shall consider the viscose-solution costs, and in the next the acid-bath costs.

Cellulose (wood pulp or cotton linters) is the most important input in the viscose solution, accounting for approximately two-thirds of the total at any time; for most of the period of our study unit cellulose costs were between 4.00 and 4.50 cents per pound of rayon. The second most important input—caustic soda—amounted to approximately 1.75 cents per pound during our period, and carbon bisulphide, a third important ingredient, to approximately 1.10 cents.[28] Unit viscose-solution costs declined from 9.87 cents in 1929 to 7.63 cents in 1957.

The following major changes have occurred in unit viscose-solution costs (Table, 4.2):

*1930–1932:* Large reductions in unit viscose-solution costs occurred in the years 1930, 1931, and 1932, amounting to 12.3, 3.5, and 8.6 per cent,

---

[27] The .20 cent reduction, 1951–1953, is largely attributable to several minor direct technical changes. The remaining decline of 1.14 cents, 1953–1960, resulted largely from the major direct technical changes of the late 1950s.

[28] Certain minor materials are excluded from the discussion of viscose-solution costs and also from that of acid-bath costs.

respectively. These reductions were the result of reductions in the unit cellulose costs of 17.9, 8.9, and 14.9 per cent. These changes can be accounted for by the improvements in process control (referred to in our discussion of operating-labor costs) in the early 1930s. Moreover, there occurred an increase in the alpha-cellulose content of wood pulp and a corresponding increase in yield of approximately 1 per cent in the period 1930–1934.[29] The adoption of constant-index systems (means of controlling the viscosity of the solution), with a consequent reduction in viscose losses, and better filtration were also responsible for economies in the use of cellulose in the early 1930s.

*1934:* Unit viscose-solution costs declined by 6.1 per cent in 1934 after an increase of 2.4 per cent, as a consequence, largely, of a major reduction in caustic-soda requirements. Unit caustic-soda costs declined by 17.1 per cent following the introduction of caustic-soda–recovery equipment— known as "dializers"—and the use of waste caustic soda at the mixing stage.

*1940:* Unit viscose-solution costs fell by 3.4 per cent in 1940 upon a unit-cost reduction in the case of the carbon-bisulphide constituent of 5.1 per cent, and of cellulose by 3.9 per cent. (Unit carbon-bisulphide costs declined by a further 2.7 per cent in 1941.) Carbon-bisulphide– recovery equipment was introduced in the late 1930s and helps account for the reduction in the costs of the former input. Cellulose costs tended to decline upon the substitution of wood pulp for the more expensive cotton linters during the late 1930s; cotton linters had been completely displaced by 1939. Moreover the alpha-cellulose content was further increased and the yield rose by approximately 1 per cent.

*1951:* Unit viscose-solution costs fluctuated somewhat during the 1940s, and declined by 2.4 per cent in 1951 to 6.91 cents. Thereafter, unit costs tended to rise. The reduction of 1951 was due, in part, to further increases in the yield of cellulose by approximately 1.5 per cent, and to efforts to reduce the caustic-soda requirements per pound of cellulose.

*1956–1957:* Unit viscose-solution costs increased in 1956 and 1957. The increases resulted from the temporary substitution of cotton linters for wood pulp during these years: all cellulose was derived from wood pulp from 1939 until 1955; in 1956 wood pulp fell to 83 per cent of total cellulose and in 1957, to 61 per cent. In 1958, however, the wood pulp constituent rose again to 79 per cent and in 1959 to 100 per cent of the total.

*Summary, 1929–1957:* The reductions in unit viscose-solution costs during the period 1929–1957 were due to minor technical improvements,

---

[29] In Appendix B the nature of the cellulose input is discussed in greater detail; essentially the yield or productivity of one pound of cellulose depends, all things constant, upon the alpha-cellulose or "pure" element in the cellulose.

of which the most important were the use of improved cellulose and of improved recovery mechanisms. Improvements in process control also permitted reductions in waste, and higher yields.

*Variations in Standard Unit Costs:* (3) *Acid Bath*

The principal constituents of the acid bath are sulphuric acid, glucose, and zinc sulphate. Unit acid-bath costs declined from 1.87 cents in 1929 to 1.02 cents in 1957 (Table 4.1). We turn now to discuss particular changes during the period (Table 4.2).

*1936–1940:* Most of the decline in unit acid-bath costs occurred in the period 1936–1940. Table 4.4 summarizes the annual reductions in the unit

*Table 4.4 Annual Reductions in Unit Costs of Acid-Bath Constituents, and Total Acid Bath (Corrected), Old Hickory Rayon Operations, 1936–1940*

| | Sulphuric Acid | | Glucose | | Zinc Sulphate | | Total | |
|---|---|---|---|---|---|---|---|---|
| Year | Unit Costs (in cents) | Per cent Change | Unit Costs (in cents) | Per cent Change | Unit Costs (in cents) | Per cent Change | Unit Costs (in cents) | Per cent Change |
| 1935 | 1.05 | — | .83 | — | .16 | — | 2.04 | — |
| 1936 | .97 | −7.6 | .69 | −16.9 | .13 | −18.8 | 1.79 | −12.3 |
| 1937 | 1.01 | +4.1 | .69 | 0 | .13 | 0 | 1.83 | + 2.2 |
| 1938 | .96 | −5.0 | .57 | −17.4 | .12 | − 7.7 | 1.65 | − 9.8 |
| 1939 | .87 | −9.4 | .40 | −29.8 | .10 | −16.7 | 1.37 | −17.0 |
| 1940 | .84 | −3.5 | .34 | −15.0 | .08 | −20.0 | 1.26 | − 8.0 |

costs of production of each constituent of the acid bath and of the total acid bath. The behavior of the unit acid-bath costs during the years 1936 to 1940 can be explained in terms of the introduction of improved bath-recovery equipment. In the original French process installed at Du Pont plants in the 1920s, "evaporators" had been employed to remove water from the "spent bath" so that the acid could be used again. This procedure was restricted in effectiveness because of the accumulation of sodium sulphate in the bath after spinning. In the middle and late 1930s improved evaporation was supplemented by "crystallization"; crystallizers removed the sodium sulphate from the spent bath and, to some extent, also removed water. At the same time excelsior filters were replaced by coal filters. The effect of these changes was a considerable reduction in unit acid-bath costs. Moreover, during the same period a constant effort was exerted to prevent leaks and similar losses and thereby to cut zinc-sulphate costs in particular.

*1943:* A unit acid-bath cost reduction of 18.0 per cent in 1943 was the result largely of a 38.2 per cent reduction in the unit glucose cost constituent. This reduction resulted from minor modifications to the spinning equipment which tended to reduce crystallization and the need for glucose.

*1948–1950:* Unit acid-bath costs fell 2.0 per cent in 1948 and 3.1 per cent in 1950. These decreases were due to small reductions in the sulphuric-acid and glucose requirements per pound. These latter changes were in part the result of improvements in the wood pulps used in the process: the pulps were more soluable and, as a consequence, less caustic soda was required in the formation of the viscose solution; but bath is consumed to some extent in neutralizing the effect of caustic soda, so that reductions in the latter had the beneficial effect of permitting reductions in unit acid-bath costs. There were no further net reductions of importance after 1950.

*Summary, 1929–1957:* The entire reduction in unit acid-bath costs was due to minor technical changes, the most important of which were the improvements in recovery mechanisms and improvements in the quality of inputs.

*Variations in Standard Unit Costs:* (4) *Direct Maintenance*

Unit costs in the case of direct maintenance—which includes both labor and materials—declined from 5.86 cents in 1929 to 1.70 cents in 1957, or at an average annual rate of 4.3 per cent (Table 4.1).

Unit direct-maintenance costs tended to be significantly influenced by changing volume, and attained their lowest level in the late 1940s and early 1950s, when volume was relatively high. Unit costs increased somewhat thereafter, when volume tended to decline. It should also be borne in mind that maintenance expenditures, unlike expenditures relating to operating labor and materials, can in any year be "postponed" or "accelerated." Total maintenance costs can be assumed to remain unchanged upon increases in volume.

*1929–1936:* We have seen that capacity output at Old Hickory was increased in 1934 by the installation of 51 additional spinning machines; the number of nozzles increased by 28.3 per cent. Actual output increased from 15,695,000 to 25,464,000 pounds between 1929 and 1936 or by 62.2 per cent. The number of nozzle positions per machine was increased somewhat in 1935 and 1936, and the spinning speed was increased on a number of machines from 46 to 100 yards per minute in 1933–1934; as a consequence, the expansion in volume was significantly greater than the increase in spinning machines alone would have permitted. At the same time, *total* direct maintenance costs declined by 13.4 per cent from $920,000 to $797,000 between 1929 and 1936. It is probable that after the extensive remodeling incurred during the installation of the cake-to-cone process, somewhat less maintenance was required.

Unit direct-maintenance costs declined by 2.73 cents from 5.86 to 3.13 cents. Assuming the 1929 output level and the 1936 level of total direct-maintenance costs, we obtain an estimate for unit costs of 5.08 cents; this estimate reflects the level of unit costs if the only change had been the reduction in total costs. Of the remaining reduction—namely 1.95 cents—approximately one-half,[30] or 0.97 cent, can be attributed to simple expansion and one-half to the increase in spinning speed. The reduction from 5.86 to 5.08 cents, that is, of .78 cent, resulted largely from process simplification over time, and in particular from simplification due to the cake-to-cone process.

*1936–1940:* Output increased further from 25,464,000 to 32,379,000 pounds between 1936 and 1940, or by 27.1 per cent; total direct-maintenance costs, however, declined from $797,000, to $618,000, or by 22.5 per cent. The increase in volume was largely the consequence of the replacement program which occurred in 1937 and which permitted a higher volume from a given number of spinning machines.

We can ascribe the .51 cent of the unit-cost reduction from 3.13 to 1.91 cents to an expansion in volume due to the replacement program. The remaining reduction of .71 cent was due, probably, to simplifications of process which allowed reductions in total costs despite increased output; the cake-to-cone process was largely responsible for the simplifications.[31]

*1940–1951:* Total direct-maintenance costs declined throughout the 1940s and until 1951 from $618,000 to $499,000, or by 19.4 per cent; volume increased, however, from 32,379,000 to a maximum level of 52,022,000 pounds, or by 60.7 per cent. Unit direct-maintenance costs declined during the period from 1.91 to .96 cent: of this reduction, .37 cent can be explained by minor process simplification and the remaining .58 cent to routine increases in denier over time.[32]

---

[30] The number of nozzles increased by 28.3 per cent upon the addition of 51 spinning machines in 1934; output should have increased in proportion; in fact, output increased by 62.2 per cent, or at approximately twice the rate of expansion, as a result of increased spinning speed.

[31] Unit direct-maintenance costs declined by 1.22 cents in the period 1936–1940, from 3.13 to 1.91 cents. Had output remained unchanged but total costs declined, unit costs would have been 2.42 cents. Our estimate of the reduction in unit costs due to process simplification is 3.13 *minus* 2.42 or .71 cent; the remaining .51 cent resulted from the introduction of Type 10 machines.

[32] Unit costs declined from 1.91 to .96 cent between 1940 and 1951. Had output remained unchanged at 32,379,000 pounds and had total costs declined to the level attained in 1951 or $499,000, unit costs would have been 1.54 cents. Therefore, 1.91 *minus* 1.54 cents is our estimate of unit-cost reduction due to process simplification permitting reductions in total costs; the remaining reduction of .58 cent was due to the effect of increased volume, which in turn resulted in large part from higher denier. Most of the reductions occurred prior to the introduction of tube spinning in 1949–1951.

*Summary: 1929–1951:* Unit direct-maintenance costs tended to increase after 1951 as volume declined. We shall center our attention mainly upon the behavior of costs from 1929 until the "peak" year.

Of the reduction in unit direct-maintenance costs between 1929 and 1951—4.90 cents—approximately .37 cent (8 per cent) can be explained by minor process simplifications, an example of minor direct technical change; 1.48 cents (30 per cent) by minor indirect technical changes, especially increased spinning speed; 1.49 cents by simplifications in process owing to a major technical change (the cake-to-cone process); .97 cent (20 per cent) by "plant-expansion"; and finally .58 cent (12 per cent) by routine increases in denier.

### B. UNIT OVERHEAD COSTS

Even a small plant requires heavy investment in overhead facilities. Overhead costs—which include certain maintenance and superintendence expenditures, as well as costs relating to the power plant and the

*Table 4.5  Overhead Costs in Selected Years (Corrected), Old Hickory, 1929–1960*

| Year | Total Overheads (S000) | Per cent Change | Volume (000 lb) | Per cent Change | Unit Costs (in cents) | Per cent Change | Per cent Capacity Utilization | Denier |
|---|---|---|---|---|---|---|---|---|
| 1929 | 1,917 | — | 15,695 | — | 12.21 | — | 100.0 | 157.0 |
| 1940 | 1,874 | − 2.2 | 32,379 | +106.3 | 5.79 | −52.6 | 93.2 | 148.3 |
| 1951 | 1,857 | − 0.9 | 52,022 | + 60.7 | 3.57 | −38.3 | 98.4 | 204.1 |
| 1960 | 1,124 | −39.5 | 19,962 | − 61.6 | 5.63 | +57.7 | *n.a.* | 221.1 |

laboratory—remain relatively constant upon increases in volume.

The effect of an increased spinning speed or denier and the introduction of all-active spinning will tend to have an even greater effect upon unit overhead costs than upon unit "direct-factory" costs. Moreover, even if volume is increased by means of the installation of additional spinning machines, the overhead costs will not, normally, be increased in proportion.

In Table 4.5, total overhead costs, volume, unit overhead costs, denier, and the percentage of capacity utilized are shown for a number of years. Unit overhead costs declined at an average annual rate of 5.4 per cent during the period 1929–1951.

*1929–1940:* Unit overhead costs declined by 6.42 cents between 1929 and 1940; output more than doubled, whereas total overhead costs declined very slightly. Of the increase in volume, approximately one-third can be ascribed to the spinning machines installed in 1934, and the remaining two-thirds to the increases in spinning speed of 1934 and 1937 and to added nozzle positions on existing machines.[33] The unit-cost reduction can be ascribed to these two causes in simlar proportion, 2.14 cents to simple expansion of plant, and 4.28 cents to increased spinning speed and added nozzle positions; that is, to "minor indirect technical change."

*1940–1951:* Unit overhead costs declined by 2.22 cents between 1940 and 1951, again as the consequence of increased volume. Denier increased substantially during the period: correcting output in 1951 for the change in denier since 1940, we obtain an estimate for unit costs of 3.78 cents. Of the reduction in unit costs by 2.22 cents, .21 cent (3.78 *minus* 3.57, the level of unit costs in 1951) can be ascribed to a substantially increased denier, and the remaining 2.01 cents to increased spinning speed. The increased spinning speed is an instance of major indirect technical change (tube spinning), but the increase in denier was of a routine nature.

After 1951, unit overhead costs tended to increase as volume declined and total overhead costs declined but in lesser proportion. Unit costs would have increased even more steeply had denier remained unchanged throughout the period.

*Summary, 1929–1951:* Of the total reduction between 1929 and 1951 of 8.64 cents in the case of unit overhead costs, 2.14 cents (25 per cent) can be ascribed to the expansion in volume due to added spinning machines, 4.28 cents (50 per cent) to minor indirect technical change, 2.01 cents (23 per cent) to major indirect technical change, and .21 cent (2 per cent) to routine increases in denier.

### C. SUMMARY OF TOTAL UNIT COSTS

Table 4.6 contains a summary of the "causes" of the unit-cost reductions which we have already considered, for the period 1929–1951. Each row contains the unit-cost reductions relating to the relevant category—operating labor, materials, direct maintenance, and overheads—and classifies them according to "cause." The column headings allow for minor technical changes, both direct and indirect, major technical changes, direct and indirect, and simple duplication of plant as "causes" of the unit-cost reductions. The proportion of the total unit-cost reduction for each group of inputs attributable to each "cause" is given in parentheses. Thus, as we have already noted in our discussion of operating-labor costs, 64 per cent of the total reduction in unit operating-labor costs was due to minor technical changes acting directly on unit costs, 10 per cent to minor

[33] No more than 28.3 per cent of the increased volume can be ascribed to the additional spinning machines (see Note 19 in the present chapter). But output approximately doubled during the period 1929–1940. As a rough estimate we ascribe one-third of the increased volume to the expansion of plant and the remainder to increased nozzles per existing machine and to increased spinning speed.

Table 4.6  Reductions in Corrected Unit Costs, and Causes, Old Hickory Rayon Operations, 1929–1951

| (1)<br>Input Group | (2)<br>Reductions Due to<br>Minor Technical Change<br>(in cents)<br>Direct | (3)<br>Indirect | (4)<br>Reductions Due to<br>Major Technical Change<br>(in cents)<br>Direct | (5)<br>Indirect | (6)<br>Reductions<br>Due to<br>Plant Expansion<br>(in cents) | (7)<br>Reductions Due<br>to Routine<br>Increases in<br>Denier<br>(in cents) | (8)<br>Total<br>Unit-Cost<br>Reduction<br>(in cents) |
|---|---|---|---|---|---|---|---|
| 1. Operating Labor | 11.89 (64)* | 1.89 (10) | 3.29 (18) | .24 (1) | .72 (4) | .52 (3) | 18.55 |
| 2. Materials | 3.87 (100) | | | | | | 3.87 |
| 3. Direct Maintenance | .37 (8) | 1.48 (30) | 1.49 (30) | | .97 (20) | .58 (12) | 4.90 |
| 4. Direct-Factory Costs (1 + 2 + 3) | 16.13 (59) | 3.37 (12) | 4.78 (17) | .24 (1) | 1.69 (6) | 1.10 (4) | 27.32 |
| 5. Overheads | | 4.28 (50) | | 2.01 (23) | 2.14 (25) | .21 (2) | 8.64 |
| 6. Factory Costs (4 + 5) | 16.13 (45) | 7.65 (21) | 4.78 (13) | 2.25 (6) | 3.83 (11) | 1.31 (4) | 35.96 |

* Figures in parentheses show the percentage of the total unit-cost reduction relevant to each input group which resulted from the "cause" indicated in the column.

technical changes influencing unit costs *via* volume of production, 18 per cent to a major technical change—the introduction of the cake-to-cone process—acting directly upon unit costs, and 1 per cent to a major indirect technical change, namely tube spinning. Plant expansion and routine increases in denier accounted for 4 per cent and 3 per cent, respectively.

The entire reduction over time in the case of unit acid-bath and viscose-solution costs was due, as we have seen, to minor technical changes acting directly upon costs. Reductions in unit direct-maintenance costs amounting to 8 per cent were due to minor direct technical changes, 30 per cent to minor indirect technical changes, 30 per cent to major direct technical change, 20 per cent to simple expansion, and 12 per cent to routine increases in denier.

Considering total direct-factory costs per pound of rayon as a whole, we find that minor direct technical changes accounted for 59 per cent of the total reduction between 1929 and 1951, minor indirect technical changes for 12 per cent, the major direct technical change for a further 17 per cent, and the major indirect technical change for 1 per cent. Only 6 per cent of the unit-cost reduction was due to simple expansion of plant, and 4 per cent to routine increases in denier.

Simple expansion of plant played a relatively more important role in explaining the reductions in unit overhead costs, accounting for 25 per cent. A further 50 per cent can be explained by minor technical change acting indirectly upon unit costs *via* volume, 23 per cent by major indirect technical change, and 2 per cent by routine increases in denier.

Unit net factory costs—the sum of standard unit costs and unit overhead costs[34]—declined by 35.96 cents (or by 4.9 per cent annually on average between 1929 and 1951), from 53.51 to 17.55 cents. Of this reduction, 45 per cent was the consequence of minor direct technical change, 21 per cent was due to minor indirect technical change, 13 per cent resulted from a major direct technical change, and 6 per cent from a major indirect change. Simple expansion of plant (and complementary inputs) accounted for only 11 per cent of the reduction, and routine increases in denier for 4 per cent.

Our analysis suggests a number of important characteristics of the behavior of unit costs at the Old Hickory location. In the first place, technical change accounted for most of the unit-cost reduction between 1929 and 1951—namely 85 per cent—whereas plant expansion accounted for only 11 per cent. Second, technical change appears to have been directed, in many instances, at permitting a larger volume from given capacity and its labor complement; that is, 27 per cent of the total unit-cost

_____

[34] It should be borne in mind that the unit overhead costs are *actual, not standard,* costs.

reduction resulted from technical changes acting upon unit costs *via* volume. Third, the relative significance of "minor" technical changes is striking: 79 per cent—67 out of 85 percentage points—of the total unit-cost reduction explained by technical change represented the effect of "minor" technical change.

### ANALYSIS OF UNIT COSTS AT SPRUANCE PLANT I

#### A. STANDARD UNIT COSTS

In 1929, Spruance Plant I, the first of the Du Pont Company's rayon-manufacturing plants at Richmond, Virginia, was established. Standard cost calculations were not prepared at this plant before 1932.

#### Original Process

Spruance I was constructed to produce textile yarn—largely for knitting purposes and for crepes—by a small-bobbin process, involving the purification of yarn in skeins. Forty-four (Kohorn) spinning machines were installed, each with 100 nozzles. The "capacity" of the plant was, therefore, 4,400 installed nozzles; however, an "alternative-active" schedule was followed until 1932 so that each nozzle served two bobbin positions.

The plant was designed to produce a fine yarn of approximately 100 denier in size, at a spinning speed of 2,500 inches per minute. A cake one-quarter pound in weight was produced on six-inch bobbins.[35] The yarn, after spinning, was washed by a "centrifugal" method, dried, twisted, reeled to skeins of from 5,000 to 10,000 yards in length, desulphured, bleached, finished, dried, and inspected, and finally shipped from the plant in packages of ten pounds.[36]

A very large number of operations were accomplished by hand. Batch-type rather than continuous-type equipment was used at the steeping and shredding stages, for the mixing of the viscose solution (by belt-driven "French mixers"), at the ripening stage, and for the deaeration of the viscose (by vacuum tanks).

#### Variations in Standard Unit Costs; (1) Operating Labor

Unit operating-labor costs declined at an average annual rate of 5.6 per cent, from 26.32 cents in 1932 to 8.30 cents in 1952 when the plant was closed down (Table 4.7). If the period 1932–1950 is considered, then

---

[35] The cake size was increased in 1930–1931 to one-half pound on some machines.

[36] After skeining, the yarn in some instances would be transferred to cones for shipment.

*Table 4.7  Standard Costs per Pound of Rayon, Corrected for Input-Price Changes, Spruance Plant I, 1932–1952 (in cents)*

| Year | Operating Labor | Viscose Solution | Acid Bath | Total Materials | Direct-Factory Costs Excl. Maintenance | Direct Maintenance | Total Direct-Factory Costs |
|---|---|---|---|---|---|---|---|
| (1) | (2) | (3) | (4) | (5) | (6) | (7) | (8) |
| 1932 | 26.32 | 8.06 | 2.09 | 10.15 | 36.47 | 3.65 | 40.12 |
| 1933 | 23.55 | 7.97 | 2.07 | 10.04 | 33.59 | 3.40 | 36.99 |
| 1934 | 22.06 | 7.96 | 2.05 | 10.01 | 32.07 | 3.07 | 35.14 |
| 1935 | 22.15 | 7.97 | 1.72 | 9.69 | 31.84 | 3.06 | 34.90 |
| 1936 | 20.43 | 8.00 | 1.69 | 9.69 | 30.12 | 2.97 | 33.09 |
| 1937 | 16.91 | 7.97 | 1.68 | 9.65 | 25.56 | 2.79 | 29.35 |
| 1938 | 13.77 | 7.86 | 1.48 | 9.34 | 23.11 | 2.62 | 25.73 |
| 1939 | 10.64 | 7.76 | 1.18 | 8.94 | 19.58 | 2.22 | 21.80 |
| 1940 | 9.21 | 7.60 | 1.05 | 8.65 | 17.86 | 2.31 | 20.17 |
| 1941 | 9.12 | 7.76 | 0.97 | 8.73 | 17.85 | 1.40 | 19.25 |
| 1942 | 9.13 | 8.24 | 0.97 | 9.21 | 18.34 | 1.82 | 20.16 |
| 1943 | 9.78 | 7.59 | 1.03 | 8.62 | 18.40 | 1.76 | 20.40 |
| 1944 | 9.13 | 7.66 | 0.99 | 8.65 | 17.78 | 2.23 | 20.01 |
| 1945 | 8.72 | 7.58 | 0.99 | 8.57 | 17.29 | 2.03 | 19.32 |
| 1946 | 9.14 | 7.39 | 0.89 | 8.28 | 17.42 | 2.05 | 19.47 |
| 1947 | 9.02 | 7.24 | 0.88 | 8.12 | 17.14 | 1.66 | 18.80 |
| 1948 | 8.21 | 7.24 | 0.88 | 8.12 | 16.33 | 1.77 | 18.10 |
| 1949 | 7.66 | 7.23 | 0.87 | 8.10 | 15.76 | 1.72 | 17.48 |
| 1950 | 6.96 | 7.25 | 0.88 | 8.13 | 15.09 | 2.00 | 17.09 |
| 1951 | 7.29 | 7.27 | 0.85 | 8.12 | 15.41 | 1.51 | 16.92 |
| 1952 | 8.30 | 7.40 | 0.89 | 8.29 | 16.59 | 1.27 | 17.86 |

the reduction—from 26.32 cents to 6.96 cents—amounted to 7.1 per cent annually.

*1932–1935:* Unit operating-labor costs declined by 10.5 and 6.3 per cent, respectively, in 1933 and 1934 (Table 4.8). These reductions occurred as the result of an expansion in volume from 3,315,000 to 6,286,000 pounds,[37] or by 89.6 per cent during the two-year period 1933–1934 and an increase in total operating-labor costs of 59.0 per cent from $873,000 to $1,387,000. The increase in output resulted, in large part, from the introduction in 1933 of an all-active spinning schedule whereby one nozzle served one,

[37] Output, denier, and the proportion of capacity operated are shown in Appendix C (Table C.2).

*Table 4.8    Percentage Changes in Standard Costs (Corrected), per Pound of Rayon, Spruance Plant I, 1932–1952*

| Year | Operating Labor | Viscose Solution | Acid Bath | Total Materials | Direct-Factory Costs Excl. Maintenance | Direct Maintenance | Total Direct-Factory Costs |
|------|------|------|------|------|------|------|------|
| (1) | (2) | (3) | (4) | (5) | (6) | (7) | (8) |
| 1933 | −10.5 | −1.1 | − 1.0 | −1.1 | − 7.9 | − 6.9 | − 7.8 |
| 1934 | − 6.3 | 0 | − 1.0 | −0.7 | − 4.5 | − 9.8 | − 5.0 |
| 1935 | + 0.4 | 0 | −16.1 | −3.2 | − 0.7 | 0 | − 0.7 |
| 1936 | − 7.8 | +0.4 | − 1.7 | 0 | − 5.4 | − 3.0 | − 5.2 |
| 1937 | −17.2 | −0.4 | − 0.6 | −0.4 | −15.1 | − 6.1 | −11.3 |
| 1938 | −18.6 | −1.4 | −11.9 | −3.0 | − 9.6 | − 6.1 | −12.3 |
| 1939 | −22.7 | −1.3 | −20.3 | −4.3 | −15.3 | −15.3 | −15.3 |
| 1940 | −13.4 | −2.1 | −11.0 | −3.3 | − 8.8 | + 4.0 | − 7.5 |
| 1941 | − 1.0 | +2.1 | − 7.6 | +0.9 | 0 | −40.0 | − 4.6 |
| 1942 | + 0.1 | +6.2 | 0 | +5.5 | + 2.7 | +30.0 | + 4.7 |
| 1943 | + 7.1 | −7.9 | + 6.1 | −6.4 | + 0.3 | − 3.3 | + 1.2 |
| 1944 | − 6.6 | +0.9 | − 3.9 | +0.3 | − 3.4 | +27.0 | − 2.0 |
| 1945 | − 4.5 | −1.0 | 0 | −0.9 | − 2.8 | − 9.0 | − 3.5 |
| 1946 | + 4.8 | −2.5 | −10.0 | −3.4 | + 0.7 | + 1.0 | + 0.8 |
| 1947 | − 1.3 | −2.0 | − 1.1 | −1.9 | − 1.7 | −19.1 | − 3.5 |
| 1948 | − 9.0 | 0 | 0 | 0 | − 4.8 | + 6.6 | − 3.8 |
| 1949 | − 6.7 | 0 | 1.1 | −0.2 | − 3.5 | − 3.0 | − 3.5 |
| 1950 | − 9.1 | +0.3 | + 1.1 | +0.4 | − 4.3 | +16.3 | − 2.3 |
| 1951 | + 4.7 | +0.3 | − 3.4 | −0.1 | + 2.1 | −24.5 | − 1.0 |
| 1952 | +13.9 | +1.8 | + 4.7 | +2.0 | + 7.6 | −15.9 | + 5.5 |

instead of two, bobbins. As a consequence, output per spinning machine could be doubled; all nozzle positions were made use of in the new schedule so that the capacity of the plant rose from 4,400 to 8,800 *installed* nozzles, without a change in the number of spinning machines.[38] The labor crews allocated to each spinning machine would not be increased in proportion upon an increase in volume accomplished in this manner, so that total costs would not rise in proportion with output. It is important to bear in mind that the unit-cost reductions could not have been accomplished at a bobbin plant earlier since a number of unsolved technical

---

[38] The introduction of all-active spinning required, for example, the development of a wider bath trough, a new roller system in the acid bath, and new techniques for the accomplishment of the doffing operation and the restarting of the spinning machines after doffing.

problems prevented the introduction of all-active spinning prior to approximately 1933. The large expansion of 1933–1934 resulted, therefore, from technical improvement. The introduction of all-active spinning is regarded as an instance of minor (indirect) technical change.[39]

During the same two-year period "high-speed" throwing or twisting, was introduced. The speed at which the operation of twisting is accomplished is, in part, dependent upon the number of turns per inch (the twist) which must be introduced. Satisfactory yarn produced by the bobbin process required, prior to 1933, from five to seven turns per inch. As a consequence of improvements in the composition of the spinning bath, and also improvements in the traverse system (which permitted a better cake formation), it became possible to produce yarn of satisfactory quality with only four turns per inch; the throwing speed was thereby increased and a greater volume of work could be accomplished by given crews at the twisting stage.

The improvements in the formation of the cake in fact *improved the quality* of the yarn, so that fewer breakages occurred at the twisting stage; thus operating labor was also saved as an indirect consequence of the technical improvements.

The speed of spinning was increased during the same period on some of the spinning machines and further economies resulted.

Following the increase in capacity, new employees were added to the labor force and larger work assignments were allocated to each crew, as the standards of performance required were raised. Training programs reflected the increased requirements. Part of the unit-cost reduction which occurred in 1933 and 1934 can be ascribed to better-trained operators.

The denier of the yarn produced increased from 94.8 to 100.6 in 1933, and to 104.9 in 1934, and might have contributed to the unit-cost reductions. (However, in 1935 the average denier rose to 111.3 and there occurred a slight increase in unit operating-labor costs.)

It is not possible to distinguish the effect on unit operating-labor costs of the introduction of all-active spinning from that of increased spinning speed. However, it is certain that the former event was overwhelmingly of greater significance; we shall, therefore, attribute the entire increase in output during the period to all-active spinning. It is believed that serious distortion is not introduced by this procedure. Approximately 76.4 per cent, or 3.19 cents of the net reduction in unit operating-labor costs (4.17 cents) during the period 1932–1935 can be explained by the "indirect"

---

[39] However the introduction of all-active spinning, although classified here as a "minor" change, is in fact a "borderline" case.

effect on unit costs of all-active spinning.[40] A variety of minor direct technical changes, including improvements in the "quality" of labor, were responsible for the remaining reduction in unit costs of .98 cent.

*1935–1940:* The average annual reduction in unit operating-labor costs during the period 1935–1940 amounted to 16.1 per cent; the net reduction was from 22.15 (in 1935) to 9.21 cents (Table 4.9). The five annual reductions were 7.8, 17.2, 18.6, 22.7, and 13.4 per cent. The level of production

*Table 4.9   Changes in Unit Operating-labor Costs and Determinants (Corrected), Spruance Plant I, 1935–1940*

| Year | Average Denier | Per cent of Capacity Operated | Pounds Production (000) | | Total Operating-Labor Costs | | Unit Operating-Labor Costs | |
|---|---|---|---|---|---|---|---|---|
| | | | Volume | Per cent Changes | ($000) | Per cent Changes | (in cents) | Per cent Changes |
| 1935 | 111.3 | 99.3 | 6,476 | — | 1,434 | — | 22.15 | — |
| 1936 | 106.8 | 99.0 | 6,608 | + 2.0 | 1,350 | − 5.9 | 20.43 | − 7.8 |
| 1937 | 101.5 | 92.9 | 6,822 | + 3.2 | 1,154 | −16.5 | 16.91 | −17.2 |
| 1938 | 115.9 | 73.0 | 5,884 | −13.7 | 810 | −29.8 | 13.77 | −18.6 |
| 1939 | 105.9 | 92.0 | 7,475 | +27.0 | 795 | − 1.9 | 10.64 | −22.7 |
| 1940 | 98.8 | 99.5 | 7,994 | + 6.9 | 736 | − 7.5 | 9.21 | −13.4 |

in 1940 was 23.4 per cent *higher* than in 1935 (7,994,000 compared with 6,476,000 pounds) whereas total operating-labor costs were 48.7 per cent *lower* ($736,000 compared with $1,434,000).

Changes in average denier were not responsible for the unit-cost reductions for the most part; in only one year of the five, 1938, did average denier increase. In 1937, the rate of plant utilization declined from 99.0 to 92.9 per cent, and in 1938 to 73.0 per cent; in 1939 the rate increased again to 92.0 and in 1940 to 99.5 per cent. Unit costs in the case of operating labor continued to decline even during years of very sharp reduction in volume: in 1938, in particular, although output fell by 13.7 per cent, total operating-labor costs declined by 29.8 per cent. Had denier remained unchanged in 1938 at 101.5—the level attained in 1937— the volume of production would have fallen by 24.5 per cent to 5,153,000 pounds. In the other four years, unit costs declined despite *reductions* in denier: in 1940 the average denier amounted to 98.8 whereas in 1935 it has been 111.3

[40] Assuming that 25 per cent of operating labor remains constant upon an increase in volume due to the introduction of all-active spinning and that the remainder increases in proportion with volume—that is, by 95.4 per cent in this instance—total operating-labor costs would have increased from $873,000 to $1,498,000 and unit costs would have declined from 26.32 to 23.13 cents. The reduction of 3.19 cents can, therefore, be attributed to the effect of all-active spinning; the reduction amounts to 76.4 per cent of the net reduction during the period.

Table 4.9 summarizes the changes in denier, rate of plant utilization, volume, total operating-labor costs, and unit operating-labor costs during the period.

A variety of changes in technique occurred during the period which help account for the reductions in unit operating-labor costs. At the same time that research was in progress for the development of the cake-to-cone weaving-yarn process (which, as we have seen, was introduced at Old Hickory largely in 1935 and 1936), attempts were being made to perfect a similar process for installation in plants producing yarn by *bobbin* spinning machines. A new process was in fact developed—referred to as the Type 9 process—and a small amount of yarn was produced thereby in October 1935 at Spruance Plant I. As in the cake-to-cone (weaving-yarn) and the Type 1 (knitting-yarn) processes at Old Hickory, it became possible to transfer yarn to cones *without skeining:* the skeining stage, various operations undertaken hitherto in the "wash-and-bleach" area, and skein inspection were abandoned, and "drip washing" of cakes followed by coning was introduced. Coning was undertaken at Spruance Plant II but the relevant costs were charged to Spruance I. Some yarn was transferred from the cakes to skeins instead of to cones; and in the case of yarn sold to the crepe trade, the process was terminated after the cakes were purified and dried. (Yarn dispatched in cake form was referred to as "flat-wrap" production.) Whatever the form of the dispatch, labor savings were permitted by the abandonment of the supplementary stages of washing prior to skeining and of reeling to skeins, and by the replacement of the costly procedure of treatment in skein form by the less expensive treatment in cake form.[41] The introduction of the Type 9 process was for the most part accomplished during the five-year period 1936–1940.

In the late 1930s, a variety of "minor" technical changes were introduced: the six-inch bobbins were replaced by nine-inch bobbins; the half-pound cakes by one-pound cakes; and the 5,000 to 10,000 yard skeins by skeins of 22,000 yards. All three features would permit reductions in unit operating-labor costs. Moreover, the spinning speed was increased from 2,500 to 3,600 inches per minute on a number of machines as a result of increased bobbin speed; output per period of time from given spinning machines and their complementary crews was thereby increased and economies made possible. Simultaneously, a reduction in twist—in terms of turns per inch—was allowed by further minor improvements. In the same years, the first automatic skein-lacing equipment was introduced and was responsible

---

[41] Strictly speaking, the new process, producing at a *bobbin* plant yarn for *knitting* purposes and crepes, accomplished effects similar to those caused by the Type 1 process for *knitting* yarns produced by the *bucket* process.

for some unit-cost reduction in the case of labor involved in this particular operation.

Total production attained relatively high levels in 1939 and 1940 (Table 4.9); if capacity output at constant (100) denier is calculated for each year, we find that volume increased from 6,177,000 in 1934 to 8,131,000 pounds in 1940, or by 31.6 per cent; this increase in capacity can be explained largely by the increases in spinning speed and by the reduction in required twisting. As in 1933–1934, technical changes were responsible, therefore, for permitting higher volume from given equipment.

In the late 1930s, fast-working, large-size shredding churns, xanthators, and barattes were introduced at Spruance I. The time cycles required at various stages during the preparation of the viscose solution were reduced. Unit operating-labor costs declined since the size of the crews per machine was not increased.

It has been estimated that at least one-half of the unit operating-labor cost reduction of 12.94 cents, from 22.15 cents in 1935 to 9.21 cents in 1940, or at least 6.47 cents, can be attributed to the introduction of the Type 9 process, an example of a major direct technical change. Production increased between 1935 and 1940 largely because of the increase in spinning speed which we have noted earlier. Unit operating-labor costs would have declined by 1.08 cents to 21.09 cents between 1935 and 1940 as a result of the expanded volume alone: our estimate for the contribution of increased spinning speed to the net reduction during the period is, therefore, 1.08 cents. The remaining reduction of 5.39 cents would then be due to the minor *direct* technical changes which were described on p. 81.[42]

*1945–1946:* From 1940 until 1945, 1,600 nozzle positions (approximately 18 per cent of the total capacity) were allocated to the production of tire-cord yarn; unit operating-labor costs remained relatively constant until 1947, although there did occur a number of temporary changes during the war and immediate postwar period. In 1945, unit operating-labor costs declined by 4.5 per cent; in the same year, a relatively large percentage of yarn was dispatched in the form of heavy beams and this increase in package size helps to explain the cost reduction. In the following year, unit operating-labor costs increased again by 4.8 per cent upon the return to all-textile yarn production; the proportion of yarn dispatched as beams declined from 41 to 20 per cent and the denier declined from an

---

[42] Assuming that 25 per cent of the total operating-labor costs are fixed, total costs would have increased by 23.4 per cent, from $1,434,000 to $1,686,000, between 1935 and 1940 had the only change been the increase in volume, because of spinning speed. Unit costs would have declined by 1.08 cents to 21.09 cents. If half of the net reduction or 6.47 cents is explained by the major technical change, then 5.39 cents remain to be accounted for; the various minor direct technical changes that have been outlined in the text can explain these reductions.

average of 113.9 to 100.9. At 9.02 cents, unit operating-labor costs in 1947 were only 2.1 per cent below the level attained in 1940; the small decline can be explained as the result of continued process simplification.

*1948–1950:* Unit operating-labor costs continued to decline in the late 1940s: by 9.0 per cent in 1948, 6.7 per cent in 1949, and by 9.1 per cent in 1950. Denier increased from 89.0 to 98.6 in 1948, but was constant thereafter. Unit costs declined in 1949, despite a reduction in the rate of capacity utilization from 97.7 to 77.2 per cent.

Total operating-labor costs declined by 10.9 per cent from $744,000 in 1947 to $663,000 in 1950, whereas output increased by 15.3 per cent from 8,252,000 to 9,518,000 pounds. The net reduction in unit operating-labor costs of 2.06 cents cannot be explained in terms of any single major technical change; the decline resulted from minor technical changes permitting reductions in unit costs both "directly" and "indirectly" *via* volume. Of the net reduction of 2.06 cents, .31 cent can be attributed to minor indirect technical change, and 1.75 cents to minor direct technical change.[43] The reduction of .19 cent between 1940 and 1947 should be added to the 1.75 cents to obtain the total net reduction in unit operating-labor costs between 1940 and 1950 which was due to minor direct technical changes.

*1951–1952:* Unit operating-labor costs increased during the final two-year period of operations at Spruance Plant I. The rate of plant utilization declined from 99.9 to 87.0 per cent in 1951, and to 38.1 per cent in 1952. The level of output was maintained, however, by an increase in denier from 97.8 to 110.1 in 1951 and to 186.8 in 1952. If output is corrected for changes in denier, volume of production of constant (100)-denier yarn would have declined from 9,732,000 pounds in 1950 to 8,587,000 pounds in 1951, and to 3,541,000 pounds in 1952; in fact, however, actual output amounted to 9,454,000 pounds in 1951 and 6,615,000 in 1952.

The increase in denier was a "routine" response to the market demand for high-denier textile yarn. The upward trend in unit costs resulted from the relatively low level of production. The equipment at Spruance Plant I proved inadequate to meet the demands for high-quality yarn and the decision was made to abandon production at the plant. The plant was closed in April 1953, and the chemical building and coagulating bath facilities were reserved for use in other plants at the location.

---

[43] Assuming, once more, that the ratio of fixed to total labor—in the case of expansion of volume owing to minor indirect technical change—is 25 per cent, total operating-labor costs would have increased from $744,000 in 1947 to $829,000 in 1950 upon the increase in volume of 15.3 per cent; unit costs would have declined by .31 cent to 8.71 cents, leaving 1.75 cents to be accounted for by the minor direct technical changes.

*Summary, 1932–1950:* The net reduction in unit operating-labor costs during the eighteen-year period 1932–1950 amounted to 19.36 cents. We have seen that of this net reduction, 8.31 cents (43 per cent) resulted from minor direct technical change, 4.58 cents (23 per cent) from minor indirect technical change, and 6.47 cents (33 per cent) from major direct technical change. Minor technical changes account for approximately two-thirds of the entire cost reduction.

*Variations in Standard Unit Costs:* (2) *Viscose Solution*

The reduction in unit viscose-solution costs between 1932 and 1952 amounted to only 0.4 per cent annually on average; the cost reduction was from 8.06 to 7.40 cents (Table 4.7).

*1933–1936:* Although viscose-solution costs per pound were constant during the period 1933–1936, changes in unit costs in the case of various constituent inputs did occur: unit *cellulose* costs increased during the four-year period as a consequence of increases in the percentage of cotton linters to total cellulose; these unit-cost increases sufficed to balance reduction in the unit *caustic-soda* costs which resulted from the introduction of caustic-soda recovery mechanisms.

*1938–1940:* Relatively small reductions occurred in unit viscose-solution costs of 1.4 per cent in 1938, 1.3 per cent in 1939, and 2.1 per cent in 1940. The reduction of 1938 was in large part the consequence of a 5.0 per cent reduction in unit carbon-bisulphide costs, which in turn resulted from the introduction of recovery equipment; unit caustic-soda costs declined by 2.2 per cent in 1938. In 1939, unit cellulose costs declined by 1.6 per cent, and in 1940 by 2.9 per cent; these reductions were due to the introduction of better grades of wood pulp and to gradual increases in the yields of first-quality yarn obtained from the plant. A similar pattern of unit-cost behavior was encountered in our discussion of Old Hickory during the same period.

*1946–1947:* Unit viscose-solution costs declined by 2.5 per cent in 1946 and by 2.0 per cent in 1947, solely as a consequence of an increase in the proportion of wood pulp to total cellulose: wood pulp relative to total cellulose increased from 49 to 77 per cent in 1946, and to 100 per cent in 1947.

*1952:* Unit viscose-solution costs increased by 1.8 per cent in 1952 as a consequence of poorer yields during a period of low volume.

*Summary, 1932–1950:* The entire reduction in unit viscose-solution costs between 1932 and 1950 of .81 cent was due to minor direct technical changes; in particular, recovery mechanisms allowed reductions in the unit caustic-soda and carbon-bisulphide costs, and improved wood pulps permitted the substitution of wood pulps for the more expensive cotton linters.

### Variations in Standard Unit Costs: (3) Acid Bath

The reduction in unit acid-bath costs between 1932 and 1952, from 2.09 to 0.89 cent (Table 4.7), averaged 4.2 per cent annually.

1935: Unit acid-bath costs declined by 16.1 per cent in 1935 as a consequence of reductions in the requirements of all the major constituents: thus, unit glucose costs declined by 29.1 per cent (from .86 to .61 cent), unit zinc-sulphate costs declined by 28.6 per cent (from .21 to .16

Table 4.10  Annual Reduction in Unit Costs of Acid-Bath Constituents. and Total Acid Bath (Corrected), Spruance Plant I, 1938–1941

| | Sulphuric Acid | | Glucose | | Zinc Sulphate | | Total | |
|---|---|---|---|---|---|---|---|---|
| Year | Unit Costs (in cents) | Per cent Change | Unit Costs (in cents) | Per cent Change | Unit Costs (in cents) | Per cent Change | Unit Costs (in cents) | Per cent Change |
| 1937 | .95 | — | .58 | — | .15 | — | 1.68 | — |
| 1938 | .89 | −6.3 | .47 | −19.0 | .12 | −20.0 | 1.48 | −11.9 |
| 1939 | .93 | +4.5 | .13 | −72.3 | .12 | 0 | 1.18 | −20.3 |
| 1940 | .89 | −4.3 | .06 | −53.8 | .10 | −16.7 | 1.05 | −11.0 |
| 1941 | .82 | −7.9 | .08 | +33.8 | .07 | −30.0 | 0.97 | − 7.6 |

cent), and unit sulphuric-acid costs declined by 2.0 per cent (from .98 to .96 cent). Improvements in recovery mechanisms accounted for these changes.

1938–1941: Unit acid-bath costs declined by large percentage amounts in each year during the period 1938–1941, because of the more extensive use of improved bath-recovery equipment (crystallizers and evaporators) and the introduction of excelsior filtration as at Old Hickory.[44] Table 4.10 summarizes the main changes.

1946: Unit acid-bath costs declined by 10.0 per cent in 1946 as the result of a 75.0 per cent reduction in unit glucose costs from .12 to .03 cent. In the following year glucose was no longer used. The reduction in unit costs in the case of glucose was, in part, the result of the use of alternative means of controlling crystal formation; to this extent there would be little if any net cost reduction if all inputs are taken into consideration. In addition, however, the introduction of small improvements in the nature

[44] Improved filtration would actually be of greater significance in accounting for improved quality than for reduced costs.

of the equipment—such as sprays—permitted net reductions in unit costs.[45]

There occurred no further net changes of importance in the acid-bath requirements after 1946.

*Summary, 1932–1950:* The entire reduction in unit acid-bath costs of 1.21 cents between 1932 and 1950 was due to the introduction of improved bath-recovery equipment and means for the control of crystal formation, both instances of minor direct technical change.

*Variations in Standard Unit Costs:* (4) *Direct Maintenance*

The annual average reduction in unit direct-maintenance costs from 3.65 cents in 1932 to 2.00 cents in 1950 amounted to 3.3 per cent (Table 4.7).

*1932–1935:* Between 1932 and 1935, total direct-maintenance costs increased by 65.0 per cent from $121,000 to $198,000; during the same four-year period, output increased from 3,315,000 to 6,476,000, or by 95.4 per cent. Unit costs declined by .59 cent from 3.65 to 3.06 cents. The increase in output was due mainly to the transition from alternative-active to all-active spinning; the reductions in unit costs by 6.9 per cent in 1933 and by 9.8 per cent in 1934 can be accounted for by the relatively large increase in output. (Also responsible for the higher output were the increases in spinning speed and in throwing speed, referred to earlier.)

*1935–1940:* Unit direct-maintenance costs declined further in the five-year period 1935–1940 by .75 cent; of particular significance was a reduction of 15.3 per cent in 1939. Production increased by 23.4 per cent from 6,476,000 pounds in 1935 to 7,994,000 pounds in 1940. Both increased spinning speed and the possibility of inserting fewer turns per inch into the yarn were responsible for a large part of the increased volume. Total direct-maintenance costs declined slightly, from $198,000 to $185,000.

*1940–1950:* Unit direct-maintenance costs tended to fluctuate throughout the 1940s, and in 1950 were 2.00 cents, .31 cent below the level attained in 1940. Total direct-maintenance costs increased by 2.7 per cent to $190,000 between 1940 and 1950, whereas output increased by 19.1 per cent to 9,518,000 pounds. The expansion, and the consequent reduction in unit costs, were due to minor changes in technique which permitted larger volume without an expansion of the plant itself.

*Summary, 1932–1950:* The introduction of all-active spinning explains

---

[45] We have seen that glucose requirements declined during the same period at Old Hickory although the chemical continued in use. Glucose is introduced to prevent the development of crystals. The centrifugal action of the bucket causes the crystals to develop on the bucket itself, and glucose cannot be dispensed with entirely. In bobbin plants, however, crystals tended to form around the edges of the bath and guides only; the introduction of water sprays sufficed to overcome the problem, and glucose could therefore be dispensed with.

.59 cent out of a net reduction of 1.65 cents in unit direct-maintenance costs between 1932 and 1950; and various means to permit the expansion of output from a given plant account for the remaining 1.06 cents. In brief, 36 per cent of the reduction can be explained by a striking minor indirect technical change, and the remaining 64 per cent by a variety of minor indirect technical changes.

### B. UNIT OVERHEAD COSTS

Unit overhead costs declined from 21.12 cents in 1932 to 5.65 cents in 1950 (Table 4.11). We will take 1950 as the terminal year, since thereafter the percentage of capacity operated was relatively low.

*Table 4.11 Overhead costs in Selected Years (Corrected), Spruance Plant I, 1932–1950*

| Year | Total Over-heads ($000) | Per cent Change | Volume (000 lb) | Per cent Change | Unit Costs (in cents) I | Per cent Change | Unit Costs* (in cents) II | Per cent Change | Per cent Capacity Utili-zation | Denier |
|---|---|---|---|---|---|---|---|---|---|---|
| 1932 | 700 | — | 3,315 | — | 21.12 | — | 21.12 | — | *na†* | 94.8 |
| 1935 | 967 | +38.1 | 6,476 | +95.3 | 14.93 | −29.3 | 14.93 | −29.3 | 99.3 | 111.3 |
| 1940 | 644 | −33.4 | 7,994 | +23.4 | 8.06 | −46.0 | 12.09 | −19.0 | 99.5 | 98.8 |
| 1950 | 538 | −16.5 | 9,518 | +19.1 | 5.65 | −29.9 | 9.68 | −19.9 | 99.9 | 97.8 |

* Unit-cost reductions after 1935 resulted largely from expansion elsewhere on Spruance location. This series shows estimates for unit costs at Spruance I if this influence is removed.
† *na*: not available.

*1932–1935:* Output increased between 1932 and 1935, as we have seen, by 95.3 per cent, and unit overhead costs therefore declined by 6.19 cents from 21.12 to 14.93 cents. The increase in volume, it will be recalled, resulted largely from the introduction of all-active spinning at Spruance I, but also from increases both in spinning speed and throwing speed.

*1935–1940:* Total costs relating to overhead facilities at the Spruance location were allocated between the various plants in proportion to the relative value of investment at each plant. From 1929 until 1935 the total costs of all the overhead facilities were borne by Spruance I. Upon the establishment of Sprunace II in 1935 and of Spruance III in 1936, it was not necessary to increase overhead facilities at the location as a whole proportionately; moreover, total costs could now be shared between the three plants so that Spruance I enjoyed considerable reductions in the total allocated to it and unit costs declined as a result. The large reduction in total overhead costs at Spruance I from $967,000 in 1935 to $644,000 in 1940 was for the most part the result of the construction of Spruance II and III. Output increased during the period, mainly as a result of increased spinning speed, by 23.4 per cent and unit costs declined from 14.93 cents to 8.06 cents.

Since our interest lies in the efficiency of Spruance Plant I—a bobbin plant producing textile yarn—in isolation, it is illuminating to estimate

Table 4.12  Reductions in Corrected Unit Costs, and Causes, Spruance Plant I, 1932–1950

| (1) Input Group | Reductions Due to Minor Technical Change (in cents) | | Reductions Due to Major Technical Change (in cents) | | Reductions Due to Plant Expansion (in cents) | Reductions Due to Other Causes (in cents) | Total Unit-Cost Reduction (in cents) |
| | (2) Direct | (3) Indirect | (4) Direct | (5) Indirect | (6) | (7) | (8) |
|---|---|---|---|---|---|---|---|
| 1. Operating Labor | 8.31 (43) | 4.58 (23) | 6.47 (33) | | | | 19.36 |
| 2. Materials | 2.02 (100) | | | | | | 2.02 |
| 3. Direct Maintenance | | 1.65 (100) | | | | | 1.65 |
| 4. Direct-Factory Costs (1 + 2 + 3) | 10.33 (45) | 6.23 (27) | 6.47 (28) | | | | 23.03 |
| 5. Overheads | | 10.32 (90) | | | | 1.12 (10)* | 11.44 |
| 6. Factory Costs (4 + 5) | 10.33 (30) | 16.55 (48)† | 6.47 (19) | | | 1.12 (3) | 34.47‡ |

* Resulting from reductions in total overhead costs because of expected shutdown of Plant I.
† This figure includes the effect of the introduction of all-active spinning, 1933. If classified as a major technical change, then 29 per cent of the unit factory cost reduction could be ascribed to major indirect technical change and 19 per cent to minor indirect technical change (see text).
‡ This figure is based on the assumption that Spruance I can be considered in isolation. If the effect of Plants II and III on unit overhead costs at I is taken into account, a further reduction of 4.03 cents would be added and the proportion resulting from expansion elsewhere would be 4.03/38.50 = 10 per cent approximately (see text).

the level of unit costs if in fact other plants had not been constructed at the location. If we assume that the overhead costs allocated to the plant in 1935 would have been retained at least until 1940, then unit overhead costs would have fallen only to 12.09 cents in 1940 rather than to 8.06 cents. This reduction was the result of higher volume from given facilities made possible by the increased spinning speed.

*1940–1950:* Unit overhead costs declined from 8.06 cents to 5.65 cents during the period 1940–1950, as output increased by 19.1 per cent and total overhead costs declined by 16.5 per cent. Unit costs would have declined to 6.77 cents if the total costs had remained unchanged: only 1.29 cents of the 2.41-cent reduction can, therefore, be explained by increased volume due to minor (indirect) technical change. Total costs declined when in the late 1940s the end of operations at the plant was envisaged.[46] Unit overhead costs would have been approximately 9.68 cents if the plant is considered in isolation.[47]

*Summary, 1932–1950:* If we assume that the effect of the establishment of Spruance plants II and III on Spruance I is removed, unit overhead costs would have declined by 11.44 cents during the period 1932–1950, from 21.12 to 9.68 cents. Of the total reduction, 6.19 cents, or 54 per cent, can be explained largely by the expansion in volume due to the introduction of all-active spinning. The increased spinning speed of the late 1930s accounted for 2.84 cents; during the 1940s further minor indirect technical change occurred and led to a reduction of 1.29 cents, so that minor indirect technical change explains a total of 10.32 cents, or 90 per cent. The remaining reduction in unit costs resulted from a decline in the total overhead costs toward the end of the plant's expected lifetime.

In actuality, unit overhead costs were only 5.65 cents in 1950, for in fact total overhead costs were shared with other plants at the same location. Thus, of a reduction amounting to 15.47 cents, expansions elsewhere at the location accounted for 4.03 cents, or 26 per cent. We shall, however, continue with the assumption that Spruance I can be considered in isolation.

### C. SUMMARY OF TOTAL UNIT COSTS

The "causes" of the unit-cost reductions at Spruance Plant I during the period 1932–1950 are summarized in Table 4.12. Plant expansion did not

---

[46] Very sharp reductions occurred in the total expenditures relating to laboratory and assistance during the period 1945–1950 (from $87,000 to $29,000), superintendence (from $88,000 to $57,000), and in the category "all other plant burden" (from $198,000 to $142,000).

[47] Unit overhead costs declined by 2.41 cents between 1940 and 1950. It is assumed that the same net reduction would have occurred when Spruance I is treated as an isolated plant.

play a role at the plant;[48] almost the entire reduction of 34.47 cents can be attributed to the effect of technical change. Moreover, as in the case of Old Hickory, *indirect* technical changes were of considerable importance: of the net reduction in unit direct-factory costs, 27 per cent resulted from technical changes which permitted a larger volume from almost unchanged plant facilities; when unit factory costs are considered, the proportion rises to 48 per cent. "Minor" technical changes were of particular importance, accounting for 78 per cent of the net reduction in unit factory costs. "Major" technical change accounted for 19 per cent.

It is probable that consideration of unit costs in the three-year period 1930–1932 would show reductions resulting mainly from the effect of minor direct technical changes of the kind introduced at Old Hickory in the same period. The cumulative effect of these numerous minor technical changes would probably raise to some extent the relative significance of minor technical changes in explaining the increased efficiency of production over the entire lifetime of the plant.[49] The most effective technical changes at the plant were the introduction of all-active spinning in the period 1933–1934, and of the Type 9 process in 1936–1940. The former case of minor technical change falls within the "indirect" category and was of especial significance in leading to a reduction in unit *overhead* costs of 6.19 cents, unit direct-maintenance costs of .59 cent, and unit operating-labor costs of 3.19 cents by means of devices permitting the production of twice the output without the duplication of existing facilities. It is important to repeat that, although it is classified as a "minor" technical change, the introduction of all-active spinning is a "borderline" case.[50] A reclassification of the process would lead to the result that 49 per cent of the unit-cost reductions were due to "minor" technical change and

[48] However, if the 4.03 cent reduction in unit overhead costs due to expansion elsewhere is taken into account, plant expansion can be said to explain approximately 10 per cent, or 4.03 cents out of a decline in unit factory costs amounting to 38.50 cents rather than 34.47 cents.

[49] Our estimate probably *understates* the contribution of minor technical change. First, 1932 was a depression year, so that the reduction in unit operating-labor costs would have been greater still had output remained high; second, we have not considered the reductions of 1931: actual unit operating-labor costs declined in 1931 by 35.5 per cent, from 54.73 to 35.30 cents. The exceptionally high figure for 1930 is simply due to the fact that 1930 was the first full year of operations at the plant. Some part of the reduction, however, was probably due to true technical change. It is believed, for example, that the cake size was increased in the early 1930s.

*Actual* cost data are available prior to 1932: unit operating-labor costs declined by 3.36 cents (9.5 per cent) from 35.30 to 31.94 cents in 1932 despite a sharp reduction in volume, and unit materials costs declined by 1.05 cents (8.6 per cent) from 12.14 to 11.09 cents, a net reduction of 4.41 cents.

[50] Informants were uncertain about the true classification of all-active spinning. In these circumstances it is least misleading to classify the change as "minor," bearing in mind the qualification.

48 per cent to "major" technical change. Even in the latter case the contribution of "minor" changes is considerable.

## ANALYSIS OF UNIT COSTS AT SPRUANCE PLANT II

### A. STANDARD UNIT COSTS

Operations at Spruance Plant II began in 1935 and terminated in 1954. Standard cost data are presented in this section for the period 1937–1953.

*Original Process*

Spruance II was designed to produce textile yarn for weaving purposes by the small-bucket process. The cake-to-cone method—similar to that introduced at Old Hickory—was used from the outset. Sixty spinning machines, with approximately 100 nozzle positions each, were installed in 1935. One-pound cakes of 150-denier yarn were produced at a spinning speed of 3,600 inches per minute. The yarn was "drip-washed" in cake form, and wound to cones two to four pounds in weight.

*Variations in Standard Unit Costs:* (1) *Operating Labor*

The reduction in unit operating-labor costs at Spruance II, from 7.45 cents in 1937 to 5.78 cents in 1953 (Table 4.13), amounted to an average rate of decline of 1.6 per cent annually. If 1951 is taken as the terminal year, the average annual decline would be 2.4 per cent, from 7.45 to 5.29 cents.

*1937–1940:* Unit operating-labor costs increased by 4.8 per cent in 1938 (Table 4.14). In this year the rate of plant utilization fell from 96.5 to 55.0 per cent of capacity, and the average denier from 150.0 to 130.9. A plant-expansion program had been started during 1938, however, so that the decline in actual output was somewhat less than is suggested by reference to denier and capacity utilization alone.[51] Approximately one-half of the expansion program—involving the installation of 30 out of 60 additional spinning machines—had been completed by the end of 1938: *in pounds of 150-denier yarn*, 55.0 per cent of capacity represented approximately 6.9 million pounds, or an output 14.6 per cent below the level attained in 1937. Actual output in 1938 (6,042,000 pounds) was 25.4 per cent below actual output in 1937 (8,103,000 pounds). Total operating-labor costs declined by 21.9 per cent only, from $604,000 to $472,000 and, as we have seen, unit operating-labor costs increased by 4.8 per cent.

[51] Series of output, denier, and rate of plant utilization are given in Appendix C (Table C.3).

*Table 4.13 Standard Costs per Pound of Rayon, Corrected for Input-Price Changes, Spruance Plant II, 1937–1953 (in cents)*

| Year | Operating Labor | Viscose Solution | Acid Bath | Total Materials | Direct-Factory Costs Excl. Maintenance | Direct Maintenance | Total Direct-Factory Costs |
|------|------|------|------|------|------|------|------|
| (1) | (2) | (3) | (4) | (5) | (6) | (7) | (8) |
| 1937 | 7.45 | 7.61 | 1.96 | 9.57 | 17.02 | 1.46 | 18.48 |
| 1938 | 7.81 | 7.41 | 1.35 | 8.76 | 16.57 | 1.91 | 18.48 |
| 1939 | 6.36 | 7.04 | 1.41 | 8.45 | 14.81 | 1.60 | 16.41 |
| 1940 | 5.08 | 6.87 | 1.28 | 8.15 | 13.23 | 1.62 | 14.85 |
| 1941 | 5.14 | 6.86 | 1.08 | 7.94 | 13.08 | 1.08 | 14.16 |
| 1942 | 5.05 | 6.88 | 1.01 | 7.89 | 12.94 | 1.19 | 14.13 |
| 1943 | 5.19 | 6.93 | 1.07 | 8.00 | 13.19 | 1.15 | 14.34 |
| 1944 | 5.59 | 6.77 | 1.09 | 7.86 | 13.45 | 1.37 | 14.82 |
| 1945 | 5.91 | 6.74 | 1.08 | 7.82 | 13.73 | 1.93 | 15.66 |
| 1946 | 5.96 | 6.79 | 1.01 | 7.80 | 13.76 | 1.91 | 15.67 |
| 1947 | 5.33 | 6.90 | 0.96 | 7.86 | 13.19 | 1.22 | 14.41 |
| 1948 | 5.58 | 6.89 | 0.96 | 7.85 | 13.43 | 1.36 | 14.79 |
| 1949 | 5.73 | 6.94 | 0.97 | 7.91 | 13.64 | 1.57 | 15.21 |
| 1950 | 5.29 | 7.11 | 0.98 | 8.09 | 13.38 | 1.91 | 15.29 |
| 1951 | 5.29 | 7.27 | 0.99 | 8.26 | 13.55 | 1.70 | 15.25 |
| 1952 | 5.76 | 7.29 | 0.96 | 8.25 | 14.01 | 1.51 | 15.52 |
| 1953 | 5.78 | 7.38 | 0.98 | 8.36 | 14.14 | 1.52 | 15.66 |

Unit operating-labor costs declined in 1939 by 18.6 per cent and in 1940 by 20.1 per cent. Denier remained relatively constant at approximately 130.0 during both years. The rate of plant utilization increased from 55.0 to 91.0 per cent in 1939, and to 99.8 per cent in 1940. The plant-expansion program, begun in 1938, was completed in 1939: capacity output in constant (150) denier reached 17,016,000 pounds, or approximately twice the level of capacity output in 1937.

The added section was almost identical to the original section except for the use of a cake 1.5 pounds, rather than 1.0 pound, in weight.

Since the plant-expansion program had been largely completed by the close of 1939, it is convenient to consider the years 1937–1939 as a unit. Output increased from 8,103,000 to 13,678,000 pounds, or by 68.8 per cent, whereas total operating-labor costs increased from $604,000 to $870,000 or by 44.0 per cent. If it is assumed that 20 per cent of the total operating-labor costs are "fixed" with respect to changes in volume, as in fact we have suggested earlier, and that the remaining 80 per cent vary in

*Table 4.14  Percentage Changes in Standard Costs (Corrected), per Pound of Rayon, Spruance Plant II, 1938–1953*

| Year | Operating Labor | Viscose Solution | Acid Bath | Total Materials | Direct-Factory Costs Excl. Maintenance | Direct Maintenance | Total Direct-Factory Costs |
|------|------|------|------|------|------|------|------|
| (1) | (2) | (3) | (4) | (5) | (6) | (7) | (8) |
| 1938 | + 4.8 | −2.6 | −31.1 | −8.5 | − 2.6 | +30.8 | 0 |
| 1939 | −18.6 | −5.0 | + 4.4 | −3.6 | −10.7 | −16.2 | −11.2 |
| 1940 | −20.1 | −2.5 | − 9.3 | −3.6 | −10.7 | + 1.2 | − 9.5 |
| 1941 | + 1.2 | −0.2 | −15.6 | −2.6 | − 1.2 | −33.4 | − 4.7 |
| 1942 | 1.8 | +0.2 | − 6.5 | −0.7 | − 1.1 | +10.1 | − 0.2 |
| 1943 | + 2.8 | +0.7 | + 5.9 | +1.3 | + 1.9 | − 3.4 | + 1.5 |
| 1944 | + 7.7 | −2.3 | + 1.9 | −1.8 | + 1.9 | +19.2 | + 3.3 |
| 1945 | + 5.7 | −0.4 | − 1.0 | −0.6 | + 2.0 | +40.8 | + 5.7 |
| 1946 | + 0.8 | +0.7 | − 6.5 | −0.3 | + 0.2 | − 1.0 | + 0.1 |
| 1947 | −10.6 | +1.6 | − 5.0 | +0.7 | − 4.2 | −36.2 | − 8.0 |
| 1948 | + 4.7 | −0.1 | 0 | −0.1 | + 1.8 | +11.4 | + 2.6 |
| 1949 | + 2.7 | +0.7 | + 1.0 | +0.7 | + 1.5 | +15.4 | + 2.8 |
| 1950 | − 7.7 | +2.4 | + 1.0 | +2.3 | − 1.9 | +21.6 | + 0.5 |
| 1951 | 0 | +2.2 | + 1.0 | +2.1 | + 1.3 | −11.0 | − 0.3 |
| 1952 | + 8.8 | +0.2 | − 3.0 | −0.1 | + 3.3 | −11.2 | + 1.8 |
| 1953 | + 0.3 | +1.2 | + 2.1 | +1.3 | + 0.9 | + 0.6 | + 0.9 |

proportion to volume, we obtain an estimate for unit operating-labor costs of 6.84 cents in 1939, or .61 cent below the level existing in 1937, which was 7.45 cents. On these assumptions, approximately 56.0 per cent of the reduction in unit costs between 1937 and 1939 can be ascribed to the effect of plant expansion.

In 1940, output increased further by 9.6 per cent, largely as a consequence of an increase in the rate of capacity utilization of 8.8 per cent. Total operating-labor costs, however, declined by 12.4 per cent to $761,000. Unit operating-labor costs, as we have seen, fell by 20.1 per cent from 6.36 to 5.08 cents. This latter reduction can be ascribed mainly to the effect of technical change, but also to the effect of higher volume due to an increase in plant utilization.

Considering the period 1937–1940, we find that only .61 cent out of a net reduction of 2.37 cents, or 25.7 per cent of the decline in unit operating-labor costs, was due to the increase in capacity. This estimate is based on an assumption that as much as 20 per cent of operating labor falls into a "fixed" input category. The remaining three-quarters of the reduction in unit operating-labor costs between 1937 and 1940 can be ascribed to influences other than the plant expansion.[52] In the first place, the expanded section of the plant made use of cakes 1.5 pounds in weight rather than 1.0 pound in weight. Moreover, as at Spruance I and Old Hickory, improved equipment for the preparation of the viscose solution was introduced in the late 1930s, permitting, for example, treatment of the solution at various stages in large batches. Numerous small improvements permitted higher yields. The unit operating-labor cost reductions of the years 1937–1940 can be explained in terms of the cumulative effect of several relatively small changes.

*1944:* Unit operating-labor costs remained almost unchanged after 1940 until an increase of 7.7 per cent in 1944. In this year, the 60 spinning machines added in 1938–1939 (Spruance II-A) were used for the production of tire-cord rayon; Spruance II referred thereafter to the *original* section of the plant only. It should be borne in mind, however, that a large number of facilities were still shared between Spruance II and II-A, so that unit costs rose less than would have been the case had Spruance II-A simply been closed down.

*1947:* Unit operating-labor costs declined by 10.6 per cent in 1947, after temporary increases in 1945–1946. The reduction was the net result of an increase in output by 6.1 per cent (due in part to an increase in denier from 131.5 to 138.1, and in part to a small increase in the rate of capacity utilization from 97.9 to 99.5 per cent), and a *reduction* in total operating-labor costs of 5.0 per cent, from $484,000 to $460,000. A variety of improvements in organization of operations developed by industrial engineering personnel were responsible for the behavior of costs in 1947.

After 1947, unit operating-labor costs tended to fluctuate but did not decline at any time significantly below the level attained in 1947. In fact, unit costs rose in 1952 by 8.8 per cent upon a sharp reduction in the rate of plant utilization from 99.4 to 74.6 per cent.

*1953:* Unit operating-labor costs remained unchanged in 1953. Nevertheless, a change in technique was introduced in that year; textile warp beams were used in place of cones. The change was not designed to reduce unit costs, however, but to improve the form of delivery. (Unit costs at the plants converting the yarn would tend to fall.) A similar change was introduced at Old Hickory in 1950.

---

[52] Unit operating-labor costs would have declined somewhat more steeply in 1939 and less steeply in 1940 if in fact the rate of plant utilization had attained almost 100 per cent in the earlier year. Thus, whereas part of the reduction in unit costs in 1940 was due to the increased utilization of capacity, when we consider the entire period 1937–1940 we can lay most emphasis on the added spinning machines and on the technical changes rather than upon increased plant utilization: in fact, the capacity-utilization rate was 96.5 per cent in 1937, not significantly lower than that of 1940.

*Summary, 1937–1953:* Unit operating-labor costs declined, as we have seen, from 7.45 cents in 1937 to 5.29 cents in 1951, and increased thereafter to 5.78 cents in 1953.

Of the net reduction of 2.16 cents between 1937 and 1951, .61 cent or 28 per cent, can be explained by plant expansion. Although the additional spinning machines were no longer part of Spruance II after 1944, many of the benefits of scale were enjoyed at the original section. The remaining reduction of 1.55 cents was due to minor direct technical change. This latter decline is somewhat less than the reduction of 1.76 cents which was attributed to minor direct technical change during the period 1937–1940; the difference can be explained by the fact that the remaining section of Plant II made use of cakes 1.0 pound in weight, whereas the added section had used 1.5 pound cakes.

*Variations in Standard Unit Costs:* (2) *Viscose Solution*

Unit viscose-solution costs declined from 7.61 cents in 1937 to 7.38 cents in 1953 (Table 4.13). However, unit costs declined more steeply in the early years of the period.

*1938–1940:* Unit viscose-solution costs declined in the three-year period 1938–1940 by 2.6, 5.0, and 2.5 per cent.

The changes in unit costs are summarized in Table 4.15. The reduction in unit cellulose costs of 1939 and 1940 resulted from an increase in the

*Table 4.15   Annual Reductions in Unit Costs of Viscose-Solution Constituents, and Total Viscose Solution (Corrected), Spruance II, 1938–1940*

| | Cellulose | | Caustic Soda | | Carbon Bisulphide | | Total | |
|---|---|---|---|---|---|---|---|---|
| Year | Unit Costs (in cents) | Per cent Change | Unit Costs (in cents) | Per cent Change | Unit Costs (in cents) | Per cent Change | Unit Costs (in cents) | Per cent Change |
| 1937 | 4.68 | — | 1.79 | — | 1.14 | — | 7.61 | — |
| 1938 | 4.56 | −2.6 | 1.73 | −3.4 | 1.12 | −1.8 | 7.41 | −2.6 |
| 1939 | 4.22 | −7.5 | 1.70 | −1.7 | 1.11 | −0.9 | 7.04 | −5.0 |
| 1940 | 4.08 | −3.3 | 1.70 | 0 | 1.09 | −1.9 | 6.87 | −2.5 |

proportion of wood pulp relative to total cellulose from 56 to 86 per cent. Moreover, throughout these years—as at Spruance Plant I and Old Hickory—cellulose of higher yield was introduced. At the same time relatively small improvements permitted increases in yield. Carbon-bisulphide recovery mechanisms were also relevant in this period.

Unit viscose-solution costs tended to rise in the late 1940s and early 1950s.

*Variations in Standard Unit Costs:* (3) *Acid Bath*

Unit acid-bath costs declined from 1.96 cents in 1937 to .98 cent in 1953. an average annual rate of decline of 4.2 per cent (Table 4.13).

*1938–1942:* Large annual reductions during the five-year period 1938–1942 lowered the level of unit acid-bath costs from 1.96 cents to 1.01 cents. These unit-cost changes are shown in Table 4.16. The large annual reductions in unit acid-bath costs were the result of the introduction of improved bath-recovery and filtration mechanisms; it will be recalled that a similar pattern of unit-cost reductions in the case of the acid bath occurred during this period, both at Spruance I and at Old Hickory.

*Table 4.16    Annual Reductions in Unit Costs of Acid-Bath Constituents, and Total Acid-Bath Costs (Corrected), Spruance II, 1938–1942*

|  | Sulphuric Acid | | Glucose | | Zinc Sulphate | | Total | |
|  | Unit | | Unit | | Unit | | Unit | |
|  | Costs | Per cent | Costs | Per cent | Costs | Per cent | Costs | Per cent |
| Year | (in cents) | Change | (in cents) | Change | (in cents) | Change | (in cents) | Change |
| 1937 | 1.06 | — | .75 | — | .15 | — | 1.96 | — |
| 1938 | .89 | −16.0 | .37 | −50.7 | .09 | −40.0 | 1.35 | −31.1 |
| 1939 | .89 | 0 | .42 | +13.5 | .10 | +11.1 | 1.41 | + 4.4 |
| 1940 | .84 | − 5.6 | .36 | −14.3 | .08 | −20.0 | 1.28 | − 9.3 |
| 1941 | .78 | − 7.1 | .24 | −33.3 | .06 | −25.0 | 1.08 | −15.6 |
| 1942 | .74 | − 5.1 | .23 | − 4.2 | .04 | −33.3 | 1.01 | − 6.5 |

*1947:* Unit acid-bath costs declined by 5.0 per cent in 1947 as a result of a reduction in unit glucose costs by 29.5 per cent. (Glucose had also declined by 32.0 per cent in the previous year.) Small alterations in the spinning machines permitted these reductions in glucose requirements. However, the complete elimination of glucose from the process was—unlike the case at Spruance Plant I—not possible, since the formation of crystals in a bucket process presents a more critical problem.

*Variations in Standard Unit Costs:* (4) *Direct Maintenance*

Unit direct-maintenance costs tended to fluctuate over time between one and two cents. The largest increase occurred in 1938 when the rate of capacity utilization was only 55.0 per cent, and in 1944–1945 when Spruance Plant II-A was detached and volume declined.

In 1951, when volume attained its highest level, unit direct-maintenance costs were 1.70 cents. Whereas output increased from 8,103,000 pounds in 1937 to 10,127,000 pounds in 1951, or by 24.9 per cent, total direct-maintenance costs increased from $118,000 to $172,000, or by 45.8 per cent.

B. UNIT OVERHEAD COSTS

Unit overhead costs declined from 8.70 cents in 1937 to 4.42 cents in 1951, or by 4.7 per cent annually on average (Table 4.17).

Table 4.17   Overhead   Costs   in   Selected   Years   (Corrected),   Spruance
Plant II, 1937–1951

| Year | Total Over- heads ($000) | Per cent Change | Volume (000 lb) | Per cent Change | Unit Costs (in cents) | Per cent Change | Per cent Capacity Utili- zation | Denier |
|---|---|---|---|---|---|---|---|---|
| 1937 | 705 | — | 8,103 | — | 8.70 | — | 96.5 | 150.0 |
| 1940 | 825 | +17.0 | 14,990 | +84.9 | 5.50 | −36.8 | 99.8 | 131.9 |
| 1944 | 495 | −40.0 | 9,085 | −39.4 | 5.45 | − 0.9 | 99.6 | 134.2 |
| 1951 | 448 | − 9.5 | 10,127 | +11.4 | 4.42 | −18.9 | 99.4 | 159.3 |

The principal reductions occurred between 1937 and 1940: whereas output increased by 84.9 per cent, from 8,103,000 to 14,990,000 pounds, upon the installation of sixty additional spinning machines (Spruance II-A), total overhead costs increased by only 17.0 per cent, from $705,000 to $825,000.

In 1944, when Spruance II-A was separated, volume recorded at Spruance II alone declined to 9,085,000 pounds, 39.4 per cent below the level recorded in 1940; total overhead costs also declined, however, by a similar percentage amount from $825,000 in 1940 to $495,000 in 1944, that is, by 40.0 per cent. Unit overhead costs, therefore, scarcely changed between 1940 and 1944. The reduction in total overhead costs in 1944 simply reflected the fact that the relevant facilities were, henceforth, allocated between Plants II and II-A and recorded separately.

If it is assumed that Spruance II-A had not in fact been constructed at the location, then it is probable that there would have occurred no reduction in unit overhead costs of any significance at Spruance II.[53]

### C. SUMMARY OF TOTAL UNIT COSTS

We have seen that 1.55 cents (72 per cent) of the net reduction in unit operating-labor costs during the period 1937–1951 resulted from minor direct technical change, whereas .61 cent of the reduction (28 per cent) was due to simple duplication of plant. The entire reduction of unit materials costs by 1.31 cents resulted from minor direct technical changes, in particular the use of improved recovery mechanisms and raw materials. Unit overhead costs declined by 4.28 cents as a result of plant expansion. Unit direct-maintenance costs increased slightly over time.

Of a net reduction of 7.51 cents in total unit costs—standard unit costs *plus* unit overhead costs—we find that 2.86 cents (35 per cent) can be explained by minor direct technical change, and 65 per cent by plant expansion (Table 4.18).

[53] Changes in average denier do not play a role of importance except in 1953, when denier rose from 158.3 to 212.5; output remained relatively high although the rate of plant utilization had declined to 71.1 per cent in that year.

Table 4.18  Reductions in Corrected Unit Costs, and Causes, Spruance II, 1937–1951

| Input Group | Reductions Due to Minor Technical Change (in cents) Direct | Indirect | Reductions Due to Major Technical Change (in cents) Direct | Indirect | Reductions Due to Plant Expansion (in cents) | Total Unit-Cost Reductions (in cents) |
|---|---|---|---|---|---|---|
| (1) | (2) | (3) | (4) | (5) | (6) | (7) |
| 1. Operating Labor | 1.55 (72) | | | | .61 (28) | 2.16 |
| 2. Materials | 1.31 (100) | | | | | 1.31 |
| 3. Direct Maintenance | | | | | | −0.24 |
| 4. Direct-Factory Costs (1 + 2 + 3) | 2.86 (81) | | | | .61 (19) | 3.23 |
| 5. Overheads | | | | | 4.28 (100) | 4.28 |
| 6. Factory Costs (4 + 5) | 2.86 (35) | | | | 4.89 (65) | 7.51 |

It may be repeated at this point that the technology at Spruance II—a plant producing weaving yarn by the cake-to-cone process—was from the beginning of operations in 1935 very similar to that introduced at Old Hickory during the 1930s. Whereas the unit-cost behavior at Old Hickory during the 1930s was to a significant extent governed by the introduction of the new technology, Spruance II was constructed to produce weaving yarn by the cake-to-cone process, and unit costs were relatively low from the start of operations.

## ANALYSIS OF UNIT COSTS AT SPRUANCE PLANT III

### A. STANDARD UNIT COSTS

Spruance Plant III was established in 1936. It was the first plant in the United States built solely for the production of tire-cord rayon, and the only Du Pont plant designed especially for this product. Standard data are available for the period 1938–1955. The plant was closed in 1957.

*Original Process*

Six large-bobbin machines were installed in 1936, each with 2,000 nozzle positions. Yarn of approximately 275 denier was produced on cakes of 1.4 pounds, at a spinning speed of 3,500 inches per minute. The yarn, after the operations of spinning and doffing, was washed automatically by a "centrifugal" technique while still on the bobbins; it was next twisted and dried by "down-twister" or "twister-dryer" machines during the passage from the bobbins to spools, and then—after transfer to multiple-end creels—collected (via beam warpers) on beams 1,000 pounds in weight. An alternative-active spinning schedule was followed.[54]

*Variations in Standard Unit Costs:* (1) *Operating Labor*

Standard unit costs, in the case of operating labor, declined at an average annual rate of 6.6 per cent during the period 1938–1955, from 5.31 cents to 1.66 cents (Table 4.19). If 1952 is chosen as the terminal year, the average annual reduction—from 5.31 to 1.51 cents—would be 8.6 per cent.[55]

*1939–1943:* The reductions in unit operating-labor costs in the four-year period 1939–1942 were respectively 22.0, 18.6, 8.0, and 11.3 per cent (Table 4.20). The level of costs was almost halved by these reductions.

[54] The nature of the acid bath is of particular importance in the production of tire-cord yarn. Initially a "high-sulphate" bath was used; in 1943 an "iron" bath was introduced, but was replaced in 1945 by a "high-zinc" bath. Each one of these changes involved significant effort, but were largely of relevance for the quality of the product.

[55] As we shall see, major changes in the nature of the product occurred after 1952 so that unit costs—in particular costs of materials—increased. Our main interest is in the efficiency of producing a substantially "unchanged" product.

*Table 4.19    Standard Costs per Pound of Rayon, Corrected for Input-Price Changes, Spruance Plant III, 1938–1955*

| Year | Operating Labor | Viscose Solution | Acid Bath | Total Materials | Direct-Factory Costs Excl. Maintenance | Direct Maintenance | Total Direct-Factory Costs |
|------|-----------------|------------------|-----------|-----------------|----------------------------------------|--------------------|----------------------------|
| (1) | (2) | (3) | (4) | (5) | (6) | (7) | (8) |
| 1938 | 5.31 | 8.06 | 1.34 | 9.40 | 14.71 | 1.48 | 16.19 |
| 1939 | 4.14 | 8.07 | 1.38 | 9.45 | 13.59 | 1.46 | 15.05 |
| 1940 | 3.37 | 7.99 | 1.26 | 9.25 | 12.62 | 1.13 | 13.75 |
| 1941 | 3.10 | 8.22 | 1.05 | 9.27 | 12.37 | .91 | 13.28 |
| 1942 | 2.75 | 8.06 | 1.06 | 9.12 | 11.87 | .78 | 12.65 |
| 1943 | 2.75 | 8.00 | 1.02 | 9.02 | 11.77 | .73 | 12.50 |
| 1944 | 2.54 | 7.85 | .78 | 8.63 | 11.17 | .74 | 11.91 |
| 1945 | 2.31 | 7.95 | .79 | 8.72 | 11.03 | .65 | 11.68 |
| 1946 | 2.18 | 7.97 | .79 | 8.78 | 10.96 | .55 | 11.51 |
| 1947 | 2.03 | 7.70 | .89 | 8.59 | 10.62 | .39 | 11.01 |
| 1948 | 1.89 | 7.84 | .88 | 8.72 | 10.61 | .41 | 11.02 |
| 1949 | 1.74 | 7.94 | .88 | 8.82 | 10.56 | .35 | 10.91 |
| 1950 | 1.56 | 7.81 | .88 | 8.70 | 10.26 | .46 | 10.72 |
| 1951 | 1.51 | 7.46 | .87 | 8.33 | 9.84 | .47 | 10.31 |
| 1952 | 1.51 | 7.07 | .87 | 7.94 | 9.45 | .46 | 9.91 |
| 1953 | 1.51 | 7.35 | .97 | 8.32 | 9.83 | .45 | 10.28 |
| 1954 | 1.88 | 7.53 | 1.04 | 8.57 | 10.45 | .51 | 10.96 |
| 1955 | 1.66 | 8.00 | 1.12 | 9.12 | 10.78 | .53 | 11.31 |

In 1938, capacity output in constant denier doubled as a consequence of a change from alternative-active to all-active spinning.[56] In the following year, capacity output increased by one-third, from 1,200 to 1,800 nozzle positions, upon the installation of three additional large-bobbin spinning machines. The expansion program, therefore, had been accomplished by 1939.

Major changes in technique were introduced at Spruance III in the late 1930s. The plant was redesigned for the production of 1,100-denier yarn, and in fact denier increased each year from 1938 until 1943 by substantial percentage amounts;[57] the increases were particularly large in 1940 (48.2 per cent), 1941 (40.9 per cent), and 1942 (53.6 per cent).

During the same period, mechanisms were introduced into Plant III to allow the "direct slashing" of yarn from the bobbins to beams, thereby

[56] The output, denier, and rate of plant utilization are shown in Appendix C (Table C.4).

[57] Although yarn of 1,100 denier was introduced in 1938–1939, yarn of 250 denier continued to be produced. The average denier increased over time as more heavy yarn was produced at the expense of the lighter yarn.

avoiding the use of down-twisting equipment. This change in technique was made possible by the fact that certain customers were willing to accept yarn from the plant in untwisted form. The yarn was washed on the bobbins by a newly developed pressure-washing system, and then passed on through "slashing machines" to the beam warper for transfer to the beams.[58] The yarn was wound in parallel form onto the beams. A main feature of the process was the elimination of the use of down-twisting equipment, allowing considerable reductions in labor cost and a convenient method of drying. The replacement program was not, however, completed until the mid-1940s.

The "direct-slashing" process was also a feature of the technology underlying the production of heavy-denier yarn. To permit increased volume (by raising the denier) from a given plant area, and to avoid the

Table 4.20  Percentage Changes in Standard Costs (Corrected), per Pound of Rayon, Spruance Plant III, 1939–1955

| Year | Operating Labor | Viscose Solution | Acid Bath | Total Materials | Direct-Factory Costs Excl. Maintenance | Direct Maintenance | Total Direct-Factory Costs |
|---|---|---|---|---|---|---|---|
| (1) | (2) | (3) | (4) | (5) | (6) | (7) | (8) |
| 1939 | −22.0 | +0.1 | +2.9 | +0.5 | −7.7 | − 1.3 | −7.1 |
| 1940 | −18.6 | −1.0 | −8.7 | −2.1 | −7.0 | −22.7 | −8.6 |
| 1941 | − 8.0 | +2.8 | −16.7 | +0.2 | −2.0 | −19.5 | −3.4 |
| 1942 | −11.3 | −2.0 | + 0.9 | −1.6 | −4.1 | −14.3 | −4.8 |
| 1943 | 0 | −0.7 | − 3.8 | −1.1 | −0.9 | − 6.5 | −1.2 |
| 1944 | − 7.6 | −1.9 | −23.5 | −4.3 | −5.1 | + 1.4 | −4.8 |
| 1945 | − 9.1 | +1.0 | + 1.2 | +1.0 | −1.3 | −12.2 | −2.0 |
| 1946 | − 5.6 | +0.5 | 0 | +0.7 | −0.6 | −15.4 | −1.5 |
| 1947 | − 6.9 | −3.4 | +12.6 | −2.2 | −3.2 | −29.1 | −4.4 |
| 1948 | − 6.9 | +1.8 | − 1.1 | +1.5 | −0.1 | + 5.0 | +0.1 |
| 1949 | − 7.9 | +1.3 | 0 | +1.1 | −0.5 | −14.7 | −1.0 |
| 1950 | −10.3 | −1.6 | 0 | −1.4 | −2.9 | +31.4 | −1.8 |
| 1951 | − 3.2 | −4.5 | − 1.2 | −4.3 | −4.1 | + 2.2 | −3.8 |
| 1952 | 0 | −5.2 | 0 | −4.7 | −4.0 | − 2.1 | −3.9 |
| 1953 | 0 | +3.9 | +11.5 | +4.8 | +4.0 | − 2.1 | +3.7 |
| 1954 | +24.5 | +2.4 | + 7.2 | +3.0 | +6.3 | +13.3 | +6.6 |
| 1955 | −11.7 | +6.2 | + 7.7 | +6.3 | +3.2 | + 3.9 | +3.2 |

[58] Essentially, the "twisting-drying" stage, followed by the beaming stage, was replaced by a process where the yarn was slashed immediately after the automatic wash; at the slashing stage "size" was applied to cause the parallel filaments to adhere together, the yarn was stretched, dried, and beamed. All these operations occurred continuously without the intervention of labor.

need for a major expansion of plant, a change in process was required. By 1943 all yarn produced at Spruance III was of 1,100 denier; yarn of 250 denier was no longer produced. Cakes weighing 2.1 pounds were introduced in 1939 as part of the conversion. The period 1938–1943 can conveniently be considered as one unit.

Production increased by 484.8 per cent from 2,832,000 pounds in 1938 to 16,563,000 in 1943, whereas total operating-labor costs increased by only 203.3 per cent, from $150,000 to $455,000; unit operating-labor costs declined, as a result, by 48.2 per cent, from 5.31 to 2.75 cents, that is, by 2.56 cents (Table 4.19). Of the entire net reduction, the increase in capacity itself attributed approximately .28 cent (11 per cent); a further .11 cent (4 per cent), can be explained by the fact that the rate of plant utilization was relatively low in 1938, and increased in the following years. The major part of the net reduction, however, can be attributed to the increase in denier and to the introduction of the "direct-slashing" process: the increase in average denier from 264.3 to 1,100.0, that is by 416.1 per cent, led to a reduction in unit operating-labor costs of 1.63 cents (64 per cent of the total net reduction), and the remaining .54 cent (21 per cent) can be explained by the new process. The increase in denier and the "direct-slashing" process were, we have argued, part of the *same* development program; both are considered to be "major" technical changes, the increase in denier acting upon unit costs *indirectly*, and the direct-slashing process permitting *direct* unit-cost reductions, and also making possible the production of high-denier yarn without an expansion of plant.[59]

[59] The fixed element of operating labor is again taken as 20 per cent for variations in volume due to increases in capacity utilization or in size of plant. In the case of a tire-cord plant, approximately 40 per cent of operating labor can be considered "fixed" upon variations in output due to denier, spinning speed and added nozzles.

Average denier increased by 416.1 per cent from 1938 to 1943; assuming the only change to be the increase in denier, total operating labor costs would have increased from $150,000 to $434,000 and output from 2,832,000 to 11,784,000 pounds. Unit costs would have declined from 5.31 to 3.68 cents or by 1.63 cents.

Capacity in terms of nozzle positions increased by one-third upon the addition of spinning machines. All things constant, increased capacity would have led to an increase in total costs from $150,000 to $190,000 and of output from 2,832,000 to 3,775,000 pounds. Unit costs would have declined to 5.03 cents, a reduction of .28 cent.

The rate of capacity utilization increased by 10 per cent during the period. Total costs would have increased to $162,000 and output to 3,115,000 pounds had this been the sole event. Unit costs would have declined to 5.20 cents, or by .11 cent. Since the rate of capacity utilization occurred while capacity itself was increasing, it is convenient to consider this "cause" together with increased scale itself. A reduction of .39 cent is therefore attributed to plant expansion for simplicity.

Of the net reduction amounting to 2.56 cents we have accounted for 2.02 cents; the remaining .54 cent can be explained by the direct effect on unit costs of the new process.

Strictly speaking, direct slashing constitutes both a major direct and indirect technical change, but for convenience the effect of volume is attributed to the increase in denier, its proximate cause.

The effect of the increase in cake size from 1.4 to production of 2.1 pounds —in itself a "minor" change—is included as part of the effect of the "direct-slashing" process, since there is no way of distinguishing the two.

*1943–1946:* Unit operating-labor costs continued their decline in 1944, falling by 7.6 per cent in 1944, 9.1 per cent in 1945, and 5.6 per cent in 1946. Average denier remained unchanged at 1,100 until 1946 when it increased to 1,206.2. In 1944–1945, capacity itself was increased by the installation of additional spinning machines; capacity output was increased by over 25 per cent. Moreover, in 1943–1944 the cake size was increased by 2.5 pounds, and in 1946 to 3.1 pounds.

The net reduction in unit operating-labor costs between 1943 and 1946 amounted to .57 cent. Of this reduction .15 cent (26 per cent), was due to the increase in plant size, and the remaining .42 cent (74 per cent) to the introduction of larger cakes. (It may be noted that in 1946, whereas output increased slightly, total operating-labor costs declined to 4.1 per cent.)[60]

*1946–1949:* Unit operating-labor costs declined by 6.9 per cent in 1947, 6.9 per cent in 1948, and by 7.9 per cent in 1949. The only changes of importance during the period were a further increase in denier of 36.4 per cent, from 1,206.2 in 1946 to 1,644.9 in 1949, an increase in cake size from 3.1 to 3.9 pounds in 1948–1949, and a small increase in the rate of capacity utilization from 94.2 to 99.1 per cent. The increase in the rate of capacity utilization accounted for only .02 cent, or 4.5 per cent of the net reduction in unit operating-labor costs of .44 cent, the increased denier for .23 cent, and the increased cake size for .19 cent.[61]

Whereas the increase in denier from approximately 250.0 to 1,100.0 was, we have pointed out, a major indirect technical change, the tendency for higher denier *after 1943* should not be considered in this category.[62]

---

[60] Denier increased by 9.6 per cent in 1946, but the rate of plant utilization declined by approximately 6.0 per cent. The actual increase in output resulting from increased denier was not of significance.

Capacity itself increased during the period. Assuming the entire increase to have resulted from the expanded capacity, and that no other changes occurred, total costs would have increased from $455,000 to $587,000 and unit costs would have declined from 2.75 to 2.60 cents; scale would then account for .15 cent of the net reduction. The remaining reduction of .42 cent can be ascribed to the increased cake size.

[61] Assuming that there is an unchanged denier, total costs would have increased to $514,000 upon the increase in the rate of capacity utilization, and output to 23,847,000 pounds. Unit costs would have declined to 2.16 cents or by .02 cent. The remaining increase in volume was due to increased denier: total costs would have increased to $599,000 upon the 36.4 per cent increase in denier (assuming 40 per cent fixed labor), and output to 30,764,000 pounds, so that unit costs would have fallen by .23 cent, to 1.95 cents. The remaining reduction by .19 cent can be accounted for by increased cake size.

[62] The upward trend in denier reflected the expansion of Type 146 yarn, first introduced in 1945. Type 146 yarn was characterized by a change from an iron to a zinc bath.

*1950–1951:* Unit operating-labor costs declined in the early 1950s, by 10.3 per cent in 1950, and by 3.2 per cent in 1951. Output increased by 8.8 per cent, in part because of increases in denier during the period amounting to 2.8 per cent, but largely because of increased spinning speed. At the same time, the effect of increased cake size was still being felt and, total operating-labor costs declined by 6.5 per cent during the period. Of a net reduction in unit operating-labor costs of .23 cent, .06 cent (26 per cent) can be explained by the increased volume, which resulted in turn from minor indirect technical change, and .17 cent by the minor direct technical change.[63]

*1952–1956:* There occurred no further net unit-cost reductions in the case of operating labor after 1951 although the cake size was raised in 1952 to 4.5 pounds. A number of important process changes were introduced, however, designed to improve the quality of the product. In 1952, the Type 146 process was replaced by a process characterized by a low proportion of solids and a high proportion of zinc in the acid bath (Type 156 yarn); and in 1955 the plant was converted to the production of "Super-Cordura" (Type 168 yarn). As a result of the latter change in process it became necessary to reduce the spinning speed. The upward trend in unit operating-labor costs, particularly after 1955, can in part be ascribed to the more expensive processes required to accomplish the product improvements. However, the increase of 24.5 per cent in 1954 was largely the result of a decline in the rate of plant utilization from 95.9 to 51.6 per cent. In 1955, part of the plant was closed down, and in 1957, operations ceased at Spruance III.

*Summary, 1938–1952:* Unit operating-labor costs declined by 3.65 cents between 1938 and 1955, and by 3.80 cents if 1952 is chosen as the terminal year. Our attention will be centered upon the period 1938–1952.

We have seen that .78 cent out of the net reduction of 3.80 cents between 1938 and 1952 (21 per cent) can be explained by minor direct technical change, .31 cent (8 per cent) by minor indirect technical change, .54 cent (14 per cent) by major direct technical change, 1.63 cents (43 per cent) by major indirect technical change (intimately related to the major direct technical change), and .54 cent (14 per cent) by expansions of plant.

*Variations in Standard Unit Costs:* (2) *Viscose Solution*

As we have already noted, the nature of the product was substantially altered after 1952 at Spruance III. Since our main interest lies in the

---

[63] As a result of increased spinning speed and denier alone, total costs would have increased from $566,000 to $596,000, and output from 32,520,000 to 35,398,000 pounds; unit costs would have declined to 1.68 cents, or by .06 cent. The remaining decline by .17 cent to 1.51 cents can be explained by increased cake size.

efficiency of producing a "given" product, we shall only consider the period 1938–1952. The average annual reduction in unit materials costs—from 9.40 to 7.94 cents—amounted to 1.2 per cent (Table 4.19).

*1947:* Unit viscose-solution costs declined by 3.4 per cent in 1947 as a result of a 7.1 per cent reduction in unit cellulose costs, which in turn was caused by an increase in the proportion of wood pulp to total cellulose from zero to 42 per cent. (The small increases in unit viscose-solution costs in 1948 and 1949 were due to a temporary reduction in the proportion of wood pulp from 42 to 16 per cent during these years.)

*Table 4.21   Annual Reductions in Unit Costs of Viscose-Solution Constituents and Total Viscose Solution (Corrected), Spruance Plant III, 1950–1952*

| Year | Cellulose | | Caustic soda | | Carbon Bisulphide | | Total | |
| | Unit Costs (in cents) | Per cent Change | Unit Costs (in cents) | Per cent Change | Unit Costs (in cents) | Per cent Change | Unit Costs (in cents) | Per cent Change |
|---|---|---|---|---|---|---|---|---|
| 1949 | 5.13 | — | 1.72 | — | 1.09 | — | 7.94 | — |
| 1950 | 5.06 | −1.4 | 1.70 | −1.2 | 1.05 | − 3.7 | 7.81 | −1.6 |
| 1951 | 4.84 | −4.3 | 1.69 | −0.6 | 0.93 | −11.4 | 7.46 | −4.5 |
| 1952 | 4.47 | −7.6 | 1.71 | +1.1 | 0.89 | − 4.3 | 7.07 | −5.2 |

*1950–1952:* Unit costs in the case of both the cellulose and the carbon-bisulphide constituents declined in the three-year period 1950–1952 and, as a consequence, unit viscose-solution costs fell by 1.6, 4.5, and 5.2 per cent, respectively, in these years. The changes are summarized in Table 4.21. The behavior of unit cellulose costs can be accounted for by the increase in the proportion of wood pulp to total cellulose from 16 per cent in 1949 to 26 per cent in 1950, 40 per cent in 1951, and 78 per cent in 1952; unit cellulose costs in 1951 are approximately at the same level as those in 1947 when the proportion had been 42 per cent. The reductions in unit carbon-bisulphide costs resulted from the introduction of recovery equipment.

The entire reduction of .99 cent between 1938 and 1952 can be explained by minor direct technical change.

*1953–1956:* Unit viscose-solution costs tended to rise after 1953 as a consequence of the changes in process designed to alter the quality of the tire cord: in particular, the proportion of wood pulp to total cellulose declined from almost 80 per cent to 52 per cent in 1953. The production of "Super-Cordura" in 1955 was even more costly than that of Type 156 rayon.

*Variations in Standard Unit Costs:* (3) *Acid Bath*

Unit acid-bath costs declined from 1.34 cents in 1938 to 1.12 cents in 1955. In 1952 unit costs were .87 cent (Table 4.19).

*1940–1944:* Large reductions in unit acid-bath costs of 8.7 and 16.7 per cent occurred in 1940 and 1941 (Table 4.20), and further reductions of 3.8 and 23.5 per cent are recorded in 1943 and 1944. Table 4.22 summarizes the main features of the reductions:

*Table 4.22    Annual Reductions in Unit Costs of Acid-Bath Constituents, and Total Acid Bath (Corrected), Spruance III, 1940–1944*

| Year | Sulphuric Acid | | Glucose | | Zinc Sulphate | | Total | |
|---|---|---|---|---|---|---|---|---|
| | Unit Costs (in cents) | Per cent Change | Unit Costs (in cents) | Per cent Change | Unit Costs (in cents) | Per cent Change | Unit Costs (in cents) | Per cent Change |
| 1939 | .99 | — | .39 | — | .10 | — | 1.38 | — |
| 1940 | .85 | −14.1 | .32 | −17.9 | .08 | −20.0 | 1.26 | − 8.7 |
| 1941 | .79 | − 7.1 | .21 | −34.4 | .05 | −37.5 | 1.05 | −16.7 |
| 1942 | .78 | − 1.3 | .22 | + 4.7 | .06 | +20.0 | 1.06 | + 0.9 |
| 1943 | .77 | − 1.3 | .19 | −13.6 | .06 | 0 | 1.02 | − 3.8 |
| 1944 | .73 | − 5.2 | | | .05 | −16.7 | 0.78 | −23.5 |

The reductions of 1939–1942 were in part the result of minor improvements in process which permitted the re-use of solutions in the bath, but were primarily the result of recovery and filtration equipment.

The reductions of 1943–1944 are closely related to the introduction of Type 146 yarn, referred to earlier. The denier of this new-type yarn was higher than that of earlier yarns. Glucose was no longer required in the production of heavy-denier yarns.

The entire reduction of .47 cent which occurred between 1938 and 1952 resulted from minor direct technical changes. Increases in unit acid-bath costs in 1947 and in the years after 1953 can be explained in terms of the requirements of a changing product.

*Variations in Standard Unit Costs:* (4) *Direct Maintenance*

Unit direct-maintenance costs declined from 1.48 cents in 1938 to .46 cent in 1952 (Table 4.19). Volume declined after 1952, and we shall center our attention upon the preceding period. Output increased by 1,176.9 per cent between 1938 and 1952, from 2,832,000 to 36,164,000 pounds, whereas total maintenance costs increased by only 133.3 per cent from $42,000 to $98,000. The large increase in volume was almost entirely the consequence of increased denier. In general, the reduction by .75 cent between 1938 and 1943 can be ascribed to the increase in denier to 1,100, a "major" indirect technical change, and the reduction by .27 cent between 1943 and 1952 can be explained by further increases in denier to 1,650; this latter trend has been classified as an example of "minor" indirect technical change.

### B. UNIT OVERHEAD COSTS

Unit overhead costs declined from 7.38 cents in 1938 to 1.76 cents in 1952 when output at Spruance III was at a maximum level of 36,164,000 pounds (Table 4.23). Whereas the increase in output between 1938 and 1952 amounted to 1,176.9 per cent, total overhead costs increased by only 204.3 per cent from $209,000 to $636,000.

Unit overhead costs increased somewhat after 1952 as volume declined, and as part of the total overhead costs were reallocated from Spruance I and II. It may be noted that if volume is corrected to a denier of 264.3—the denier existing in the base year—volume in 1952 would have been only 5,541,000 rather than 36,164,000 pounds, and unit overhead costs in 1952

*Table 4.23  Overhead Costs in Selected Years, Spruance Plant III, 1938–1952*

| Year | Total Over- heads (S000) | Per cent Change | Volume (000 lb) | Per cent Change | Unit Costs (in cents) | Per cent Change | Per cent Capacity Utili- zation | Denier |
|------|------|------|------|------|------|------|------|------|
| 1938 | 209 | — | 2,832 | — | 7.38 | — | 88.0 | 264.3 |
| 1940 | 314 | + 50.2 | 6,538 | +130.9 | 4.80 | −35.0 | 97.7 | 447.2 |
| 1945 | 773 | +146.2 | 22,174 | +239.1 | 3.49 | −27.3 | 99.5 | 1,100.9 |
| 1952 | 636 | − 17.7 | 36,164 | + 63.1 | 1.76 | −49.6 | 99.9 | 1,691.4 |

would have been over 11.0 cents per pound. Almost the entire behavior of unit overhead costs can be explained in terms of the continually rising denier at Spruance III: thus the reduction of 3.18 cents between 1938 and 1943 can be explained by the increase in denier to 1,100, a "major" technical change, and the reduction of 2.44 cents by the increase in denier to 1,650, a "minor" technical change.

### C. SUMMARY OF TOTAL UNIT COSTS

Thus far—in the case of Old Hickory, Spruance Plant I, and Spruance Plant II—we have found that the contribution of minor technical change to increased efficiency over time has been considerably greater than that of major technical change. At Spruance Plant III, 44 per cent of the reduction in unit factory costs can be accounted for by minor technical change, 51 per cent by major technical change and 4 per cent by plant expansion (Table 4.24). Thus, 46 per cent—44 out of 95 percentage points—of the increased efficiency *attributable to technical change alone* resulted from minor technical change. The first year for which standard cost data are available, however, is 1939, whereas the plant was established in 1936. In other plants at the same location and at Old Hickory, considerable minor direct technical change occurred after 1937, and it is probable that

*Table 4.24   Reductions in Corrected Unit Costs, and Causes, Spruance III, 1938–1952*

| Input Group | Reductions Due to Minor Technical Change (in cents) | | Reductions Due to Major Technical Change (in cents) | | Reductions Due to Plant Expansion (in cents) | Total Unit-Cost Reduction (in cents) |
| | Direct | Indirect | Direct | Indirect | | |
| (1) | (2) | (3) | (4) | (5) | (6) | (7) |
| 1. Operating Labor | .78 (21) | .31 (8) | .54 (14) | 1.63 (43) | .54 (14) | 3.80 |
| 2. Materials | 1.46 (100) | | | | | 1.46 |
| 3. Direct Maintenance | | .27 (26) | | .75 (74) | | 1.02 |
| 4. Direct-Factory Costs (1 + 2 + 3) | 2.24 (36) | .58 (9) | .54 (9) | 2.38 (38) | .54 (9) | 6.28 |
| 5. Overheads | | 2.44 (43) | | 3.18 (57) | | 5.62 |
| 6. Factory Costs (4 + 5) | 2.24 (19) | 3.02 (25) | .54 (4) | 5.56 (47) | .54 (4) | 11.90 |

the significance of minor technical changes would appear somewhat larger if the entire period could be taken into account.[64] Moreover, it will be recalled that the effect of increased cake size in 1939, from 1.4 to 2.1 pounds, a "minor" change, was included in that of the "direct-slashing" process, a "major" change.

The major technical changes which have been identified above were the introduction of "direct slashing" and the increase in denier from 250 to 1,100. The increased denier is a striking example of *indirect* technical change which was directed at permitting the production of increased pounds of yarn without duplication of plant facilities. Changes of this nature play a considerable role in determining the level of unit overhead and maintenance costs.

### ANALYSIS OF UNIT COSTS AT SPRUANCE PLANT II-A

#### A. STANDARD UNIT COSTS

The 60 spinning machines added by Spruance Plant II-A to the existing 60 machines at Spruance II in 1938–1939, were used after 1944 for the production of tire cord. The required conversions were carried out in 1943–1944.

*Original Process*

The plant was designed in 1943 for the production of tire-cord yarn of 1,100 denier at a spinning speed of 3,708 inches per minute, compared with 3,600 inches per minute at Spruance II. The cake remained 1.5 pounds in weight. After spinning, doffing, and cake wrapping, the yarn was "drip washed," desulphured, and finished and dried while in cake form, and then wound to cones; after coning the yarn was stretched during transfer to beams.[65] The number of nozzles per machine was reduced to 34 from the original 100, since it was necessary at the outset to follow a spinning schedule involving the use of every third nozzle position. The

[64] Actual unit operating-labor costs declined in 1938 by 38 per cent, from 11.16 to 6.92 cents. Since 1937 was the first *full* year of operations at the plant, the entire reduction cannot be explained by technical change. Nevertheless, it is probable that some part was due to minor technical change occurring in 1937–1938.

[65] The process can be described in greater detail: the yarn, after spinning, doffing, and wrapping, was drip washed, desulphured, given a second wash, finished, wrung, dried, wound to cones, and transferred to beams. The process differed from the cake-to-cone process used at the plant prior to the conversion in three main respects: first, the yarn was not bleached; second, whereas as many as 20 hand operations were required at different stages between doffing and wrapping, and drying in the textile-yarn process, no more than 12 were needed in the new process; third, the yarn was transferred to beams after coning.

development of a process which allowed the production of tire cord in a plant designed initially for the production of textile yarn required in itself considerable effort.

*Variations in Standard Unit Costs:* (1) *Operating Labor*

Reductions of relatively large magnitude occurred in each year during the period 1946–1951 in the case of unit operating-labor costs. After 1952,

*Table 4.25   Standard Costs per Pound of Rayon, Corrected for Input-Price Changes, Spruance Plant II-A, 1945–1955 (in cents)*

| Year | Operating Labor | Viscose Solution | Acid Bath | Total Materials | Direct-Factory Costs Excl. Maintenance | Direct Maintenance | Total Direct-Factory Costs |
|------|------|------|------|------|------|------|------|
| (1) | (2) | (3) | (4) | (5) | (6) | (7) | (8) |
| 1945 | 3.50 | 7.69 | .78 | 8.47 | 11.97 | .89 | 12.86 |
| 1946 | 3.26 | 7.55 | .81 | 8.36 | 11.62 | .82 | 12.44 |
| 1947 | 2.80 | 7.48 | .85 | 8.13 | 10.93 | .53 | 11.46 |
| 1948 | 2.65 | 7.54 | .85 | 8.39 | 11.04 | .46 | 11.50 |
| 1949 | 2.43 | 7.63 | .86 | 8.49 | 10.92 | .50 | 11.42 |
| 1950 | 1.80 | 7.64 | .86 | 8.50 | 10.30 | .61 | 10.91 |
| 1951 | 1.73 | 7.49 | .87 | 8.36 | 10.09 | .55 | 10.64 |
| 1952 | 1.73 | 7.45 | .82 | 8.27 | 10.00 | .59 | 10.59 |
| 1953 | 1.85 | 7.53 | .84 | 8.37 | 10.22 | .61 | 10.83 |
| 1954 | 1.93 | 8.34 | .99 | 9.33 | 11.26 | .62 | 11.88 |
| 1955 | 1.78 | 8.43 | .99 | 9.42 | 11.20 | .72 | 11.92 |

however, unit costs tended to rise; the increase reflected the introduction of "Super-Cordura" yarn at the plant. Our attention will be centered largely upon the period 1945–1952: unit operating-labor costs declined from 3.50 cents to 1.73 cents during the seven-year period, or at an average annual rate of 9.6 per cent (Table 4.25).

*1946–1947:* The annual reductions in unit operating-labor costs in 1946 and in 1947 were 6.9 and 14.1 per cent, respectively (Table 4.26). Capacity output corrected for denier (1,000) remained at approximately 22 million pounds during the period, and the proportion of capacity in operation declined from 94.0 to 88.9 per cent in 1946 and rose to 95.8 per cent in 1947. Actual output, however, increased significantly during the two-year period, from 22,081,000 to 28,106,000 pounds, or by 27.3 per cent as a result of an increase in denier of 13.2 per cent (from 1,104.9 to 1,251.0) in 1946, and of 6.4 per cent (to 1,332.2) in 1947.[66] Total operating-labor costs remained almost unchanged during the period, increasing by only 1.8 per cent from $773,000 to $787,000. The unit-cost reductions can be explained in part by the increase in denier, but the constancy of total operating-labor costs suggests that other improvements were at play.

In fact, during the immediate postwar period a number of relatively minor changes were made in the process which permitted the elimination of the stage of desulphuring, hitherto part of the purification procedure,

Table 4.26   Percentage Changes in Standard Costs (Corrected), per Pound of Rayon, Spruance Plant II-A, 1946–1955

| Year | Operating Labor | Viscose Solution | Acid Bath | Total Materials | Direct-Factory Costs Excl. Maintenance | Direct Maintenance | Total Direct-Factory Costs |
|------|------|------|------|------|------|------|------|
| (1) | (2) | (3) | (4) | (5) | (6) | (7) | (8) |
| 1946 | − 6.9 | − 1.9 | + 3.8 | − 1.3 | − 3.0 | − 7.9 | −3.3 |
| 1947 | −14.1 | − 1.0 | + 4.9 | − 2.8 | − 6.0 | −35.4 | −7.9 |
| 1948 | − 5.4 | + 0.8 | 0 | + 3.2 | + 1.0 | −13.3 | +0.3 |
| 1949 | − 8.3 | + 1.1 | + 1.1 | + 1.2 | − 1.1 | + 8.6 | −0.7 |
| 1950 | −25.9 | + 0.1 | 0 | + 0.1 | − 5.7 | +22.0 | −4.5 |
| 1951 | − 3.9 | − 2.0 | + 1.2 | − 1.7 | − 2.1 | − 9.8 | −2.5 |
| 1952 | 0 | − 0.6 | − 5.7 | − 1.1 | − 0.9 | + 7.2 | −0.5 |
| 1953 | + 6.9 | + 1.1 | + 2.4 | + 1.2 | + 2.2 | + 3.3 | +2.3 |
| 1954 | + 4.3 | +10.7 | +17.9 | +11.5 | +10.1 | + 1.6 | +9.7 |
| 1955 | − 7.8 | + 1.1 | 0 | + 1.0 | − 0.6 | +16.1 | +0.3 |

and a stage of washing, hitherto required after desulphuring. Operating labor.was therefore economized.

Of the net reduction in unit operating-labor costs of .70 cent, approximately .30 cent can be explained by the increase in volume owing to the higher denier, an example of minor indirect technical change, and .40 cent by the minor direct technical changes.[67]

[66] Volume, denier, etc., are shown in Appendix C (Table C.5).

[67] Assuming, as we have assumed in the case of Plant III, that upon an increase in output owing to denier, approximately 40 per cent of total operating-labor costs can be taken as "fixed" and the remaining 60 per cent as varying in proportion with volume, we obtain an estimate for total costs after the increase in volume, ceteris paribus, of $900,000, an increase of $127,000 over the level of costs in 1945, namely $773,000; dividing by the higher volume we obtain an estimate of 3.20 cents for unit operating-labor costs. Thus of the .70 cent reduction, .30 cent can be ascribed to the effect of denier, and the remainder to the improved process. An inaccuracy enters, in that output increased in slightly greater proportion than denier as a result of small additions

*1948:* Unit operating-labor costs declined further from 1948 until 1951; the annual reductions were 5.4, 8.3, 25.9, and 3.9 per cent. A variety of events account for the reductions. In the first place the average denier continued to increase in 1948, by 7.1 per cent (from 1,525.1 to 1,625.1). Thereafter, average denier remained relatively constant. The unit-cost reduction of 1948 (.15 cent) can be explained largely in terms of the increase in volume from 28,106,000 to 31,918,000 pounds, or by 11.4 per cent, which resulted from the increased denier and other minor indirect technical changes; total operating labor costs in 1948 increased by only 7.5 per cent from $787,000 to $846,000.[68]

*1949–1951:* In 1948–1949, the plant was converted to a "wet-slashing" process: cakes of yarn were transported by conveyers to be purified in automatic washers (centrifugal washing); the wet cakes were then creeled, and the yarn "slashed" to beams while still in a wet state. At the slashing stage, the filaments were treated with "size," stretched, and dried. The essential features of the new process were the avoidance of the stages of *cake drying* and of *coning,* and the introduction of conveyers and automatic washers.[69] A further feature was an increase in the size of the cake from 1.5 to 4.5 pounds; this increase would permit large reductions in unit operating-labor costs.

The mechanical handling of packages, the new method of purification (automatic washing), the direct slashing to beams of yarn in a wet state, and the increase in size of the cakes, were integral parts of a single major technical change designed specifically to reduce labor costs and to increase the quality of the yarn.

At the same time, capacity was increased from 2,040 to 3,000 nozzles upon the introduction of an alternative-active spinning schedule. This event is considered to be a minor indirect technical change.

As a consequence of these technical changes, output *increased* by 36.5 per cent, whereas total operating-labor costs *declined* by 10.9 per cent

---

[68] It is important to note that whereas the plant was *designed* for the production of 1,100-denier yarn, minor changes enabled the production of yarn of over 1,600 denier. The plant was *redesigned* for 1,650-denier yarn during the conversion program relating to "Super-Cordura" in 1953–1954.

[69] It may be added that the wrapping of the cakes prior to purification, as in the original process, was replaced by "insertion." The slashing procedure paralleled the process at Spruance III; the application of "size" to cause the adherence of filaments was, however, less crucial at Spruance II-A, a bucket plant, than at Spruance III, where the yarn was spun without twist.

---

to nozzle positions per machine. Both the increase in denier and in nozzle positions, however, are in the present instance examples of minor indirect technical change.

It may be added that in 1945–1946 the "iron bath" hitherto in use at the plant was replaced by a "zinc bath" in an effort to improve the quality of the yarn; the changeover is an example of major technical change designed to improve the *quality* of the product.

during the period 1949–1951. Of a net reduction in unit operating-labor costs amounting to .92 cent, the increase in capacity due to the introduction of alternative-active spinning accounted for .28 cent and the major direct technical changes for the remaining .64 cent.[70]

*1952–1955:* Unit operating-labor costs tended to rise somewhat in the early 1950s. The annual increases were 4.0 per cent in 1952, 2.7 per cent in 1953, and 4.3 per cent in 1954. In September 1953, 20 of the 60 spinning machines were converted to the production of "Super-Cordura." In 1954, the remaining machines were converted and the spinning speed was raised from 3,708 to 4,212 inches per minute. The tendency toward increased unit costs can largely be accounted for by the changes in the nature of the product. In 1955 unit operating-labor costs declined, however, by 7.8 per cent, almost restoring the level of costs existing in 1951. The reduction resulted from an increase in volume from 51,341,000 to 56,105,000 pounds, by 9.3 per cent, resulting in turn from the increase in spinning speed and a less-than-proportional increase in total operating-labor costs of 0.9 per cent, from $991,000 to $1,000,000. Once again, we note a tendency for technical change to take the form of the introduction of means to permit a larger volume from given "capacity."

*Summary, 1945–1952:* Our main concern is with the efficiency of production of a substantially unchanged product; we shall therefore be mainly concerned with the period prior to the introduction of "Super-Cordura" yarn. Unit operating-labor costs declined by 1.77 cents during the seven-year period. Of this reduction we can ascribe .40 cent (23 per cent) to minor direct technical change (occurring in 1946–1947); .73 cent (41 per cent) to minor indirect technical change (1946–1947, 1948, and 1949–1950); and .64 cent (36 per cent) to the major direct technical changes (occurring in the late 1940s).

*Variations in Standard Unit Costs:* (2) *Viscose Solution*

Unit viscose solution costs remained relatively stable until 1954 (Table 4.25). A number of changes in the unit costs of various constituent inputs did occur, however.

*1946–1947:* Unit viscose-solution costs declined by 1.9 per cent in 1946 and by 1.0 per cent in 1947; unit cellulose costs, however, declined by 3.3

[70] Total operating-labor costs in 1948 amounted to $846,000. Assuming that 40 per cent remained unchanged and that the remaining 60 per cent increased by 36.5 per cent—proportionately with volume—we obtain an estimate for total costs in 1951 of $1,031,000. Actual output in 1951 was 43,554,000 pounds (compared with 31,918,000 in 1948) and unit costs would have amounted to 2.37 cents if the only change had been the expansion of volume. There remains .64 cent which can be explained by the major direct technical changes.

and by 6.8 per cent in these years as a consequence of an increase in the proportion of wood pulp to total cellulose from zero to 12 per cent in 1946 and to 40 per cent in 1947. Unit carbon-bisulphide costs increased in 1946 by 1.9 per cent and in 1947 by 3.7 per cent; and unit caustic-soda costs increased by 2.4 per cent in 1947. On balance the changes in unit viscose-solution costs as a whole were very small.

*1954–1956:* In 1954 unit viscose-solution costs increased by 10.7 per cent, in 1955 by 1.1 per cent, and in 1956 by 10.6 per cent. These increases were directly related to the improvements in quality—namely the introduction of "Super-Cordura"—in these years. In particular, the proportion of wood pulp in total cellulose declined in 1954 from 53 per cent to zero.

*Variations in Standard Unit Costs:* (3) *Acid Bath*

There were no important reductions in unit acid-bath costs at Spruance II-A. The nature of the product determined in large measure the direction of change.

*1946–1947:* Unit acid-bath costs rose by 3.8 per cent and by 4.9 per cent in 1946 and in 1947, respectively: these increases resulted from an upward trend in the use of zinc sulphate and sulphuric acid.

*1954:* Unit acid-bath costs rose by 17.9 per cent as a consequence of an increase in unit sulphuric-acid costs by 12.8 per cent and the replacement of zinc sulphate by the more expensive zinc oxide. In 1956 zinc sulphate was reintroduced and unit acid-bath costs declined by 8.0 per cent.

*Variations in Standard Unit Costs:* (4) *Direct Maintenance*

Unit direct-maintenance costs declined from .89 cent in 1945 to .59 cent in 1952, and tended to increase thereafter (Table 4.25). Output increased (1945–1952) by 103.7 per cent, and total direct-maintenance costs increased by 105.7 per cent, from $196,420 to $403,960.

The large increases in output over time at Spruance II-A resulted in part from substantial increases in denier until 1949 and in 1954 to an increase in spinning speed from 103 to 117 yards per minute. In 1948–1949, capacity in terms of installed nozzles increased, as we have seen, from 2,040 to 3,000 upon the introduction of alternative-active spinning. The reduction in unit costs of .30 cent during the period 1945–1952 can be attributed in equal proportions to the increase in denier and the transition to the alternative-active schedule, both instances of minor, indirect technical change.[71]

[71] Denier increased by approximately 50 per cent during the period and nozzle capacity, as a consequence of alternative-active spinning, similarly increased by 50 per cent. The net reduction of .30 cent can therefore be attributed equally to these two changes.

### B. UNIT OVERHEAD COSTS

Unit overhead costs declined from 3.60 cents in 1945 to 2.05 cents in 1952 (Table 4.27). The 103.7 per cent expansion in volume was accompanied by an increase in total overhead costs of 15.8 per cent, from $796,000 to $922,000.

The behavior of total overhead costs after 1952 was influenced by external events: in 1952–1954 Spruance Plants both I and II were closed down and the remaining overhead facilities allocated to Spruance II-A and III. An increase in total overhead costs of 64.3 per cent at Spruance II-A between 1952 and 1955—a period when output increased by only 24.7 per cent—reflects this reallocation. If we assume, in our study of efficiency at Spruance II-A in isolation, that total overhead costs would have

*Table 4.27 Overhead Costs in Selected Years (Corrected), Spruance Plant II-A, 1945–1955*

| Year | Total Over-heads ($000) | Per cent Change | Volume (000 lb) | Per cent Change | Unit Costs (in cents) | Per cent Change | Per cent Capacity Utili-zation | Denier |
|---|---|---|---|---|---|---|---|---|
| 1945 | 796 | | 22,081 | | 3.60 | | 94.0 | 1,104.9 |
| 1952 | 922 | +15.8 | 44,977 | +103.7 | 2.05 | −43.2 | 99.8 | 1,635.5 |
| 1955 | 1,515 | +64.3 | 56,105 | + 24.7 | 2.70 | +31.7 | 100.0 | 1,661.6 |

remained unchanged after 1952 if other plants had remained in operation, unit overhead costs would have declined to 1.64 cents in 1955, since volume increased as a consequence of higher spinning speed. Unit overhead costs were in fact 2.70 cents in 1955.

If the average denier in 1955 would have been no higher than in 1945, unit overhead costs would have tended to remain unchanged and possibly to have increased somewhat between 1945 and 1955. Our estimate of unit overhead costs in these circumstances is 4.06 cents as compared with 2.70 cents, which is in fact the level recorded in 1955.

The net reductions in unit overhead costs of 1.55 cents, 1945–1952, can be attributed equally to the increase in denier and the transition to alternative-active spinning, both cases of minor, indirect technical change.[72]

### C. SUMMARY OF TOTAL UNIT COSTS

Technical change accounted for the entire reduction in unit factory costs at Spruance Plant II-A during the period 1945–1952; plant expansion played no part. Minor technical change was responsible for 83 per cent of the net reduction of 3.82 cents (Table 4.28). Minor indirect technical

[72] See preceding note.

Table 4.28  Reductions in Corrected Unit Costs, and Causes, Spruance II-A, 1945–1952

| (1) Input Group | Reductions Due to Minor Technical Change (in cents) Direct (2) | Indirect (3) | Reductions Due to Major Technical Change (in cents) Direct (4) | Indirect (5) | Reductions Due to Plant Expansion (in cents) (6) | Total Unit-Cost Reduction (in cents) (7) |
|---|---|---|---|---|---|---|
| 1. Operating Labor | .40 (23) | .73 (41) | .64 (36) | | | 1.77 |
| 2. Materials | .20 (100) | | | | | .20 |
| 3. Direct Maintenance | | .30 (100) | | | | .30 |
| 4. Direct-Factory Costs (1 + 2 + 3) | .60 (26) | 1.03 (45) | .64 (28) | | | 2.27 |
| 5. Overheads | | 1.55 (100) | | | | 1.55 |
| 6. Factory Costs (4 + 5) | .60 (16) | 2.58 (67) | .64 (17) | | | 3.82 |

change accounted for 67 per cent of the net reduction; the increased denier—from 1,100 to 1,600—was of particular importance.

The reduction in unit costs by .64 cent which we have attributed to "major" technical change was due, it will be recalled, to the introduction of wet slashing, mechanized means of handling packages, larger cakes, and automatic purification.

### CAPITAL-USING TECHNICAL CHANGES VERSUS NET REDUCTIONS IN UNIT FACTORY COSTS

A distinction may be drawn between technical change which permits *net* reductions in unit costs, and technical change which is "capital using" and which offsets all or at least part of the savings in labor or materials by the necessity of installing additional equipment. In this section we shall argue on the basis of qualitative evidence that technical change *which permitted net savings* predominated. In Chapter 6 this conclusion will be supported by data relating to investment expenditures required by technical change: we shall show that *replacement* investment was considerably more important than additions to the capital stock.

*Simplifications in Process*

Most of the "major" technical changes which have been encountered— namely, the cake-to-cone process, the Type 9 process, direct slashing and wet slashing—simplified the sequence of rayon production and permitted savings in *both* equipment and complementary labor. Replacement of spinning equipment to embody certain "minor" technical changes, in particular the introduction of Type 10 spinning machines, also simplified the sequence and allowed *net* economies.

*Improved Equipment in Viscose Preparation*

The larger, faster-acting units of equipment introduced at the shredding, xanthation and mixing stages, and the introduction of continuous-steeping and continuous-shredding equipment also permitted reductions in the total stock of capital (in constant dollars), as well as savings in the operating-labor input, in the production of given levels of output.[73]

*Larger Packages*

Larger packages would depend upon the use of larger buckets and other collecting devices. Such changes were capital using but only to a very

---

[73] For example a given number of small pieces of equipment might be replaced by a smaller number of larger units; in constant dollars it was not usual for the capital stock to increase.

Table 4.29  Summary of "Causes" of Reductions in Corrected Unit Factory Costs

| | | Cumulative Avg. Annual Reduction | Percentage of Net Reduction Due to Technical Change | | | | | | Minor as Fraction of Major and Minor | Percentage of Net Reduction Due to | |
| | | | Minor | | | Major | | | | Plant | |
| Plant | Period | Per cent | Direct | Indirect | Total | Direct | Indirect | Total | Per cent | Expansion | Other |
|---|---|---|---|---|---|---|---|---|---|---|---|
| (1) | (2) | (3) | (4) | (5) | (6) | (7) | (8) | (9) | (10) | (11) | (12) |
| 1. Old Hickory | 1929–1951 | 4.9 | 45 | 21 | 66 | 13 | 6 | 19 | 79 | 11 | 4* |
| 2. Spruance I | 1932–1950 | 4.5 | 30 | 48 | 78 | 19 | | 19 | 80 | | 3† |
| 3. Spruance II | 1937–1951 | 2.3 | 35 | | 35 | | | 0 | 100 | 65 | |
| 4. Spruance III | 1938–1952 | 4.9 | 19 | 25 | 44 | 4 | 47 | 51 | 46 | 4‡ | |
| 5. Spruance II-A | 1945–1952 | 3.7 | 16 | 67 | 83 | 17 | | 17 | 83 | | |

\* Routine denier increases.
† Reduced total overheads towards end of plant's expected lifetime.
‡ Adds to 99 per cent due to rounding.

small extent. The use of larger buckets or bobbins is not a *significant* instance of capital-using technical change.

### *"Indirect" Technical Change*

Increased denier and spinning speed of major dimension frequently required additions to the viscose-making equipment. The addition of nozzles to existing spinning machines upon the introduction of all-active spinning or upon a transition from the use of every third nozzle position to alternative-active spinning, would also require additional equipment.

The "indirect" technical changes were, however, directed at obtaining larger output from *almost* unchanged facilities. Both output per unit of labor *and "per unit of equipment"* would be increased. The additional equipment required by the changes would not suffice to offset these intended benefits.

### *Recovery Equipment*

The most significant instance of "capital-using" technical change can be found in the devices introduced to permit the recovery of materials used in the acid bath and the viscose solution; unit materials costs declined as a result, but the savings were offset to a considerable extent by the required additions to the capital stock.

Considering the technical changes as a whole we can say that for the most part, *net* reductions in unit costs were permitted; there were, however, certain instances of technical change which can be considered "capital using."

### SUMMARY

The contributions of technical change and of plant expansion to increased efficiency—as measured by reductions over time in unit factory costs—are summarized for each of the Spruance Plants and for Old Hickory in Table 4.29. A number of characteristics may be noted.

In the first place, technical change was of overwhelming significance in explaining the reduction in unit factory costs. In two instances, Spruance I and Spruance II-A, plant expansion played no role; at Spruance III it accounted for only 4 per cent of the net reduction and at Old Hickory for 11 per cent. An exception is Spruance II, where 65 per cent of the reduction was due to plant expansion. It should not be inferred from the first four instances that size of plant is not relevant to the production of rayon yarn. The theoretical relationship between plant expansion and unit costs has been discussed in Chapter 3; it was seen that plant size was of significance as a variable in the determination of unit costs. It is probable that consideration of cost data during the period 1925–1929 at Old Hickory when substantial expansions in capacity occurred would raise the contribution of plant growth to the total cost reduction over time. Moreover, it will be recalled that substantial reductions in unit overhead costs occurred at Spruance I during the period 1935–1940 as a result of the establishment at the Spruance location of Plants II, III, and II-A; certain overhead facilities were, henceforth, shared between a larger number of plants. Our main interest has been with individual plants considered in isolation, but if the reduction in overhead costs at Spruance I attributable to the establishment of other plants is taken into account, it would be found that scale of plant accounted for approximately 10 per cent of the net reduction in unit factory costs at that plant.

Second, the contribution of *"minor" technical change* to increased efficiency over time has been of great importance in the cases analyzed. The contribution of minor technical change as a proportion of the contribution of both "minor" and "major" technical change amounted to 100 per cent at Spruance II, 83 per cent at Spruance II-A, 80 per cent at Spruance I, 79 per cent at Old Hickory, and 46 per cent at Spruance III. We have pointed out above the likelihood that consideration of the period prior to 1932 at Spruance I would reveal further substantial reductions in unit costs attributable to minor technical changes. Similarly, consideration of the years 1937–1938 at Spruance III would probably show that substantial unit-cost reductions occurred which could be attributed to minor technical changes. It is also probable that minor technical changes occurred during years when unit-cost reductions have been attributed to major changes; for although it is possible that the major changes explain the entire unit-cost reductions, minor changes— poorly documented—may at the same time have played a role.

A third feature of importance is the significance of *indirect* technical change, both minor and major. Effort has been exerted continually to obtain a higher volume of output from a substantially unchanged capacity, measured in terms of spinning machines or installed nozzles. This has been particularly true at Spruance II-A and III, where tire-cord yarn was produced: it was necessary to devise methods of reducing the unit overhead costs in order to permit the product to compete with cotton in the industrial market. In the case of Spruance III 75 per cent of the unit-cost reductions *resulting from technical change* were attributed to technical change which we have categorized as "indirect." At Spruance II-A the proportion amounted to 67 per cent. But even in textile-yarn plants the proportion was quite high, amounting to 49 per cent at Spruance I and to 32 per cent at Old Hickory.

Chapter Five


# Interplant Analysis of Standard Costs per Pound of Rayon


In this chapter the differences in unit standard costs among the four Spruance plants will be considered.[1] The data, it will be recalled, have been corrected to reflect productivity movements. The tables presented in Chapter 4 show that unit direct-factory costs were highest at Spruance Plant I, followed in order of magnitude by costs at Spruance Plants II, II-A, and III. First, we shall attempt to account for the cost differential between the two textile-yarn plants; then we shall consider the differential between the two tire-cord plants; and finally, we shall turn to the cost differential between the tire-cord and textile-yarn plants.

### TWO TEXTILE-YARN PLANTS COMPARED

Table 5.1 summarizes unit costs in a number of years at the two textile-yarn plants. In 1937, unit direct-factory costs at Spruance I were

*Table 5.1   Standard Costs per Unit, in Selected Years, Spruance I and II*

|  | Operating Labor (in cents) (1) | Per cent I $\overline{\text{II}}$ (2) | Viscose Solution and Acid Bath (in cents) (3) | Per cent I $\overline{\text{II}}$ (4) | Direct Main- tenance (in cents) (5) | Per cent I $\overline{\text{II}}$ (6) | Total Direct- Factory Costs (in cents) (7) | Per cent I $\overline{\text{II}}$ (8) |
|---|---|---|---|---|---|---|---|---|
| 1937 Spruance I | 16.91 | | 9.65 | | 2.79 | | 29.35 | |
| II | 7.45 | 227.0 | 9.57 | 100.8 | 1.46 | 191.1 | 18.48 | 158.8 |
| 1940 Spruance I | 9.21 | | 8.65 | | 2.31 | | 20.17 | |
| II | 5.08 | 181.3 | 8.15 | 106.1 | 1.62 | 142.6 | 14.85 | 135.8 |
| 1945 Spruance I | 8.72 | | 8.57 | | 2.03 | | 19.32 | |
| II | 5.91 | 147.5 | 7.82 | 109.6 | 1.93 | 105.2 | 15.66 | 123.4 |
| 1950 Spruance I | 6.96 | | 8.13 | | 2.00 | | 17.09 | |
| II | 5.29 | 131.6 | 7.99 | 101.8 | 1.91 | 104.7 | 15.19 | 112.5 |

[1] Old Hickory is not discussed in this chapter: Spruance II was very similar to plants at Old Hickory and unit costs were almost identical.

58.8 per cent higher than at Spruance II, largely because of higher unit operating-labor costs at the former plant; unit direct-maintenance costs were also higher at Spruance I.

The differential between the two plants declined considerably over time: in 1950, unit operating-labor costs at Spruance I were only 31.6 per cent higher than at Spruance II, and unit direct-maintenance costs scarcely differed at the two plants. As a result of these trends, unit direct-factory costs at Spruance I were only 12.5 per cent higher than at Spruance II.

*Operating Labor:* One explanation for the higher level of unit operating-labor costs at Spruance I in 1937 is the fact that the denier of the yarn was lower than at Spruance II. However, the difference between the denier spun at the plants was not sufficient to exert a great influence.[2]

A more important consideration is the fact that the technique of production differed at Spruance I from that at Spruance II. The use of the bucket at Spruance II avoided the necessity for a separate stage of twisting the filaments; and the use of the "cake-to-cone" process avoided the stage of skeining and permitted a more convenient method of yarn purification.

We have seen in the preceding chapter that the Type 9 process was introduced at Spruance I between 1935 and 1940. Skeining was avoided in this method, which was similar in many respects to the cake-to-cone process with the difference that preliminary washing and preliminary drying were still required. In 1937, however, most yarn at Spruance I was still produced by the original skein-reeling method.

A higher spinning speed and a larger cake size at Spruance II were also important determinants of the relatively low level of unit operating-labor costs at that plant.

By 1940, both the spinning speed and the cake size at Spruance I had been raised to the levels existing at Spruance II; moreover, the Type 9 process was in general use at the former plant. Unit operating-labor costs declined considerably at Spruance I. At the same time, however, 60 additional spinning machines (Spruance II-A) were installed at Spruance II; cakes of 1.5 pounds were used, compared with cakes of 1.0 pound at the original section of the plant. Unit operating-labor costs on all yarn at the bucket plant, therefore, declined too. On balance, the differential between the two plants in the case of unit operating-labor costs was reduced between 1937 and 1940 from 127.0 per cent (in favor of Spruance II) to 81.3 per cent.

---

[2] The difference between the denier at the two plants remained relatively constant over time, whereas the cost differential fell very sharply; denier cannot, therefore, explain *changes* in the cost differential *over time*.

A further reduction in the unit-cost differential between 1940 and 1945 resulted largely from an *increase* in costs at Spruance II, which in turn resulted from the separation of Spruance II-A. A number of minor technical changes at both plants tended to reduce costs during the period 1945–1950, although unit operating-labor costs declined more steeply at Spruance I.

In 1950, unit operating-labor costs were only 37.0 per cent higher at the bobbin plant than at the bucket plant. This remaining differential was due

*Table 5.2   Capacity Output, Spruance I and II*

|  | Spruance I | | | Spruance II | | |
|  | Capacity Output (000 lb) (1) | Denier (2) | Capacity Output* Corrected for Denier (000 lb) (3) | Capacity Output (000 lb) (1) | Denier (2) | Capacity Output Corrected for Denier (000 lb) (3) |
|---|---|---|---|---|---|---|
| 1937 | 7,343 | 101.5 | 7,234 | 8,397 | 150.0 | 5,598 |
| 1940 | 8,034 | 98.8 | 8,131 | 15,020 | 131.9 | 11,387 |
| 1945 | 10,132 | 113.9 | 8,894 | 8,352 | 132.4 | 6,308 |
| 1950 | 9,528 | 97.8 | 9,741 | 9,782 | 151.2 | 6,470 |

* Corrected to denier = 100.

in part to the higher denier at the bucket plant, but was mainly the result of the fact that the Type 9 process did not possess all the advantages of the cake-to-cone process.

*Direct Maintenance:* Substantially the same reasons for the cost differential between the two plants, and changes therein, that were given in the case of operating labor apply in that of direct maintenance.

The original skein-reeling process, still in extensive use at Spruance I in 1937, involved more stages than the cake-to-cone process and correspondingly more equipment.[3] By 1940, the Type 9 process was in extensive use at Spruance I; many of the stages typical of the original process were rendered unnecessary by the new process and the requisite equipment was reduced. Unit direct-maintenance costs were 91.1 per cent higher at Spruance I than at II in 1937, but the differential had fallen to 42.6 per cent by 1940.

The difference between the denier of the plants and the spinning speed also contribute to the explanation of the cost differential. In Table 5.2,

[3] Specifically, the process involved additional dryers, throwing machines, reels, and spooling equipment, compared with the process at Spruance II.

capacity output at Spruance I and II is shown. The maximum output which can be obtained at each plant annually is recorded, first *in pounds of rayon of the particular denier actually produced* in each year, and next, *in pounds of constant (100) denier.* Capacity output at Spruance II in 1937 exceeded that at Spruance I despite the fact that the capacity defined in terms of the number of nozzles was larger at Spruance I (8,800 compared with 6,000). This can be explained by the higher spinning speed at Spruance II and the higher denier (150.0 compared with 101.5). If all pounds of yarn are corrected to rayon of standard denier, capacity output at Spruance I would be greater than at Spruance II, in spite of the higher spinning speed at the latter plant. The fact that a larger number of pounds was obtained from a smaller nozzle capacity at Spruance II would explain the lower maintenance costs per unit at that plant compared with Spruance I in 1937.

The doubling of capacity output between 1937 and 1939 at Spruance II resulted from an increase in the spindle capacity, which would not exert an influence upon unit maintenance costs. In 1938, the spinning speed at Spruance I was increased to that already existing at Plant II, and in fact the differential declined between 1937 and 1940. Because of the higher spindle capacity at Spruance I, and because the spinning speed had been increased, capacity output (even uncorrected for denier), was greater at Spruance I than at Spruance II after 1944. The fact that the maintenance costs per pound at Spruance I remained somewhat higher than at Spruance II must be explained by the remaining difference in the processes used at the plants.

*Summary:* In summary, the differential between the unit direct-factory costs at the two plants was largely the result of the differences between the techniques used. The difference in denier played some part, particularly in the explanation of the maintenance-cost differential. Finally, the difference in spinning speed prior to 1938 was partly responsible for the difference in unit costs.

Spruance I was constructed in 1929 and Spruance II in 1936. However, the bucket process was available for use and had been installed in certain Du Pont rayon plants before 1929, so that the question arises why Spruance I was built to produce yarn by the more expensive bobbin process. It should be borne in mind, however, that the cake-to-cone process, which greatly improved the bucket method, was not yet available in 1929; the cost differential between bucket and bobbin plants in 1929 would certainly have been smaller than that in 1937.

The answer lies largely in the fact that Spruance I was designed to produce a relatively fine-denier yarn. In the late 1920s it would have been technologically impossible to produce low-denier yarn by means of the bucket process.[4] In this sense, the cost differential between the bucket and bobbin plants can be considered as (indirectly) the result of the difference between the two products. During the 1930s the bucket-producing companies developed buckets capable of a sufficiently high speed for use even in the production of fine-denier yarn. At the same time, however, the introduction of the Type 9 process did much to reduce the advantage of the bucket process over the bobbin process. The remaining cost advantage was too small to justify the replacement of existing facilities at Spruance I.[5]

## TWO TIRE-CORD PLANTS COMPARED

Unit costs at Spruance II-A, the bucket plant producing tire-cord yarn, were somewhat higher than at Spruance III, where tire cord was produced by bobbin process (Table 5.3). In 1945, unit direct-factory costs at

*Table 5.3 Standard Costs per Unit, in Selected Years, Spruance II-A and III*

| | Operating Labor (in cents) (1) | Per cent II-A / III (2) | Viscose Solution and Acid Bath (in cents) (3) | Per cent II-A / III (4) | Direct Maintenance (in cents) (5) | Per cent II-A / III (6) | Total Direct-Factory Costs (in cents) (7) | Per cent II-A / III (8) |
|---|---|---|---|---|---|---|---|---|
| 1945 Spruance II-A | 3.50 | | 8.47 | | .89 | | 12.86 | |
| III | 2.31 | 151.5 | 8.72 | 97.1 | .65 | 136.9 | 11.68 | 110.1 |
| 1950 Spruance II-A | 1.80 | | 8.50 | | .61 | | 10.91 | |
| III | 1.56 | 115.4 | 8.70 | 97.7 | .46 | 132.6 | 10.72 | 101.8 |

Spruance II-A were 10.1 per cent higher than at Spruance III, largely because of higher unit operating-labor costs at the bucket plant; higher unit direct-maintenance costs at Spruance II-A also contributed to the net difference. However, the differential almost disappeared between 1945 and 1950.

*Operating Labor:* Spruance Plant III was the only Du Pont plant designed especially for the production of tire cord; it contained only those features required by the product. Many stages typical of textile-yarn production could be avoided from the outset. Moreover, further improvements were introduced with the development of the direct-slashing process in the late 1930s. Spruance II-A, however, was a *converted* plant and made use of features installed earlier when textile yarn was produced. With the passage of time, technical changes—in particular, the introduction of

[4] The bucket speed (in terms of revolutions per minute) was relatively slow, so that the centrifugal force of the bucket failed to build a satisfactory cake of low-denier yarn. It was physically necessary, therefore, to use a bobbin process for low-denier yarn.

[5] Yarn of 50 denier was in fact produced by the bucket process at Old Hickory.

wet slashing (entailing the abolition of coning)—brought about relatively large reductions at II-A, so that the differential between the two plants declined.

Moreover, Spruance III made use of more recently developed equipment, whereas in 1945 Spruance II-A used equipment which was older and less efficient. With time this disadvantage too was overcome.

Finally, it will be recalled that the spinning package at Spruance III (2.5 pounds in weight) exceeded that at Spruance II-A in 1945 (1.5 pounds). The limitation on the size of the cake was in part a technological phenomenon, but in part because the smaller cake was a feature of the "heritage" with which Spruance II-A began the production of tire-cord yarn. By 1950, however, the cake size at Spruance II-A had increased to 4.5 pounds, whereas that at Spruance III had increased to 3.9 pounds.

*Direct Maintenance:* Both the denier and the spinning speed were similar at the two tire-cord plants between 1945 and 1950. Unit direct-maintenance costs were somewhat lower at Spruance III, however; bobbin machines are said to be technically easier to maintain than bucket machines.

### TEXTILE-YARN AND TIRE-CORD PLANTS COMPARED

We turn now to compare the costs of production at plants producing different products. It is convenient to consider the cost differential between the two bucket plants, Spruance II-A (which produced tire-cord rayon) and Spruance II (which produced textile yarn), and that between the two bobbin plants, Spruance I (a textile-yarn plant) and Spruance III (a tire-cord plant).

Some justification for an attempt to compare production costs at plants producing different products may be in order at this point. The main requirements which must be met by a satisfactory textile-filament yarn are efficient "running" on textile-making equipment, freedom from broken filaments, uniform whiteness, and evenness of dyeing, whereas tenacity is of relatively small importance beyond the attainment of some minimum standard. Tenacity, however, is a requirement of prime significance in the case of tire cord, together with fatigue resistance, while color and mechanical quality are of lesser importance. If fatigue resistance and tenacity are high, then the filaments will "run" well on cord-making equipment. Evenness of dyeing is not a requirement; indeed the procedure of developing greater tenacity (by stretching the filaments under controlled circumstances) would render dyeing, were it required, more difficult.

In comparing the unit costs at the textile-yarn plants with those at the plants where tire cord is produced, we are not implying that some rationalization must be found for the fact that "low-cost" and "high-cost" plants exist side-by-side. The fact that tire cord is produced at lower cost per unit than textile yarn should not be surprising, since these are "different" products (with different price structures). Our purpose, however, is limited: we shall point out below that costs at the *textile-yarn plants* might have been reduced by the introduction of certain mechanisms. The extent to which unit costs would probably have been reduced can be seen by considering the cost differential between these plants and those where the mechanisms were installed. The cost differential is by no means a

*Table 5.4   Standard Costs per Unit, in Selected Years, Spruance I and III*

| | Operating Labor (in cents) (1) | Per cent $\frac{I}{III}$ (2) | Viscose Solution and Acid Bath (in cents) (3) | Per cent $\frac{I}{III}$ (4) | Direct Main-tenance (in cents) (5) | Per cent $\frac{I}{III}$ (6) | Total Direct-Factory Costs (in cents) (7) | Per cent $\frac{I}{III}$ (8) |
|---|---|---|---|---|---|---|---|---|
| 1938 Spruance I | 13.77 | | 9.34 | | 2.62 | | 25.73 | |
| III | 5.31 | 259.3 | 9.40 | 99.4 | 1.48 | 177.0 | 16.19 | 158.9 |
| 1940 Spruance I | 9.21 | | 8.65 | | 2.31 | | 20.17 | |
| III | 3.37 | 273.3 | 9.23 | 93.7 | 1.13 | 204.4 | 13.73 | 146.9 |
| 1945 Spruance I | 8.72 | | 8.57 | | 2.03 | | 19.32 | |
| III | 2.31 | 377.5 | 8.72 | 98.3 | .65 | 312.3 | 11.68 | 165.4 |
| 1950 Spruance I | 6.96 | | 8.13 | | 2.00 | | 17.07 | |
| III | 1.56 | 446.2 | 8.70 | 93.4 | .46 | 434.7 | 10.72 | 159.4 |

precise measure, since certain features in the tire-cord plants which were partly responsible for the cost differential would have been unfeasible in textile-yarn production.[6]

In 1938, unit direct-factory costs were 58.9 per cent higher at Spruance I than at Spruance III (Table 5.4). The differential was due almost entirely to the higher unit operating-labor costs at the textile-yarn plant, for unit materials costs were almost identical in that year. Unit direct-maintenance costs were also considerably lower at Spruance III. The differential between total costs per pound at the two plants remained relatively stable over time, in spite of the increase in the differential between unit operating-labor costs, and between unit direct-maintenance costs. Material costs per unit at Spruance I remained slightly lower throughout than material costs at Spruance III.

In the case of production by the bucket process (Table 5.5) we find once more that costs at the textile-yarn plant were higher than at the tire-cord plant. The differential, however, was smaller than that between Spruance I and III. In 1945, for example, unit direct-factory costs at Spruance II were only 21.8 per cent higher than at Spruance II-A. The differential rises slightly over time as a result of relatively large reductions in unit operating-labor costs at Spruance II-A.

[6] It may also be mentioned that tire-cord yarn can be considered a product improvement rather than a new and different product, insofar as it resulted from an attempt to improve the tenacity of textile yarn.

*Operating Labor:* The main reason for the lower unit operating-labor costs at the tire-cord plants lies in the nature of the product. We have already noted the principal requirements of tire-cord yarn compared with those of textile yarn: simpler control in spinning, easier standards of purification, and less severe standards of mechanical quality typified the production of industrial yarn. It was therefore feasible to install processes which avoided many steps in the spinning and postspinning operations, and which dispensed both with equipment and complementary labor.

*Table 5.5    Standard Costs per Unit, in Selected Years, Spruance II and II-A*

| | Operating Labor (in cents) (1) | Per cent II II-A (2) | Viscose Solution and Acid Bath (in cents) (3) | Per cent II II-A (4) | Direct Main- tenance (in cents) (5) | Per cent II II-A (6) | Total Direct- Factory Costs (in cents) (7) | Per cent II II-A (8) |
|---|---|---|---|---|---|---|---|---|
| 1945 Spruance II | 5.91 | | 7.82 | | 1.93 | | 15.66 | |
| II-A | 3.50 | 168.9 | 8.47 | 92.3 | .89 | 216.8 | 12.86 | 121.8 |
| 1950 Spruance II | 5.29 | | 7.99 | | 1.91 | | 15.19 | |
| II-A | 1.80 | 293.9 | 8.50 | 94.0 | .61 | 313.1 | 10.91 | 139.2 |

Thus, for example, bleaching and desulphuring were not required in the production of tire cord and "compensation spinning" was unnecessary. The trend towards simplification of process at tire-cord plants culminated in the installation of automatic washing at both tire-cord plants, of direct slashing at Spruance III and wet slashing at Spruance II-A. Large-size "beams" were a further feature peculiar to tire-cord production.[7]

Substantial differences in denier and in cake size also contributed to the unit-cost differential between textile and tire-cord plants. Large size buckets could have been installed in textile-yarn plants, but only with the development of entirely new purification and drying procedures, and new-type spinning machines.

The viscose-making equipment tended to be larger in the case of tire-cord plants, and this permitted certain economies in the use of operating labor in the chemical building. The larger units were introduced in the newer plants and could have been installed in the original textile-yarn plants.

Nickel piping replaced iron piping in tire-cord plants, in the viscose-preparation rooms and in the installations from the viscose rooms to the spinning baths. The use of iron piping had been responsible for the contamination of the solution, the consequent blockage of piping, and the necessity for frequent stoppages; upon recommencement of operations,

---

[7] The slashing processes embodied means for rapid drying, and avoided coning or skeining. Alternative-active spinning at Spruance II-A avoided all waste at the doffing stage.

several weeks might be required before first-grade yarns could be produced. The nickel piping could have been installed in textile-yarn plants.

*Materials:* Unit materials costs were higher at the tire-cord plants than at the textile-yarn plants. The differential can be explained by the fact that more expensive cellulose sources were used in the production of tire cord. Although all cost data have been corrected for input-price changes, we have not assumed that the *base year* price of cellulose was the same at each plant, for tire-cord production demanded purer cellulose than that used in textile-yarn production, and the prices paid for such pulps and linters were higher than those of regular sources of cellulose. Strictly

*Table 5.6   Capacity Output, Spruance I and III*

| | Spruance I | | | Spruance III | | |
|---|---|---|---|---|---|---|
| | Capacity Output (000 lb) (1) | Denier (2) | Capacity Output* Corrected for Denier (000 lb) (3) | Capacity Output (000 lb) (1) | Denier (2) | Capacity Output* Corrected for Denier (000 lb) (3) |
| 1938 | 8,060 | 115.9 | 6,954 | 3,218 | 264.3 | 1,219 |
| 1940 | 8,034 | 98.8 | 8,131 | 6,692 | 447.2 | 1,496 |
| 1945 | 10,132 | 113.9 | 8,894 | 22,285 | 1,100.9 | 2,024 |
| 1950 | 9,528 | 97.8 | 9,741 | 33,587 | 1,650.0 | 2,035 |

* Corrected to denier = 100.

speaking, "cellulose" at the tire-cord plants is a different input from "cellulose" at the textile-yarn plants, and the *intraplant price differential has been retained* to reflect this fact. Although the physical productivity of the highly purified cellulose sources exceeded that of regular pulp, the price differential is such that unit costs were higher in the case of Spruance II-A or III than at I or II.

*Direct Maintenance:* Two facts account for the lower unit direct-maintenance costs at tire-cord plants. First, less equipment was required in the production of any given volume of output as a result of the simplifications in process introduced at Spruance II-A and III. Second, the denier was substantially higher at the tire-cord plants. Consequently, although the *installed-nozzle capacity* was smaller at the tire-cord plants, volume of output was considerably greater (Tables 5.6 and 5.7).[8]

[8] Installed-nozzle capacity at Spruance I was 8,800, whereas that at Spruance III amounted to 1,800 after the expansion, 1938–1940. Installed-nozzle capacity at Spruance II was 6,000, whereas at Spruance II-A the figure was 2,040 until 1947–1948, and 3,120 thereafter.

SUMMARY

The unit-cost differential that existed between the two textile-yarn plants at Spruance declined radically over time. The introduction of the Type 9 process permitted reductions in unit costs at Spruance I which, although not as marked as those resulting from the cake-to-cone process, were sufficient to justify the continuation of production by bobbin process.

The differential between unit costs at the two tire-cord plants also declined sharply with the passage of time. By 1950, Spruance II-A—a

*Table 5.7   Capacity Output, Spruance II and II-A*

| | Spruance II | | | Spruance II-A | | |
|---|---|---|---|---|---|---|
| | Capacity Output (000 lb) (1) | Denier (2) | Capacity Output* Corrected for Denier (000 lb) (3) | Capacity Output (000 lb) (1) | Denier (2) | Capacity Output* Corrected for Denier (000 lb) (3) |
| 1945 | 8,352 | 132.4 | 9,462 | 23,490 | 1,104.9 | 3,189 |
| 1950 | 9,782 | 151.2 | 9,705 | 41,171 | 1,609.3 | 3,837 |

* Corrected to denier = 150.

converted textile-yarn plant—was able to produce tire cord almost as cheaply as Spruance III, which had been designed especially for the new product. Any remaining differential in favor of Spruance III did not justify the wholesale replacement of the bucket techniques used at Spruance II-A.

Finally, we have considered the unit-cost differential that existed between the tire-cord and the textile-yarn plants. The major part of the differential resulted simply from the fact that different products were produced at the different plants; the nature of the product determined to a large degree the processes which could be introduced. Highly simplified methods were installed in tire-cord plants which could not be introduced at the textile-yarn plants. However, there were certain features of tire-cord production which, if applied to textile yarn, would have permitted reductions in unit costs: in certain instances, significant development would have been required before application to textile-yarn production would have been feasible; in every instance, investment outlays would have been required.

# Chapter Six

# Technical Change and Investment

In this chapter the relationship between the particular changes in technique of production, enumerated in the preceding chapters, and investment in plant and equipment will be considered. As a preliminary, it may be helpful to recall the well-known principles governing the decision to replace existing equipment by new equipment, since the later discussion will be intimately concerned with this problem.

It is widely recognized that the mere existence of new-type technology is not a guarantee that it will in fact be introduced in an old plant. In any decision to allocate funds for the purchase of plant and equipment, management can be conceived of as estimating the present value of the net benefits expected from various projects, ranking the projects according to the magnitude of the expected rate of return on the investment involved, and choosing those projects promising a rate of return in excess of some "rejection rate." But how are the net benefits permitted by the introduction of new-type equipment arrived at? When considering the introduction of cost-reducing equipment, for example, a comparison would be made between the *total* costs relevant to the new equipment and the *variable* costs relevant to the existing equipment. Cost comparisons limited to operating costs may be misleading. But even when the new method is found to offer advantages over the existing method, there is no assurance that the rate of return on the necessary investment expenditures needed to accomplish the replacement will suffice to overcome the competition for scarce financial resources which any particular project must meet. Moreover, the calculation of the rate of return depends upon the *expectations* of management respecting various future relationships; we are not usually in a position to recreate these expectations, and what appears after the event to be a cost advantage may not have been evident at the time a decision was made.

Of particular relevance in this respect is the possibility that despite the satisfaction of the test which must be made before new equipment will be introduced, that is, despite the fact that the average total costs of using the new equipment are below the average variable costs of continuing the use of the existing equipment, a company may practice what has been called "anticipatory retardation." The company may expect that the new-type equipment will shortly be superseded by a superior alternative; rather than install the currently available equipment it may, therefore, decide to wait upon events.[1]

In considering the question why techniques installed in certain rayon plants are in fact not installed in others despite the fact that a cost advantage appears to exist, great care must be exercised in the definition of the product "rayon"; certain mechanisms might be inapplicable to certain categories of rayon. Moreover, relative factor prices may conceivably differ between plants and, therefore, be partly responsible for the existence at the same time of different technologies.

In some instances a change in technology undertaken in order to reduce production costs may of necessity involve an alteration in the nature of the end product, so that the introduction of such improvements depends upon the willingness of the customers of the plant to accept the altered product. Certain technologies may not be applied for this reason. However, all these possibilities are not exceptions to the principles of replacement, but are rather instances of certain complications which enter into the decision.

During the following discussion, the distinction may be borne in mind between two kinds of additions to the capital stock resulting from technical change. First, it is possible that a technical change brings about a unit-cost reduction (or an improvement in quality) which makes it profitable to expand production; as a result, equipment may be added to the existing stock of capital, and more labor hired and more materials purchased per period. Investment of this nature is "expansionary," but is not the *proximate* result of the technical change. Second, however, there may be instances when technical change requires added equipment; thus, a technical change may permit reductions in unit operating-labor or materials costs but only because added capital equipment is introduced: in these

---

[1] The term "anticipatory retardation" is used by William Fellner, "The Influence of Market Structure on Technological Progress," in American Economic Association, *Readings in Industrial Organization and Public Policy*, ed. Heflebower and Stocking, Richard D. Irwin, Inc., Homewood, Illinois, 1958, pp. 277–296. See also George Terborgh, *Dynamic Equipment Policy*, McGraw-Hill Book Co., Inc., New York, 1949, Ch. 4.

instances there occurs a substitution of capital for other inputs. Such changes may be termed "capital using."[2]

### TECHNICAL CHANGE REQUIRING INVESTMENT IN THE RAYON INDUSTRY AS A WHOLE

In this section we shall consider improvements in technique, *dependent upon investment in plant and equipment*, which are known to have been permitted by developments in the rayon industry *as a whole* or in industries supplying equipment to rayon plants. In the next section we shall again turn to a consideration of events at the Spruance and Old Hickory plants.

*Input-Recovery Systems*

It is interesting to recall the statement by Avram, made in 1927:[3]

Comparatively speaking, they [the raw materials used in the Viscose process] are cheap in price and are to be found in large quantities in almost every part of the world. Because of this comparative cheapness there is no necessity of an expensive recovery system with its added technical difficulties, such as the case with the other processes.

Within four or five years circumstances had changed and great attention was being centered upon recovery systems.

*Caustic Soda:* The necessity for the recovery of caustic soda became increasingly important during the early 1930s as pressure to reduce costs increased; although this input is relatively cheap per pound, large quantities are used in production. Stream pollution laws in the United States also necessitated steps to recover caustic soda. In some European plants, primitive recovery methods existed during the 1920s. In the late 1920s, the principle of "osmosis," involving the use of dializing tanks, was developed; patents were taken out by Cerini in Italy, and by Asahi in Japan.[4] During the 1930s the Cerini dializer was improved to the point where 98 per cent

---

[2] See Chapter 4, pp. 117–118.
[3] Mois H. Avram, *The Rayon Industry*, D. Van Nostrand Company, New York, 1927, p. 256.
[4] Some caustic soda is drained out before the steeping presses are operated and is stored for re-use. Much of the chemical still remains and is extruded when the pulp sheets are pressed. This caustic soda is "rich" in hemicellulose which must be removed if the chemical is to be re-used. This is done in the dializing tanks by passing the caustic soda through parchment-paper membranes.
Asahi dializers were installed at Old Hickory and both Asahi and Cerini dializers at Spruance.

of soda impurities could be removed.[5] Improvements in the dializing equipment by American engineering companies also took place in the early 1930s.[6] The introduction of dializers into a rayon plant involved the installation of new equipment.[7]

*Carbon Bisulphide:* Attempts were also made during the 1930s by engineering companies, to develop mechanisms which would permit the recovery of carbon bisulphide.[8] Recovery of carbon bisulphide was limited at Du Pont plants because of the great expense involved. Recovery equipment was introduced in the late 1930s and early 1940s in small amounts.

*Acid-Bath Recovery:* Of great importance were the efforts made to allow economies in the use of the constituent elements in the spinning bath. For example, the Swenson Evaporator Company of Illinois developed three pieces of equipment for the recovery of sulphuric acid and sodium sulphate.[9] These mechanisms were cast-lead evaporators used for the concentration of the bath (that is, for the evaporation of water from the spent bath), batch-type vacuum crystallizers for the crystallization of sodium sulphate (Glauber's Salts) from the spent bath, and rotary filters of the batch type for the filtration of the Glauber's Salts after their removal from the bath.[10] Later improvements led to the commercial development of continuous evaporators, crystallizers, and rotary-filter mechanisms.

The introduction of bath-recovery equipment called for investment expenditure; the effect would theoretically be a reduction in *net* costs of sulphuric acid and sodium sulphate per pound of rayon. Glucose requirements would also be reduced. Acid-bath reclaim became increasingly

[5] H. R. Mauersberger, "Review of Rayon Machinery Improvements," *Rayon Textile Monthly*, Vol. XX, Sept. 1939, pp. 110–113.

[6] Arthur O. Russell, "The First American Dialyzer Unit," *Rayon and Melliand Textile Monthly*, Vol. XVI, Sept. 1935, p. 87. Until the early 1930s the dializer was an offshoot of that used in the sugar industry; in this paper, a new-type dializer—patented by Russell—is described.

[7] Dializers were first introduced at Spruance and Old Hickory in 1933–1936.

[8] Williams Haynes, *American Chemical Industry*, D. Van Nostrand Company, Inc., New York, 1948, Vol. V, p. 369. Reference is made here to the new designs and apparatus for the recovery of carbon bisulphide by the Semet-Solvay Engineering Company. This particular piece of equipment was not used at Du Pont Rayon plants.

[9] The reaction of the caustic soda in the viscose and the acid in the spinning bath results in excess sodium sulphate (Glauber's Salts). For the re-use of the bath after spinning, evaporators are needed to remove water; crystallizers, to crystallize the sodium sulphate from the bath; and filters, to filter the sodium sulphate which has been removed. The sodium sulphate can be re-used rather than "ditched" and the sulphuric acid can be sold or used in the process. Glucose is needed in lesser amounts as a result of the recovery mechanisms.

[10] H. R. Mauersberger, "A Review of Rayon Machinery Developments," *Rayon and Melliand Textile Monthly*, Vol. XVI, Sept. 1935, pp. 57–68. Improved filtration is of particular relevance for *quality* improvement.

important with the development of high-tenacity yarns which demand more expensive materials than regular textile rayon.[11]

### Chemical Plant Equipment

Significant developments have taken place in techniques used in the chemical building, apart from the recovery mechanisms referred to in the preceding section.

*Steeping:* The earliest steeping (mercerizing) presses installed in United States plants were operated by mechanical screw; by about 1936, hydraulic presses had been installed in most plants. Originally, the pressed alkali cellulose sheets were removed from the presses vertically by hand; improvements by the mid-1930s permitted the automatic discharge by hydraulic ram of the pressed sheets (onto trucks or through holes in the floor).[12] The valves governing the inflow and outflow of the caustic soda, and the movement of the ram, were controlled automatically rather than manually in the more advanced steeping presses. Each press, in the older technique, was linked by pumps to a common power unit (the pump-and-accumulator system); a well-known development was that made by the Hydraulic Press Manufacturing Company whereby each press could be operated as a self-contained unit; these presses used motor-driven pressure generators and were operated by automatic control of speed and pressure. Some of these presses are known to have been installed in American plants by 1935.

In addition to the replacement of manual by automatic controls, attention was paid by equipment manufacturers to the development of continuous-steeping equipment[13] and the use of larger units. By the end of the 1930s successful mechanisms had been developed.

[11] Swenson evaporators were used at Du Pont plants; crystallizers and coal filters were also used but were designed by Du Pont. The first crystallizers to be installed at a Du Pont rayon plant were introduced in 1931 at Buffalo, and in subsequent years—particularly the period 1936–1940—at all Du Pont rayon plants.

In some cases the original batch-type mechanisms were later replaced by continuous equipment: for example, the replacement of the original filter tanks by equipment allowing continuous filtration occurred at Spruance II-A in 1954. Continuous evaporation also replaced batch-operated evaporation.

[12] One such (patented) steeping press of a relatively advanced type is described in H. B. Vollrath, "Progress in Machinery for the Chemical Plant," *Rayon Textile Monthly*, Vol. XVII, Sept. 1936, p. 55.

[13] H. B. Vollrath, "Progress in Machinery for the Chemical Plant," *Rayon Textile Monthly*, Vol. XVIII, Sept. 1937, p. 68.

Continuous-steeping equipment was installed as part of a replacement program at Du Pont's Buffalo Plant II in 1941. Continuous-steeping machines were introduced almost twenty years later at Old Hickory (1958) but were not used at any time at Spruance. Automatic controls of the time cycle were introduced at Spruance II-A in 1951.

The Hydraulic Press Manufacturing Company's equipment was not used at Du Pont plants.

*Shredding:* The earliest shredding machines were adaptations of paper making equipment; the time cycle was slow—approximately three hours—because of the danger to the process of the high temperatures generated by speed. Equipment manufacturers significantly improved the shredding machines by the complete "jacketing" of the troughs; this change allowed the use of cold water in the place of brine for cooling purposes, a faster rate of flow of the cooling liquid and, as a result, the possibility of introducing high-speed blades which reduced the time cycle. (In 1931 patents covering high speed ("Duplex") blades were taken out; these blades were installed in Baker Perkins shredding equipment. By 1936 shredding equipment had become further improved: The Baker Perkins "Size 20" Shredder, for example, reduced the pressed sheets to crumbs in one-hour cycles; maintenance costs were low and perfect temperature control was possible as a result of automatic-control mechanisms. The capacity of this machine was raised to accommodate batches of 600 pounds.)[14] Continuous shredders were developed by Baker Perkins by 1938.[15]

*Aging:* Mechanized means were introduced in most United States plants during the 1930s to convey the alkali cellulose into and out of the aging cellars.[16]

*Xanthation:* Xanthation machinery was also improved by equipment manufacturers during the 1930s. Conveyers were introduced to feed the aged crumbs into the xanthation churns, and after the completion of this stage, the contents could be discharged directly through chutes into the dissolvers. There is particular difficulty involved in rendering this stage by continuous process although ultimately continuous xanthators

[14] Reference to the 1931 development can be found in H. B. Vollrath, "Progress in Machinery for the Chemical Plant," *Rayon Textile Monthly,* Vol. XVII, Sept. 1936, p. 56; Eric Schuelke, "Recent Developments in Rayon Machinery," *Rayon and Synthetic Yarn Journal,* Vol. XIII, July 1932, pp. 12–15. These shredding machines had roller bearings, direct motor drives, better gears, automatic electrically driven tilting devices, and an increased cooling area. The patented blades permitted doubled cutting work per revolution. The main features of the "Size 20" machine were complete jacketing and increased capacity. See *Rayon Textile Monthly* for Sept. 1939, Vol. XX, pp. 110–113. The Size 20 machines were installed at Du Pont plants. Du Pont and Baker Perkins cooperated in the development of the machine.

[15] It has been argued that the cost saving permitted by the replacement of batch by continuous shredders was small and that it would probably not have been profitable to replace existing shredders. H. B. Vollrath, "Progress Towards Continuous Processing in Viscose Manufacture," *Rayon Textile Monthly,* Vol. XIX, Sept. 1938, pp. 72–74. Continuous shredding of a different type (coupled with continuous steeping) was developed by Du Pont, and introduced in Buffalo in 1941. This equipment was transferred to Old Hickory in 1958. Shredding at Spruance remained throughout a batch-operated process; automatic temperature controls, however, were introduced.

[16] Electric trucks were used in place of hand trucks at Du Pont plants. Continuous-aging machines were available but were not installed at either Old Hickory or Spruance. The only change over time at these plants was the installation of larger units.

were developed. An important development was the introduction by Baker Perkins of a completely water-jacketed churn of 900 gallons capacity, by 1935 or in 1936.[17]

*Mixing (Dissolving):* Improved dissolvers known as "Vissolvers" were developed experimentally by Baker Perkins in 1925; the time cycle was considerably reduced by these machines. Improvements in the "Vissolver" led to the "Size 20" dissolver, which treated larger batches and, at the same time, cut the time cycle from six or eight hours to three hours. Exact temperature control was maintained by means of the efficient circulation of cooling water; the finished material was discharged by means of compressed air, or vacuum. This machine was available for use in rayon plants by 1937.[18]

*Ripening:* Continuous-ripening equipment was installed at certain United States plants: the viscose solution in the process is pumped continuously through the filter presses. This method replaces the batch process, in which the viscose solution is blown from one filter press to the next.

*Deaeration:* Originally, rayon plants (including Spruance and Old Hickory) made use of vacuum tanks. Continuous-deaeration equipment replaced the batch-operated tanks in later years.

*Summary of Changes in Chemical Plant Equipment:* The improvements in the equipment used in the chemical buildings of rayon plants for the production of the viscose solution have several common features. They involved the replacement of batch by continuous process, the replacement of manual by automatic-control mechanisms, an increase in the size of the units of equipment, and a reduction in the time required for the completion of each stage in the sequence of viscose manufacture.

Continuous operation has the effect of reducing operating-labor costs per pound of rayon; this is also true of the use of automatic-control mechanisms. The introduction of larger units of equipment is a means of exploiting the indivisible nature of labor crews. Further economies may result from the increase in output per period due to reduced time cycles.

---

[17] H. B. Vollrath, "Progress in Machinery for the Chemical Plant," *Rayon Textile Monthly*, Vol. XVIII, Sept. 1937, p. 69.
This piece of equipment was installed in parts of the Spruance and Old Hickory plants. Continuous xanthation was not used at these locations.

[18] H. B. Vollrath, "Progress Towards Continuous Processing in Viscose Manufacture," *Rayon Textile Monthly*, Vol. XIX, Sept. 1938, pp. 72–74. It may be noted that some European companies made use of a combined xanthation and dissolving machine or "xantholver"; this machine was developed by Werner and Pfleiderer, the parent company of Baker and Perkins, and was patented.
The improved Baker Perkins equipment referred to above was installed at Spruance and in parts of Old Hickory. In the case of Spruance I, the "Vissolvers" replaced the original French (belt-driven) mixers. Continuous dissolving was not introduced.

Capital equipment as well as labor may, in fact, be economized on balance in the production of a given level of output when a continuous operation or an automatic-control mechanism is introduced instead of a batch operation or a manual-control mechanism. Moreover, the increase in output per period may permit reductions in "capital" per unit as well as reductions in labor per unit of output. "Capital" is economized as a result of the use of larger machines operating at faster speeds because of the expansion of output from a given "unit" of equipment.

*Spinning*

Attempts were made by equipment manufacturers to increase the "spinning speed," or the length of rayon filament spun during a given period. An important prerequisite for increased spinning speed is the attainment of higher "bucket speed," or the number of revolutions per minute made by the bucket.[19]

Various companies had succeeded by the early 1930s in their efforts to raise the number of revolutions per minute made by the bucket or bobbin.[20] Of great significance is the development of the "Textolite High Speed Spinning Pot" by General Electric; this mechanism made feasible the introduction of larger buckets of improved structure and material. Available records show that the Spruance II buckets installed in 1935 were capable of 9,000 revolutions per minute. (The mechanical spindles used in the early 1920s limited speeds to below 5,200 rpm.)

The advantage of high spinning speeds lies in the reduction in the unit costs related to fixed equipment, in unit power costs, and in "fixed" labor items per unit of output.

With the development of high bucket speeds, even fine-denier yarn could be spun by means of the bucket rather than the bobbin.

*Purification Mechanisms*

The variety of washing methods employed at Spruance and Old Hickory is representative of those available to the industry as a whole. In Spruance I "centrifugal washing" was used; Spruance III, which was also a bobbin plant, employed at first a "centrifugal-washing" technique but later installed "pressure washing." "Drip washing" was employed at Spruance

---

[19] If the bucket speed is, for example, 8,400 rpm and a twist of three turns per inch is introduced into the yarn, then the spinning speed will be 8,400/3, or 2,800 inches per minute. An increased bucket speed permits more twist without a reduction in spinning speed or increased spinning speed without a reduction in twist per inch.

[20] Companies referred to in the literature include: The Max Ams Chemical Engineering Corporation of Bridgeport, Connecticut; Dobson and Barlow of Bolton, England; The Wicaco Machine Company; H. W. Butterworth and Sons; the General Electric Company; and the Whitin Corporation. Most of the developments were patented.

II, at Old Hickory, and at Spruance II-A (from 1944–1948). Later developments include the mechanization of the pressure-washing and of the drip-washing techniques.[21]

### INVESTMENT REQUIRED BY TECHNICAL CHANGE AT INDIVIDUAL DU PONT PLANTS

*Old Hickory*

The initial establishment of rayon-producing facilities at Old Hickory in the two-year period 1925–1926 required expenditures on plant and equipment amounting to approximately $13.50 ($15.30) million.[22] The number of spinning machines was increased in 1928 from 128 to 180 at a cost of approximately $7.00 ($8.00) million.

We shall now consider chronologically the investment expenditures required at Old Hickory by the technical changes described in Chapter 4:

*1930–1932, Several "Minor" Technical Changes:* A number of "minor" technical changes were introduced in the three-year period 1930–1932, leading to reductions in unit operating-labor costs of 7.50 cents and in unit materials costs of 2.23 cents. The increase in the size of the buckets and consequently in the cakes, the increase in skein length and the introduction of improved means of yarn stretching—of particular relevance in explaining the unit operating-labor cost reductions—and better filtration required expenditures on new equipment as part of a replacement program. No *individual* technical change had a great effect upon unit costs and the investment required for the accomplishment of each change was not large. The expenditures involved alterations to the existing spinning machines. Certain of the minor changes, however, were not dependent

---

[21] Experimentation at the Du Pont plants indicated that "mechanized pressure washing" and "mechanized drip washing" did permit cost reductions, but it was not until 1958 at Old Hickory that the original drip-washing process was replaced. Centrifugal washing could have been applied to the remaining section of Spruance II, but the necessary investment expenditure could not be justified by the labor savings permitted. The cakes are put into a special compartment which spins around, while the wash solution is sprayed through from the inside; in the drip method (used at Spruance II), there is a separate section of wash racks, and labor requirements are relatively high. The effects of mechanized drip washing at Old Hickory were reduced labor costs per pound, improved working conditions, and improved quality.

Automatic centrifugal washers were installed at Spruance II-A in 1948–1949.

[22] In this chapter we shall refer to a change in unit costs exceeding one cent in the case of textile yarn and one-half cent in that of tire cord—in constant (1939) dollars—as "large" or "significant"; the entire cost structure is lower in the production of tire cord. Investment outlays exceeding $250,000 in constant (1939) dollars will be considered "significant" outlays.

The text employs current dollars, with constant (1939) dollars in parentheses.

upon investment expenditures: improved process control, improvements in the "quality" of operating labor, the adoption of a constant-index system and the use of more productive raw materials are the most important instances of technical change which did not require investment expenditures during the early 1930s at Old Hickory.

*1932–1937, Cake-to-Cone Process:* The cake-to-cone process was introduced for the first time at Old Hickory in 1932, although it was not widely used at the location until the mid-1930s. In 1934, operations were expanded by the addition of 51 spinning machines designed for the production of weaving yarn by the new process. Unit operating-labor costs declined by 3.29 cents between 1932 and 1937 and unit direct-maintenance costs by 1.49 cents as a result of the change in process.

Approximately $1.00 ($1.20) million was expended for both the replacement and the conversion of existing equipment.[23] A further $4.40 ($5.20) million was required by the expansion program. *The process change in itself* did not require net additions to equipment however.

A change in the organization of the doffing stage—itself a "minor" technical change required by the cake-to-cone process—necessitated some small investment in added equipment.

*1933–1934, Electric-Spindle Motor Drives:* In the period 1933–1934, the spinning machines were converted to electric-spindle motor drives; the spinning speed increased as a result. Unit operating-labor costs declined by 1.31 cents and unit direct-maintenance costs by .97 cent; there also occurred a reduction in unit overhead costs of approximately 2.14 cents.[24] The replacement of the belt-driven motor system required an investment outlay of $500,000 ($640,000).

*1934, Dializers:* The addition of dializers in 1934 for the recovery of caustic soda permitted a reduction in unit caustic-soda costs of .26 cent. The project involved an expenditure on new equipment of approximately $100,000 ($120,000). Essentially this expenditure represented the "substitution" of capital for materials.

[23] The expenditure of $1.0 million covered the replacement or conversion of equipment in spinning, washing, and drying; the conversion of reeling rooms into winding areas; and the abolition of the "wash-and-bleach" areas. In late 1935 and early 1936 the cloverleaf bucket used in the introduction of the new process was replaced by round buckets (and rubber dams) in the production of yarn of 150 denier or less, for "flashes" appeared on certain yarns upon the introduction of higher bucket speeds.

[24] Output increased from 1929 to 1940 by 106.3 per cent. We have seen in Chapter 4, p. 71, that this increase can be broken down as follows: (a) 28.3 per cent due to added capacity, 1934; (b) 33.9 per cent due to increased spinning-speed, 1933–1934; and (c) the remainder (or 44.1 per cent) due to the Type 10 replacement program of 1937. Unit overhead costs declined by 4.28 cents, 1929–1940, as a result of events (b) and (c), see p. 72; as an approximation, this decline can be attributed *equally* between the events, although (c) was somewhat more important. A reduction of 2.14 cents is therefore attributed to electric-spindle motor drives, and 2.14 cents to Type 10 spinning machines.

*1935–1936, Increased Nozzles per Spinning Machine:* The addition of a small number of nozzles per spinning machine permitted a reduction in unit operating-labor costs of .12 cent and required a relatively small investment expenditure.

*1937, Type 10 Spinning Machines:* Unit operating-labor costs declined by 1.74 cents, unit direct-maintenance costs by .51 cent and unit overhead costs by 2.14 cents[25] as a consequence of the replacement of 106 spinning machines by high-speed Type 10 machines which were capable of making either weaving yarn by the cake-to-cone process or knitting yarn by the Type 1 process. A replacement expenditure on new equipment amounting to $2.50 ($2.50) million was required.

*1936–1940, Acid-Bath Recovery:* In the five-year period 1936–1940, unit acid-bath costs declined by .78 cent as the result of the introduction of improved acid-bath recovery equipment. Evaporators and crystallizers were installed in 1935–1936 at an outlay of $250,000 ($290,000), and shortly thereafter a further investment of $300,000 ($300,000) on evaporators, crystallizers, and coal filters was made. The projects involved additions to existing equipment rather than replacements.[26] The added equipment represented the "substitution" of capital for materials.

*1938–1941, Several "Minor" Technical Changes:* Several minor technical changes were introduced during the late 1930s which led to a net reduction in unit operating-labor costs of 2.69 cents. Further improvements in 1940–1941 resulted in a reduction in unit viscose-solution costs by .25 cent.

The introduction of improved equipment for the preparation of the viscose solution—large-size and rapid-operating shredding churns, xanthation barattes, and mixers—required a replacement expenditure of approximately $1.70 ($1.70) million.

Very little investment was required for the increase in cake size and the continuation of the trend from dispatch in skein form to dispatch in cone form. The introduction of carbon-bisulphide recovery equipment involved an insignificant expenditure on equipment since the project was on a small scale; unit carbon-bisulphide costs declined by only .08 cent.

No investment was necessary for the reduction in unit cellulose costs of .17 cent in the early 1940s; the reduction resulted from the use of high-quality wood pulp instead of cotton linters. More rigorous cost control, improved training of labor, and subsequent reductions in waste did not involve investment outlays.

---

[25] See previous note.
[26] Filtration, however, is designed largely to improve the quality of the product rather than to reduce unit costs.

*1943-1944, Spinning-Machine Equipment:* In 1943-1944 unit acid-bath costs declined by .26 cent, largely because of a reduction in unit glucose costs of .17 cent. The latter reduction resulted in part from minor modifications to the spinning equipment, which tended to reduce crystallization somewhat, and in part because of improved humidification, which was accomplished without investment.

In the same two-year period an outlay of approximately $300,000 ($210,000) was made on additional filtration equipment; quality improvement rather than cost reduction was the principal objective.

*1948-1951, Improved Pulp:* Unit acid-bath costs declined slightly (by .05 cent) in the late 1940s as an indirect consequence of the use of more soluble wood pulps. Investment was not required.

Unit viscose-solution costs declined by .17 cent in 1951 upon an increase in the alpha-cellulose content of wood pulp and a resultant increase in yield. Moreover, improvements in the chemical processes permitted reductions in the caustic soda-cellulose ratio.

*1949-1950, Tube Spinning:* Upon the introduction of tube spinning in 1949-1950, unit operating-labor costs declined by .24 cent and unit overhead cost by 2.01 cents. An expenditure of $15,000 per machine on 50 machines, or a total replacement expenditure of $750,000 ($340,000) was required. The outlays represented substantial alteration of the existing spinning machinery.

*1950-1952, Increased Cake Size:* In the early 1950s the size of the cake was increased from 1.0 to 1.8 pounds in the production of relatively heavy-denier yarn. Unit operating-labor costs declined by .20 cent as a result.[27] Replacement expenditures of $10,000 per machine were made in the conversion of 100 machines, a total expenditure of $1.00 million ($420,000).[28]

*1950, Beams:* The beaming of textile yarn for dispatch was introduced in 1950. The project involved an outlay on added equipment of $300,000 ($130,000) designed to improve the "quality" of the product—with respect to the converters—rather than to reduce costs.[29]

*1958-1960, Dielectric Drying, Large Barattes, Continuous Steeping and Continuous Shredding, and Mechanized Purification:* In the late 1950s a

---

[27] This attributes the entire reduction in unit operating-labor costs in the late 1940s and early 1950s to tube spinning and to increased cake size. Some error is introduced since, in fact, additional crepe output also contributed to lower costs.

[28] In many instances buckets would require replacement—and a substantial investment outlay—even though unit-cost reductions would not result. The opportunity may be taken to install larger buckets and at the same time enjoy some unit-cost reduction.

[29] In 1948-1950, the cloverleaf bucket was removed in the case of yarn of at least 300 denier, because of the use of longer bath-travel. The replacement involved an expenditure of $3,000 per machine on 25 machines, a total outlay of $75,000 ($34,000).

number of major technical changes were introduced. Unit operating-labor costs declined by 1.14 cents, largely as a result of the introduction of mechanized purification, continuous steeping and continuous shredding and to a smaller degree, larger barattes. Dielectric drying was installed with the objective of improving product quality rather than reducing costs. A total replacement expenditure of approximately $5.50 ($1.70) million was required for the accomplishment of these technical improvements.[30] Very little *actual* expenditure was required for the installation of continuous steeping and shredding, however, since the relevant equipment was transferred from Buffalo.

### Spruance Plant I

Spruance Plant I was constructed with the particular aim of producing a relatively strong textile yarn of low denier. In order for the features of this plant to be incorporated in the Company's existing facilities elsewhere, extensive replacement of equipment would have been necessary. Approximately $6.70 ($7.60) million was spent in 1928–1929 on the establishment of the plant.

*1932–1934, All-Active Spinning:* The introduction of all-active spinning in the three-year period 1932–1934 led to a reduction in unit operating-labor costs of 3.19 cents, in unit direct-maintenance costs of .59 cent, and in unit overhead costs of 6.19 cents. The investment expenditures required for the transition amounted to approximately $750,000 ($1.00 million) on added equipment.

In addition to all-active spinning, high-speed throwing was introduced and contributed to the expansion of volume. The estimate of the cost reduction attributable to all-active spinning in fact is an overstatement; some part of the reduction was due to high-speed throwing. Modifications to existing equipment representing a replacement expenditure of approximately $100,000 ($120,000) was necessary for the accomplishment of this latter technical change.

*1932–1935, Several "Minor" Technical Changes:* During the same period a number of "minor" technical changes were introduced. Each in isolation had a small effect on unit costs; together, the technical changes permitted a reduction in unit operating-labor costs of .98 cent. Relatively small amounts of investment were required to implement some of the changes, such as for example, improved cake formation. The "quality" of the labor input was increased, and investment would be of no relevance in this particular case; improvements in bath composition would also not depend on investment.

[30] The relevant outlays were made largely in 1957–1958.

*1932–1936, Dializers:* Unit caustic-soda costs declined by .53 cent during the period 1932–1936 upon the introduction of dializers for the recovery of the raw material. The added equipment involved an expenditure of approximately $50,000 ($60,000). As in the case of Old Hickory, recovery equipment is an instance of a "capital-using" technical change.

*1935–1940, Acid-Bath Recovery:* In 1935, unit acid-bath costs declined by .33 cent and in 1937–1940 by a further .71 cent upon the addition to existing equipment of improved acid-bath recovery mechanisms. Expenditures totaling $300,000 ($310,000) were required by the two projects. This represented a further case of "capital-using" technical change.

In the late 1930s filtration equipment was added at Spruance I at an investment outlay of $100,000 ($100,000). The purpose of the investment in the new equipment was to improve the quality of the product, although unit costs would be somewhat reduced too.

*1935–1940, Type 9 Process:* Unit operating-labor costs declined by 6.47 cents upon the introduction of the Type 9 process, which permitted production of yarn by bobbin process without the intermediate step of skeining.

A replacement investment of only $500,000 ($520,000) was required. However, use was also made of purification facilities available at Spruance II, where the time cycles at various stages had been reduced, thereby releasing facilities and space for the treatment of yarn produced elsewhere at the location. It has been estimated that a significant investment of at least $2.0 million would have been required if the necessary equipment had not been available.

*1938, Carbon-Bisulphide Recovery:* Unit carbon-bisulphide costs declined by .06 cent in 1938 upon the introduction of additional recovery equipment; a very small outlay was required.

*1938–1940, Several "Minor" Technical Changes:* The original process involved quarter-pound cakes on six-inch bobbins; the cake size was increased somewhat, in the early 1930s, on some spinning machines. In 1938, the entire plant converted to 1.0-pound cakes on nine-inch bobbins, and the spinning speed was increased from 2,500 to 3,600 inches per minute upon the introduction of high-speed bobbins. At the same time, the first automatic skein-lacing equipment was installed, and the skein length increased to 22,000 yards. These minor technical changes required an outlay on the replacement of existing mechanisms of approximately $750,000 ($750,000).

Improved equipment for the preparation of the viscose solution was installed at Spruance I as at Old Hickory in the late 1930s: approximately $500,000 ($500,000) was spent on the necessary machines.

The introduction of larger bobbins and skeins, of automatic skein lacing and of improved viscose-making equipment led to a reduction in unit operating-labor costs of 5.39 cents. The increase in spinning speed due to the installation of higher-speed bobbins permitted a reduction in unit operating-labor costs of 1.08 cents, in direct-maintenance costs of .75 cent and in unit overhead costs of 2.84 cents.

*1939–1940, Improved Pulp:* Unit cellulose costs declined by .22 cent upon an increase in the alpha-cellulose content of wood pulp used in the preparation of the viscose solution. Investment expenditures were not required.

*1946, Spinning-Machine Equipment:* Minor additions of equipment to the spinning machines at a relatively small investment outlay led to reductions in unit glucose costs of .09 cent; in fact, as a result of the project, glucose was no longer required in the process.[31]

*1946–1947, Improved Pulp:* As a result of the increased use of wood pulp—in turn due to improvements in the quality of this input—unit cellulose costs declined by .49 cent. Investment was not required.

*1948–1950, Several "Minor" Technical Changes:* Unit operating-labor costs declined by 2.06 cents as a result of both direct and indirect technical change of a "minor" nature. Small amounts of investment would be required in most instances.[32]

### Spruance Plant II

Approximately $7.30 ( $8.60) million was spent on the initial construction of Spruance Plant II in 1935–1936. Sixty additional spinning machines were installed in 1939 at a cost of $6.60 ($6.60) million. The features of the plant differed considerably from those at Spruance I; the cake-to-cone process permitted production at lower cost per pound of rayon than was the case at the older plant.

*1937–1940, Several "Minor" Technical Changes:* As a result of the installation of cakes 1.5 pounds in weight (at the expanded section of the plant), the use of improved viscose-making equipment, and the increase in yield due to a number of small improvements, unit operating-labor costs declined by 1.76 cents.[33]

Replacement expenditures of approximately $500,000 ($500,000) were required for the installation of the improved viscose-making equipment. The increase in cake size was accomplished as part of a major expansion

[31] Sprays, for example, were installed.

[32] A number of process simplifications were introduced in the 1940s, leading to reductions in unit operating-labor costs of .19 cent. Minor indirect technical changes permitted a reduction in unit direct-maintenance costs of .31 cent and in unit overhead costs of 1.29 cents.

[33] A further reduction of .61 cent is attributable to plant expansion.

program, but replacement investment relating to sections of the spinning machines would have been required if this change had been applied to the original section of the plant. Small amounts of investment were required in most instances for the accomplishment of the improvements leading to higher yields. We have estimated, in Chapter 4, that approximately 1.55 cents of the net reduction of 1.76 cents can be explained by minor changes other than the increased cake size.

*1937–1940, Improved Wood Pulp:* Unit cellulose costs declined by .60 cent in the late 1930s upon the use of a higher proportion of wood pulp relative to cotton linters, and an increase in the alpha-cellulose content of the pulp. Investment was not required.

*1937–1940, Viscose-Solution Recovery:* Unit carbon-bisulphide costs declined by .05 cent and unit caustic-soda costs by .09 cent in the late 1930s upon the addition of recovery equipment. Minor investment expenditures were required; in particular, dializers costing $50,000 ($50,000) were installed as part of the "capital-using" technical change.

*1937–1942, Acid-Bath Recovery:* Unit acid-bath costs declined by .95 cent in the late 1930s and early 1940s upon the addition of bath-recovery equipment. The outlay required amounted to approximately $150,000 ($140,000). Once more the introduction of acid-bath recovery equipment represented a "capital-using" technical change.

*1946–1947, Spinning-Bath Equipment:* As a result of minor additions to spinning machines, it was possible to dispense somewhat with glucose; unit glucose costs declined by .13 cent.

*1947, Improved Organization:* Unit operating-labor costs declined in 1947 as the result of improved organization.

*1953, Beams:* As at Old Hickory in the early 1950s, textile-warp beams were introduced to improve the "quality" of the product dispatched from the plant, and thereby to permit reductions in the processing costs of the customers of the plant. Replacement expenditures of $150,000 ($60,000) were required.

At the same time, the plant was redesigned to produce a higher denier: large buckets, tube spinning, and acid-bath recovery equipment were introduced at a cost of $1.50 million ($600,000). Had output been maintained, some reduction in unit costs might have been apparent.

*Spruance Plant III*

An investment expenditure of approximately $3.00 ($3.40) million was required for the establishment of Spruance Plant III. The characteristics of this tire-cord plant permitted production at lower cost than at Spruance I or Spruance II, or at Old Hickory. We have argued in the previous chapter that a cost comparison between textile and tire-cord plants is justified only from a limited viewpoint, since the product requirements were so distinct. The precise technical characteristics of Spruance III required either the establishment of an entirely new plant or very extensive alterations in existing facilities.

In 1938, the plant was converted from alternative-active to all-active spinning at a cost of $570,000 ($570,000).

*1939–1943, Increased Denier and Direct Slashing:* The plant was redesigned for the production of 1,100-denier yarn in the late 1930s. To permit the production of higher-denier yarn the original process—which involved the so-called "twister-dryer" apparatus—was replaced by direct slashing. At the same time the cakes were increased from 1.4 to 2.1 pounds in weight in 1939. The effect was not felt in its entirety until 1943, when the *average* denier increased to approximately 1,100. As a consequence, during the period 1939–1943, unit operating-labor costs declined by 2.17 cents, unit direct-maintenance costs by .75 cent, and unit overhead costs by 3.18 cents.

The entire replacement project was accomplished during the period 1939–1943 at a cost of $3.50 ($3.30) million.[34] In 1938–1939, three large spinning machines were added to the existing six spinning machines as part of a general expansion program; an outlay of $1.10 ($1.10) million was involved in this expansion. These machines embodied the features required by the new process.

*1940–1944, Acid-Bath Economies:* During the five-year period 1939–1944, unit acid-bath costs declined by .60 cent. Of this reduction, .32 cent can be ascribed to the addition of acid-bath recovery equipment in 1940–1941; the outlay on this "capital-using" technical change amounted to $50,000 ($47,000). The remaining reduction of .28 cent resulted from the increase in denier in 1944 above 1,100; at this level glucose was no longer required.

*1945–1949, Increased Cake Size and Denier:* The average denier increased between 1945 and 1949 from approximately 1,100 to approximately 1,650. In 1943, the cake size was increased from 2.1 to 2.5 pounds in the case of 1,100-denier yarn. In 1946, the cake size was further increased to 3.1 pounds on all yarn produced at the plant, that is, on yarn of 1,650 denier. In 1948–1949, the cake size was again increased to 3.9 pounds. It is quite common for higher denier to be produced on larger cakes, so that in a sense the changes were part of a single project.

We have seen in Chapter 4 that unit operating-labor costs declined by .42 cent as a direct consequence of the larger cakes installed in 1943, and

---

[34] Approximately three-quarters of the expenditures were made during 1939–1940 and the remaining one-quarter in 1941–1943.

by a further .19 cent as a result of the larger cakes introduced in 1946 and 1948–1949. The increase in average denier between 1945 and 1949 led to a reduction in unit operating-labor costs of .23 cent, in unit direct-maintenance costs of .27 cent, and in unit overhead costs of 2.44 cents. An expenditure of approximately $1.00 million ($600,000) on additional equipment was required to accomplish the increase in denier.[35] The increase in cake size required relatively significant replacement outlays.

*1947, Improved Wood Pulp:* Unit cellulose costs declined by .37 cent in 1947 upon the substitution of higher-grade wood pulp for cotton linters.

*1949–1952, Improved Wood Pulp:* Further reductions in unit cellulose costs of .69 cent occurred between 1949 and 1952 as wood pulp was substituted to a greater extent. Investment played no role in this trend.

*1949–1952, Carbon-Bisulphide Recovery:* Unit carbon-bisulphide costs declined by .20 cent between 1949 and 1952 upon additions of small magnitude to recovery equipment.

*1950–1951, Several "Minor" Technical Changes:* Unit operating-labor costs declined slightly (by .06 cent) in 1950–1951 upon further small increases in denier and in spinning speed. The effect of the increased cake size—noted earlier for the years 1948–1949—was still felt in 1950–1951, and unit operating-labor costs declined by .17 cent as a result. The increase in denier, in spinning speed, and in cake size required small amounts of investment.

*1952–1955, Changes in Product:* Our main concern has been with technical changes which have resulted in unit-cost reductions. We shall briefly outline the expenditures, if any, required by significant *product* changes during the period 1952–1955. In 1952–1954, the process was changed to one characterized by a low proportion of solids and a high proportion of zinc in the acid bath. Spinning speeds tended to be reduced. Unit costs rose despite a further increase in cake size in 1952 to 4.5 pounds. Very little investment was required by the alterations in product; the improvement in quality depended largely upon the changes made in the chemical relationships involved.

In 1955, "Super-Cordura" high-tenacity yarn was introduced at the plant. Approximately $1.00 million ($360,000) was spent on conversions to permit the production of the yarn, although once again the improvement in quality depended very heavily upon changes in the chemicals used.

[35] The expenditure was made largely in 1944–1946. Increased viscose-making equipment was required by the increased volume resulting from the higher denier. Part of the equipment was used for Spruance II-A, where denier was raised during the same period. Part of the outlay—$158,000 ($80,000)—related to the introduction of the high zinc bath, which replaced the iron bath.

We shall assume that $300,000 can be allocated to Spruance III and $300,000 to Spruance II-A.

*Spruance Plant II-A*

Spruance II-A was that part of Spruance II added during the 1938 expansion program; records were kept separately after 1943, since the product at Plant II-A differed thenceforth from that at Plant II.

The initial conversion from textile to tire-cord yarn involved an expenditure of $700,000 ($520,000). An important installation was that of new-type stretching devices. The entire outlay was relatively modest.

We turn now to consider the technical changes recorded in Chapter 4:

*1946–1947, Several "Minor" Technical Changes:* In the years immediately following the conversion of Spruance II-A, the stage of desulphuring and a stage of washing after desulphuring were eliminated from the process; unit operating-labor costs declined by .40 cent as a result. Investment outlays were not required.[36]

A second feature of the period was a tendency towards higher denier, which permitted a reduction in unit operating-labor costs of .30 cent, in unit direct-maintenance costs of .15 cent and in unit overhead costs of .77 cent.[37] Additions to viscose-making equipment were required. An expansion of over $1.00 million ($600,000) was recorded in the section relating to Spruance III during the period.[38]

*1946–1947, Improved Wood Pulp:* The proportion of wood pulp increased in the years 1946–1947 and unit cellulose costs declined by .51 cent. Investment expenditures were not required.

*1948–1949, Direct-Slashing Process:* In the late 1940s a new process— "wet slashing"—was introduced. Its main feature was the "direct slashing" of yarn to beams; integral parts of the process were the mechanical handling of packages, automatic (centrifugal) washing and the use of larger cakes. Alterations in the Godet-wheel system were also required by the technical change.

As a result of the new process unit operating-labor costs declined by .64 cent. Approximately $4.80 ($2.20) million was spent on the necessary plant and equipment. Most of the outlay involved replacement of existing facilities.

*1948–1949, Alternative-Active Spinning:* The transition from the use of every third nozzle position to alternative-active spinning led to a reduction in unit operating-labor costs of .28 cent in 1948–1949, in unit direct-maintenance costs of .15 cent and in unit overhead costs of .77 cent.[39]

---

[36] Essentially the conversion from textile-yarn to tire-cord production was finally accomplished in these years.

[37] The reduction in unit costs due to increased denier occurred largely during the period 1945–1949. For the cost breakdown in the case of direct-maintenance and overhead, see pp. 114–115.

[38] One-half of the expansion, or $300,000, can be allocated to Spruance II-A.

[39] See pp. 114–115 for the allocation of direct-maintenance and overhead costs.

The addition of nozzles to each spinning machine required an expenditure of $94,000 ($43,000).

*1952–1954, Changes in Product:* The plant was converted to the production of high-tenacity "Super-Cordura" in 1953–1954. The designed denier, the spinning speed, and the bucket size were increased and the number of bucket positions per machine was slightly reduced. An investment of approximately $7.5 ($2.82) million was required by the conversion. Moreover, extensive chemical changes were necessary.

### Summary of Relation Between Technical Change and Investment at Old Hickory and Spruance

It is clear from consideration of events at Spruance and Old Hickory, that most of the cases of *cost-reducing technical change* were dependent for their introduction upon investment in plant and equipment. The exceptions, as we have seen, were unit-cost reductions owing to improved raw materials, improved "organization" of operations, and the employment of better-trained labor. We have also had occasion to note the dependence of *improvements in quality* upon investment. In attempting to judge the relation between technical changes which increase efficiency of production by lowering unit costs and investment, it is necessary to bear in mind the fact that many cost-reducing technical changes were also intended to change the nature of the product.

Our analysis of the relation between cost-reducing technical change and investment has also indicated that "significant" unit-cost reductions were dependent upon "significant" investment outlays, whereas very small outlays usually sufficed to accomplish small reductions in unit cost.[40] Moreover, the analysis has shown that replacement investments were considerably more important than expansionary investments in leading to unit-cost reductions in the plants under consideration.

### CHANGES IN THE QUALITY OF INPUTS AND IMPROVED ORGANIZATION

The most important single input in the production of rayon is cellulose. The quality of this input influenced the efficiency of production in a variety of ways.

*Proximate Influence:* Improvements in the quality of wood pulp over time permitted the substitution of pulp for the more expensive cotton linters as a source of cellulose. Although the purity and yield of cotton linters remained at all times somewhat higher than that of pulp, the price

---

[40] On this, see further pp. 155–156 and p. 163.

of linters was also higher. The possibility of substituting the cheaper input without detriment to the quality of the end product led to reductions in unit cellulose costs over time.[41] Moreover, even in the absence of substitution the improved quality of wood pulp (and linters) allowed a greater yield per pound of cellulose used.

At Old Hickory (during the period 1929–1951) only 1.3 per cent of the unit-cost reductions attributable to *technical change of all kinds* can be accounted for by improvements in the cellulose source; at Spruance I (1932–1950) the proportion was 2.1 per cent, but at Spruance II (1937–1951) the proportion was as high as 21.0 per cent. Thus at the textile-yarn plants unit-cost reductions resulting from improved pulps constituted a very small proportion of the entire reduction in unit costs, with the exception of Spruance Plant II. It will be recalled, however, that very little technical change was recorded at the latter plant; the absolute contribution of improved cellulose was substantially of the same order as at the other textile-yarn plants. A more accurate picture is suggested by reference to those plants constructed during the 1920s—namely Old Hickory and Spruance I—for which recorded data are available throughout most of the 1930s.

At the tire-cord plants the proportion of the unit-cost reductions due to technical change which is attributable to improved cellulose was higher: 9.4 per cent at Spruance III (1938–1952) and 13.3 per cent at Spruance II-A (1945–1952). Although the proportion is lower in the case of Spruance III—the older plant—the absolute contribution is in fact higher. A more accurate indication of the contribution of improved cellulose at tire-cord plants is gained by reference to the older plant.[42]

Even in those instances where it appears that a unit-cost reduction was permitted by improved pulps (or other inputs) influencing efficiency of production without the intermediary of investment outlays, it should be borne in mind that the *manufacturers of the relevant inputs* may have introduced new equipment in the production of their product.

*Influence of Improved Cellulose Via Investment:* The influence exerted by the quality of inputs has also been *indirect* and has operated, in part, *through the capital equipment of the plant.* Improved pulps have permitted

---

[41] See Appendix B for the percentage of wood pulp to total cellulose at each plant.

[42] Reference to the description of technical changes and the resultant unit-cost reductions given in detail in Chapter 4 will show that at Old Hickory (1929–1951) a reduction of .39 cent out of total net reduction in unit costs of 30.84 cents (or 1.3 per cent) was due to improved raw materials. At Spruance I (1932–1950) the relevant figures are .71 out of 33.36 cents (or 2.1 per cent); at Spruance II (1937–1951), .60 out of 2.86 cents (or 21.0 per cent); at Spruance III (1938–1952), 1.06 out of 11.29 cents (or 9.4 per cent); and at Spruance II-A (1945–1952), .51 out of 3.82 cents (or 13.3 per cent).

the production of stronger yarns and this in turn has been partly responsible for the success of mechanisms raising the spinning speed. The greater uniformity of pulp has had wide effects: it has been partly responsible for the introduction of larger units of equipment in the chemical building and for continuous methods of operation; originally the need to blend pulps of various batches to assure a minimum degree of uniformity had mitigated against continuous-flow techniques and had limited the size of the equipment in the chemical plant. Moreover, the introduction of high-alpha pulps, or pulps with a low hemicellulose content, may have tended to reduce the number of dializers required for a given volume of output.

*Abandonment of Stages:* A further instance of the feasibility of reducing costs without the prerequisite of investment expenditure is found in the opportunities open to rayon plants of abandoning stages in the process of production which had previously been carried out at the plant. The blending of the pulp at various stages of operation was abandoned when the pulp arrived at the plant in uniform bundles of strict specification. This case can be considered as an instance of a cost reduction directly resulting from an improved-quality input. Only isolated instances of cost reductions appear to have resulted from changes of this kind.

*Improved Organization and Improvements in the Quality of Labor:* An accurate estimate of the contribution of improved organization of operations, and of improvements in the quality of labor, has not been attempted so far. Such changes have been included within the designation "minor direct technical change." The most significant instances of improvement in organization and in the training of labor occurred during the early years of the 1930s and toward the close of the same decade, namely during or immediately following periods of severe depression.

One estimate for Old Hickory would attribute to improved organization and labor-training approximately 15.0 per cent of the net reduction in unit operating-labor costs during the period 1929–1951. The estimate for plants constructed at more recent dates, or plants for which data are not available during the early 1930s, would be approximately 10.0 per cent.[43]

---

[43] On the assumption that 25 per cent of the net reduction in unit operating-labor costs at Old Hickory, 1929–1932 and 1937–1940, can be attributed to the effect of improved organization and the like, and adding a further reduction of .37 cent which occurred during the 1940s as a result of improved organization, we obtain an estimate of 1.87 *plus* .67 *plus* .37 cents, or 2.91 cents, which amounts to 15.7 per cent of the entire reduction in unit operating-labor costs of 18.55 cents during the period 1929–1951. If the period 1929–1931 is disregarded, then organizational changes account for 1.04 cents out of a total net reduction of 11.05 cents, 1932–1951, that is, for 9.4 per cent.

We shall use 15 per cent as an estimate for the contribution of improved organization to reductions in unit operating-labor costs at Old Hickory, 1929–1951, and 10 per cent for the contribution at other plants which either were constructed in the mid- or late-1930s or, as in the case of Spruance I, lack data for the early 1930s.

Using these estimates, the proportion of the reduction in unit costs due to technical change of all kinds which can be accounted for by technical changes *not dependent upon investment at the plants* amounted to 10.7 per cent at Old Hickory, 7.9 per cent at Spruance I, 28.7 per cent at Spruance II, 12.7 per cent at Spruance III and 18.1 per cent at Spruance II-A.[44] As already noted, Spruance II represents a less accurate picture of events at a textile-yarn plant than either Old Hickory of Spruance I and, similarly, Spruance II-A reflects a less accurate picture of events at a tire-cord plant than Spruance III.

In summary, approximately 90.0 per cent of cost reductions owing to technical change were dependent upon investment at textile-yarn plants, and 80.0–90.0 per cent at tire-cord plants.

### DIGRESSION ON PRODUCT-QUALITY IMPROVEMENTS AND INVESTMENT

In most instances, investment in plant and equipment was a prerequisite for cost-reducing technical change.

*Cost-Reducing, Quality-Improving Technical Changes and Investment:* In many cases technical changes which tend to reduce costs also have the effect of improving the quality of the yarn. This is particularly true where the handling of the semifinished product at various stages is reduced: thus, for example, the cake-to-cone process had a significant effect upon the quality of the yarn; the Type 9 process introduced at Spruance I allowed more uniform shrinkage of the yarn; and the sharp increases in denier at Spruance III and II-A improved the product significantly from the viewpoint of the converters.[45]

*Quality Improvement and Investment:* The increase in the tenacity of yarn (designed in part to permit higher spinning speeds and lower

---

[44] Adding, except at Old Hickory, 10 per cent of the entire reduction in unit operating-labor cost—our estimate of the contribution of improved organization to increased efficiency—to the reduction in unit costs due to improved raw materials, we obtain the following estimates of the total contribution of technical change not requiring investment outlays: Old Hickory, 3.30 cents (2.91 *plus* .39 cent) out of 30.84 cents (10.7 per cent); Spruance I, 2.65 cents (1.94 *plus* .71 cent) out of 33.36 cents (or 7.9 per cent); Spruance II, .82 cent (.22 *plus* .60 cent) out of 2.86 cents (or 28.7 per cent); Spruance III, 1.44 cents (.38 *plus* 1.06 cents) out of 11.29 cents (or 12.7 per cent); and Spruance II-A, .69 cent (.18 *plus* .51 cent) out of 3.82 cents (or 18.1 per cent).

[45] The cake-to-cone process reduced operating-labor costs, increased dyeing uniformity, and permitted more thorough purification of the yarn. The increase in tenacity—brought about in part by novel mechanisms for stretching the newly-formed filaments—improved dyeing, and permitted better processing and in addition was partly directed toward permitting higher spinning speeds and lower capital costs per pound.

The benefit of high-denier yarn to converters lay in the fact that twisting of yarn—the practice in the case of low-denier yarn—to form a single cord was no longer necessary.

capital costs per pound) depended upon the introduction of both novel mechanisms and chemicals. The conversion program at Spruance II in 1943–1944 when tire cord was introduced, and the construction of a completely new plant (Spruance III) in 1936 for the production of tire cord, might be cited as instances where *product* innovation depended predominantly upon new investment. (It should be borne in mind, however, that these plants embodied mechanisms which might well have been introduced at the existing textile-yarn plants; from this viewpoint, at least part of the investment expenditures should be considered as an effort to maintain a high level of efficiency rather than alter the product.) The dryer-twister mechanism installed at Spruance III was intended to improve the quality of the product and demanded investment expenditures. Similarly the expenditures relating to textile-warp beams at Old Hickory in 1950 and at Spruance II in 1953 were specifically intended to improve the competitive position of the Company by altering the product, allowing converters to avoid the step of transferring yarn from cones to beams. Investment outlays on filtration mechanisms were designed to improve the quality of the product. Part of the heavy investment outlays at Old Hickory in the late 1950s involved the installation of equipment for dielectric drying, which improved quality rather than reduced costs. A further instance of great importance is of course the introduction of "Super-Cordura" at Spruance II-A and III; unit costs in fact tended to rise, and the heavy expenditures were solely directed at improving the product.

*Quality Improvements and Nature of Inputs:* Improved methods of dyeing and delustering and of thus achieving better quality yarn depended heavily upon advances in chemistry, although in many instances mechanical alterations would be a necessary concomitant of an improvement in quality.

The quality of the cellulose source is of profound significance for the nature of the end product. The uniformity of product, the evenness of dyeing, and tenacity are directly dependent upon the quality of the cellulose.[46] Similarly the content of the acid bath is crucial.

*Conclusion:* In summary, we must conclude that it is often impossible to distinguish an effort to increase efficiency from an effort to improve quality or introduce a new product. It follows that a unit-cost reduction may not be the sole purpose of an investment expenditure; the full benefit of the outlay cannot be judged by reference to unit-cost reductions alone.

Moreover, in those cases where *important* improvements in quality

[46] We refer, in particular, to the development of "Super-Cordura,"which was produced at Spruance II-A and III in the early 1950s, and the introduction of tire-cord yarn in general in the 1930s.

alone occurred, investment in plant and equipment was usually required. The nature of the materials used—for example, the introduction of new chemicals and improved cellulose—has also been a necessary prerequisite of many of the product changes.

## RELATIVE MAGNITUDES OF UNIT-COST REDUCTIONS AND REQUISITE INVESTMENT OUTLAY

We have seen that more than 85.0 per cent of the net reduction in unit costs, resulting from technical change of all kinds, depended upon investment in plant and equipment. The relation between unit-cost reduction and investment can be stated more precisely: "significant" reductions in unit cost owing to technical change were accompanied in most cases by "significant" investment outlays, whereas the "less-significant" unit-cost reductions were accomplished by "small" outlays.[47] It does *not* appear, however, that the *larger* the unit-cost reduction within each group, the *larger* the related investment. In particular, many technical changes—the so-called "indirect" technical changes—were designed to permit an expansion of volume and a reduction in unit overhead costs. A given investment outlay embodying technical change of this nature usually had a much greater absolute effect on total unit costs than a similar outlay embodying technical change acting directly upon unit operating-labor or unit materials costs. Striking instances of indirect technical change occurred at Spruance I (the introduction of all-active spinning in 1933–1934) and at Spruance III (the introduction of 1,100-denier yarn in 1939).

Moreover, the fact that in many instances quality improvement as well as unit-cost reduction was intended by a particular outlay clouds the relationship which may exist between the size of a unit-cost reduction and the related investment.

---

[47] A significant reduction in unit costs, it will be recalled, is considered to be any reduction exceeding one cent in the case of textile yarn and .50 cent in that of tire-cord production; a "significant" investment outlay is an outlay exceeding $250,000. These figures are in "1939 dollars."

Exceptions to the relationship between "significant" unit cost reductions (owing to technical change) and "significant" outlays on plant and equipment occurred at Old Hickory in 1936–1940 and in 1950–1952: in the former case an expenditure on acid-bath recovery and filtration equipment of $590,000 was accompanied by a unit-cost reduction of .78 cent, and in the latter instance, an expenditure on larger buckets of $420,000 was accompanied by a reduction in unit costs of only .32 cent. However, in the former case, filtration mechanisms—designed to improve *quality* rather than to reduce costs—were included and in the latter case replacement at substantial outlay would have been required in any event; that is, even in the absence of an opportunity for introducing larger buckets.

It will be noted that all the instances of "major" technical change—that is, technical change based on *technology* which had required much effort to develop—led to "significant" unit-cost reductions and were accompanied by "significant" investment outlays.[48] Several "minor" technical changes (in particular, all-active spinning at Spruance I in 1933–1934 and the introduction of Type 10 spinning machines at Old Hickory in 1937) also permitted substantial unit-cost reductions and were accompanied by "significant" investment outlays, but on the whole the "minor" changes tended to be related to smaller ("less-significant") unit-cost reductions and smaller ("less-significant") outlays.

## INTERPLANT COMPARISONS OF INVESTMENT OUTLAYS

Consideration of investment outlays at various plants suggests that relatively small investment expenditures incorporating modifications to *existing* plants are capable of generating large improvements in efficiency. Such improvements are sometimes sufficient to permit an older plant to produce at a unit cost which is not substantially higher—relative to a cost comparison prior to the modifications—than those at a *newly constructed* plant embodying the latest technology.

### Old Hickory and Spruance II

Old Hickory was under construction in 1924 and cost data are available from 1929. Spruance II was constructed in 1934–1935 and operations began in 1935. The cost of the newly built plant (in 1939 dollars) amounted to $8.60 million, and unit direct-factory costs were 18.48 cents in 1937. The capacity at Old Hickory in 1937 was four times that at Spruance II, whereas in 1929 the plant was only three times as large. Unit direct-factory costs at Old Hickory declined from 41.30 cents in 1929 to 20.12 cents in 1937. However, of this net reduction 1.68 cents is attributable to the plant-expansion program of 1934; unit costs would therefore have amounted to approximately 21.80 cents had the size of plant remained unchanged.[49] The investment data show that the outlays—apart from those reflecting the expansion—responsible for most of the unit-cost reduction totaled no more than $4.76 million.[50]

[48] The "major" technical changes were the cake-to-cone process, tube spinning, and the variety of improvements introduced as a unit in the late 1950s at Old Hickory; the Type 9 process at Spruance I; direct slashing and increased denier at Spruance III; and wet slashing and related changes at Spruance II-A. Other "major" changes occurred but were directed at improved quality.

[49] In Chapter 4, we attributed a reduction of .71 cent in unit operating-labor costs and a further reduction of .97 cent in unit direct-maintenance costs to the expansion of 1934.

[50] The expansion program required an outlay of $5.20 million. This sum is excluded from the calculations in the text.

With an expenditure at Old Hickory of only 55 per cent of the outlay required for the construction of Spruance II it was possible to reduce unit direct-factory costs to a level only 18 per cent higher than at the newer plant. Unit direct-factory costs at Old Hickory in 1929 were 123 per cent higher than those at Spruance II in 1937.

When overhead costs are included in the comparison, the effectiveness of modifications to existing plants is even more striking. If we assume that the size of plant had remained unchanged at Old Hickory during the

Table 6.1   Cost Comparison Between Old Hickory and Spruance II

| Plant | Unit Direct-Factory Costs (in cents) | Unit Overhead Costs (in cents) | Unit Factory Costs (in cents) |
|---|---|---|---|
| Old Hickory, 1929 | 41.30 | 12.21 | 53.51 |
| 1937 | 21.80 (20.12)* | 7.93 (5.79)* | 29.73 (25.91)* |
| Spruance II, 1937 | 18.48 | 8.70 | 27.18 |

* Figures in parentheses refer to the level of unit costs if the effect of plant expansion at Old Hickory, 1929–1937, is not removed.

period 1929–1937, then unit overhead costs would have declined from 12.21 cents to 7.93 cents as a consequence of technical change alone, and unit factory costs in 1937 would have amounted to 29.73 cents, only 9 per cent above the level of costs at Spruance II. Without the stream of technical changes which occurred at Old Hickory, unit factory costs would have been 97 per cent higher. The relevant data are summarized in Table 6.1.

*Spruance I and Spruance II*

Spruance I was completed in 1928–1929 and production began in 1929; data are available from 1932. Approximately $4.11 million were spent in investment outlays incorporating cost-reducing technology during the period 1932–1937, and unit direct-factory costs declined from 40.12 cents (1932) to 29.35 cents (1937). The expenditures required for the construction of the newer plant (II) were $8.60 million, and unit costs were 18.48 cents in 1937. Although it is true that costs at Spruance I were 59 per cent above those at Spruance II in 1937, there was a considerable reduction compared with the relationship which would have existed— 117 per cent—without the outlays. Moreover, if 1940 is taken as the date of comparison, and the expenditures directed at cost reduction at both plants during the years 1937–1940 taken into account, we find that unit direct-factory costs at Plant I (20.17 cents) were only 30 per cent higher than those at Plant II (15.46 cents).[51] On the other hand, the total outlays amounted to only $5.36 million at Plant I, 1932–1940, compared with $9.29 million at Plant II, 1935–1940.[52] When unit overhead costs are included, the comparisons reveal a similar pattern.

Needless to say, in neither of the comparisons are we questioning the rationale for the construction of Spruance II; obviously it was desirable to expand capacity. It does appear, however, that investment outlays—relatively small when compared with those required to construct a new plant—appear capable of generating increases in productivity of impressive magnitude. Indeed unit costs at the older plant, in one of the comparisons, declined to a level almost as low as those at the newly built plant.

*Spruance II-A and Spruance III*

Another instance of the efficacy of relatively small investments incorporating modifications to existing plants relates to the conversion of part of Spruance II (Plant II-A) from textile yarn to tire-cord yarn in 1943–1944. The cost of the conversion was only $520,000, and production of tire-cord yarn was possible at a unit direct-factory cost of 12.86 cents. On the other hand, a total outlay of $3.40 million was required in 1935 for the construction of Spruance III, which was built especially as a tire-cord plant.[53]

### THE RELATIVE IMPORTANCE OF REPLACEMENT AND EXPANSIONARY OUTLAYS

We have had occasion to remark in an earlier chapter[54] that most of the instances of technical change which have been encountered permitted *net* reductions in unit labor, materials, or overhead costs; for the most part they were not "capital-using" changes involving simply the substitution of capital for other inputs. This relationship can be confirmed by the fact that most of the investment outlays embodying technical change represented

[51] In fact, unit direct-factory costs at Spruance II in 1940 were 14.85 cents. But of the reduction in unit operating-labor costs during the late 1930s, .61 cent was attributable to plant expansion. Thus unit costs would have been 15.46 cents without the expansion.

[52] In fact total outlays at Spruance II, 1935–1940, were $8.60 million (the initial construction) *plus* approximately $.69 million (cost-reducing outlays), *plus* $6.60 million (the 1939 expansion). The latter outlay is excluded from the calculation, although strictly some part should be included because the added section of the Plant contained larger cakes which did contribute to lower unit costs somewhat.

[53] Unit direct-factory costs in 1938 at Plant III amounted to 16.19 cents, and a further outlay of $3.35 million was made during the years 1939–1943, permitting a decline in unit costs to 12.07 cents in 1945. Actually, unit costs were 11.68 cents, but .39 cent of the reduction, 1939–1943, are attributable to plant expansion and increased rate of plant utilization. An expansionary outlay of $1.10 million in 1938–1939 is excluded from the data in this note.

[54] See Chapter 4, pp. 117–118.

*replacement* investment rather than "additions" to the capital stock.[55] The proportion of replacement investment to all investment outlays required by technical change amounted to at least 90 per cent at Spruance III; 90 per cent at Old Hickory, 75 per cent at Spruance II-A, 72 per cent at Spruance II, and 58 per cent at Spruance I.[56]

[55] By "additions" we do not refer to equipment which is added as part of a general expansion program (wherein *all* inputs, including capital, are increased), even if the expansion was due to a preceding technical change which reduced unit costs; we refer specifically to equipment which is added as a "substitute" for other inputs at given levels of output.

We shall center our attention solely upon investment outlays directed at *cost-reducing* technical change and ignore "quality-improving" expenditures. However, reference to earlier sections will show that the most important quality improvements—the alterations in product at Spruance II-A and III during the 1950s—required *replacement* expenditures.

The estimates make use of expenditures in constant (1939) dollars.

[56] In the case of Old Hickory we have referred to investments (corrected), 1929–1951, amounting to $7.51 million, which relate solely to outlays required proximately by technical change; an investment of $5.20 million representing an increase in the capital stock which was part of a general expansion of all inputs is not included, although the new equipment also embodied the cake-to-cone process. Of the total expenditure, $6.80 million or 90 per cent was replacement investment; the remaining 10 per cent represented additions to the capital stock which permitted reductions in other inputs. Equipment for the recovery of raw materials was the most important instance of "capital-using" technical change at Old Hickory.

At Spruance III replacement investment amounted to $3.30 out of $3.65 million or 90 per cent; an outlay of $1.10 million on added equipment, which was part of an expansion program during the late 1930s, is ignored in the calculation, although the relevant equipment embodied the direct-slashing process.

At Spruance II-A, $2.20 out of $2.93 million, or 75 per cent, represented replacement investment. The most important instances of "capital-using" technical change at the tire-cord plants were the increases in denier which required additional viscose-making equipment and, in the case of Spruance II-A, transition to alternative-active spinning, which required added nozzles and related equipment.

At Spruance II the proportion amounted to $.50 out of $.69 million, or 72 per cent, and at Spruance I the figures were $1.89 out of $3.26 million, or 58 per cent. However, we have noted above that but for the fact that certain equipment was at hand (at Spruance II), the Type 9 process would have required the installation of additional equipment amounting to approximately $2.00 million. Material-recovery equipment represented an important instance of "capital-using" technical change at the Spruance textile-yarn plants; the introduction of all-active spinning at Spruance I is another example.

If all the investment outlays are included in the calculations—including added equipment which embodied technical change but which was part of a general expansion of all inputs—then the proportion of replacement investment is considerably lower, although it remains more important than expenditures representing "additions" of both kinds: at Spruance II-A, 75 per cent; at Spruance II, 72 per cent; at Spruance III, 69 per cent; at Old Hickory, 54 per cent; and at Spruance I, 58 per cent.

Many of the "minor" technical changes required *replacement* investments for which complete data are not available. The foregoing estimates of the significance of replacement investment are, therefore, minimum estimates.

If the decade 1951–1960 is considered, the ratios of replacement to total investment designed to introduce cost-reducing technical change rises, at Old Hickory, to $8.50 out of $9.21 million, or 92 per cent.

The statements concerning the relative importance of replacement investment have been made with reference to *existing* plants, However, we must also take into account the fact that certain plants were actually constructed either to embody cost-reducing technical changes or to produce new products. Thus Spruance II was constructed in 1935 to produce textile yarn by the new cake-to-cone process, and in the following year Spruance III was constructed to produce tire-cord yarn. Spruance II-A, on the other hand, was a converted plant.

### THE "DELAY" BETWEEN DEVELOPMENT AND APPLICATION: FURTHER EVIDENCE OF THE SIGNIFICANCE OF INVESTMENT

The pervasive influence of investment can be confirmed by indirect evidence. Our study has revealed several instances of "delay" in the introduction of existing technology. In particular, technology embodied at Spruance II was not applied in Spruance I, and that in Spruance III was not introduced in Spruance II-A. Certain features applicable both to tire-cord yarn and to textile yarn were in fact restricted to the plants producing the former product. Continuous steeping and shredding, developed in the late 1930s and in fact applied at Buffalo in 1941, was not introduced at Old Hickory until 1958.

As pointed out in the introduction to this chapter, there are sound reasons which can explain delay in the introduction of new technology. In particular, if the total costs per pound of production by means of the new technology should exceed the variable costs per unit of production by means of the existing technology, replacement will not be called for. Where plants in their entirety are concerned, it is possible to make the necessary cost comparisons.[57] We find, however, that the average total costs of production at Spruance II were *lower* than the average variable costs at Spruance I. This might suggest that it would have been profitable to replace the mechanisms installed at Plant I by those used at Plant II. It will be recalled that in the early years of the existence of Spruance I the use of a bucket process for the production of fine-denier yarn was technologically impossible; however, by the late 1930s buckets capable of sufficiently high spinning speed had been developed and this would have overcome the technological problem referred to. The question arises, therefore, why, at least in the late 1930s, a bucket process was not

[57] As an estimate of average *total* costs, we use actual, uncorrected cost figures representing net manufacturing costs; for an estimate of average variable cost we use actual, uncorrected series of net factory costs. The former series includes depreciation, insurance, and other "fixed" items. Since we are comparing different plants at the same time, correction of the cost data is not essential.

introduced to replace the existing bobbin process even for the production of fine-denier yarns.

Two principal reasons account for the continued use of the bobbin technique at Spruance I: in the first place, the Type 9 process was developed during the period 1933–1935 and installed between 1935 and 1940; the unit-cost differential between the bobbin and the bucket plant was significantly reduced. In addition, the remaining cost advantage of the bucket process did not justify the necessary heavy outlays that a complete conversion of Plant I would have entailed.

Although Spruance Plant II-A was created by the conversion of a section of Plant II to tire-cord production, we can conceive its establishment as part of an *expansion* (rather than a replacement) program relating to tire-cord yarn. From this point of view, the relevant cost comparison which should be made in attempting to account for the use of a bucket process in the production of tire cord would be between the average *total* costs of production by means of the bobbin (which can be estimated by reference to the average total costs at Spruance III) and the average total costs by means of the bucket (an estimate of which being the actual costs of production at Spruance II-A). We find in fact that the average total costs at Spruance III were below the average total costs at Spruance II-A, and the question arises why bobbin spinning was not installed. A possible explanation lies in the fact that the creation of Spruance II-A was part of a wartime emergency expansion program; the decision might have been made to utilize somewhat inferior techniques if the expansion could thereby be speeded up. On the other hand, it may be argued that the creation of Spruance II-A should not be considered as a completely expansionary project; rather, although it produced a "different" commodity from that produced at the original plant, at least part of the original equipment remained in use so that *to some extent* at least, Spruance II-A ought to be seen as a plant already in existence. From this viewpoint, fixed costs would not be considered in their entirety, and the average total costs of installing a completely new bobbin plant might not in this case fall below the unit costs relevant for the comparison at the "existing" plant. Once the bucket equipment had been installed at Spruance II-A then, in whichever way we conceive of the original establishment of the plant, the relevant costs are the variable costs; we find that average total costs at the bobbin plant exceed average variable costs at Spruance II-A so that it would not have been profitable to convert the plant to a bobbin technique (even if it were true that a bobbin plant should have been constructed in the first instance).

Operating costs at Spruance II were initially below those at Old Hickory (during the period 1936–1943). However, the average total costs at

Spruance II exceeded the average variable costs at Old Hickory, so that replacement at Old Hickory of all plant and equipment was not called for.

We have taken care in the previous chapter to distinguish, among those technical features of tire-cord technology, those which could also have been installed in textile-yarn plants. Limiting our attention to these mechanisms, the question arises why in fact their application was in many cases restricted to the tire-cord plants. The size of the bobbin or bucket, the nature of the piping, and the size of the viscose-making equipment are most relevant. In this instance we are unable to make the cost comparisons between total costs of operation with new equipment and variable costs of operation with existing equipment, because part of the cost differential between tire-cord and textile-yarn plants is due to mechanisms and techniques which were technically restricted to the former product. It has been confirmed that either average costs of continuing with existing equipment were below all costs necessary to take into account in considering replacement by the alternative equipment, or that the rate of return offered would in any event have proved insufficient.

The delay in introducing continuous-steeping, continuous-shredding and mechanized-washing equipment at Old Hickory until 1958 can be accounted for by the fact that the rate of return would have been insufficient: the installation of continuous steeping at Old Hickory became "justified" only when the requisite equipment was rendered surplus by the shutdown of the Buffalo plant.[58]

An interesting case of "delay" in the introduction of new technology was the relatively slow application of the cake-to-cone method at Old Hickory. The explanation lies in the fact that the new process would be profitable only if customers of the plant (converters) were prepared to accept the yarn in the form of cones; that is to say, the cost reductions made possible by the new technique entailed an alteration in the nature of the end product, which was dispatched in the form of cones rather than skeins. The customers would themselves find it necessary to install equipment capable of handling the altered units. The timing at Old Hickory of the installation of the new equipment was thus governed by events in another sector.

In brief, the attempt to account for the "delay" in the introduction of new technology has for the most part hinged upon the fact that such introduction would have demanded the *replacement* of existing equipment and that such replacement might not have been "profitable," either because average total costs of production by the new method exceeded

---

[58] It was not until the mid-1950s that an economical *automatic-washing* process for bucket-made cakes of textile yarn was developed.

average variable costs of continued production by the existing method, or because the rate of return was considered inadequate.

## Summary

The evidence considered in this chapter suggests that at least 80.0 per cent of the unit-cost reductions explained by technical change of all kinds depended upon investment in plant and equipment. On the whole, "significant" cost reductions depended upon "significant" outlays, whereas small outlays sufficed usually to accomplish small reductions.[59] However, it does not follow that there exists a simple relationship between the size of outlay and the size of the resultant cost reduction. We find that a given outlay incorporating *indirect* technical change—permitting larger volume from substantially unchanged plant facilities—usually has a far greater effect on unit costs than a similar outlay designed to reduce costs directly.[60]

"Major" technical changes—changes deriving from *technology* which required much effort—generally led to "significant" cost reductions and required "significant" outlays. *Individual* minor changes often required small outlays but permitted small cost reductions. However, there are important instances when even the individual minor change required "significant" investment and led to very impressive reductions: this was true particularly when the minor change fell within the *indirect* category.

Consideration of investment outlays at the various plants shows that relatively low expenditures incorporating modifications to existing plants may be capable of reducing costs to a level not substantially higher than that at a newly built plant.

Replacement investment was considerably more important than investments constituting additions to the capital stock at existing plants. In most instances well over two-thirds, and sometimes as much as nine-tenths, of all investments required by technical change represented replacements. (However, it must be remembered that the actual establishment of plants producing new products or incorporating cost-reducing techniques constituted significant instances of expansionary investment from the point of view of the Company.)

---

[59] The term "significant," when applied to cost reductions, means a decline of at least one-half cent in the case of tire-cord rayon and at least one cent in the case of textile yarn. A "significant" outlay is an outlay exceeding $250,000. All figures are in constant (1939) dollars.

[60] Many of the "indirect" technical changes were particularly profitable because replacements of certain mechanisms were required regularly, even in the absence of changed techniques.

Most instances of delay in the application of cost-reducing technology were explicable by the fact that new investment would have been required, but was not justified in terms of the relevant cost comparisons or did not promise a sufficient rate of return on the necessary outlays. Thus the significance of investment for the introduction of technical change has also been confirmed by indirect evidence.

# Chapter Seven

# The Sources of Technology Introduced at Spruance and Old Hickory

In earlier chapters we have considered the technical changes introduced at the Spruance and Old Hickory plants. We now turn to consider the source of these technical changes, that is, the technology upon which they were based. We shall be concerned with two questions: first, were the techniques based upon technology developed by the Du Pont Company itself rather than acquired from outside the Company; and second, were the techniques based upon patented technology? As a brief preliminary it may prove helpful to outline the organization of internal research and development at Du Pont.

Each of the industrial departments of the Company, such as the Textile Fibers Department, is responsible for the research necessary to support its present and future commercial interests, and each has its own research divisions. In the first place, much of the work undertaken by the individual departments, relating to improvement of the quality and reduction in the cost of production of existing products, takes place at the laboratories on the plant sites, and is performed, for example, by Technical Assistance to Production personnel. Technical Assistance members are trained chemists and engineers whose concern is the solution of problems generated by current operations at the plants; to this extent they can be viewed as technical personnel within the plant organization, although they contribute to improvements in processes actually in use. In addition, large-scale formal research relating to specific products within each department is undertaken. Thus, for example, during the period of our study Rayon Research conducted formal research relating to improved processes and products specific to rayon production. Finally, in the case of textile fibers, the Pioneering Research organization undertakes long-range research on behalf of the department as a whole.

In addition to departmental activities, there exist the Central Research Department (known as the Central Chemical Department before 1959), which is concerned with the longest-range chemical and physical research leading to new products; the Haskell Laboratory of Industrial Toxicology, which carries on research relating to toxic hazards; and the Engineering Department. These three groups do work of interest to the Company as a whole, and work of special account for individual departments. The Engineering Department contributes to new technology at two levels. First, it undertakes formal engineering and metallurgical research on equipment design, materials of construction, measurement and control methods, and the development of new equipment and machines. The Department also acts through its Service and Design section in an advisory capacity, providing consultation services based upon its backlog of experience to the individual departments and plants. In its latter function the Engineering Department is very closely linked with current plant operations, and the problems generated thereby.[1]

Construction expenditures are directed by the central Engineering Department in the case of major projects; each department may do some of its own design and construction relating to less significant projects, although Engineering Department personnel assist the department in projects designed to reduce costs and improve quality. The Company undertakes its own engineering primarily to attain close integration of research, design, construction, and manufacturing. This integration of effort makes it feasible to start certain phases of design work on a plant or process before the research and development for the entire project are completed, and to start certain construction before all design work is completed. Moreover, integration of engineering with manufacturing allows for early training of operating personnel and advance scheduling of production.[2]

The company itself stresses the results of research and development carried on internally, in accounting for observed improvements in the efficiency of operation:

> In a time of reduced economic activity, such as was experienced during the past year [1958], the problem of cost reduction, always a matter of major concern, assumes special significance. The problem has been intensified in recent years by rapidly increasing wages and salaries, reflected directly in labor costs and indirectly in the costs of purchased raw materials and services.

[1] Needless to say, in practice, the dividing line between the responsibilities of each group is often difficult to determine.
[2] *Annual Report*, E. I. du Pont de Nemours and Company, 1955, p. 7.

Prior to World War II, advances in technology made possible by research and development in the Du Pont Company's plants and laboratories more than offset increases in the elements of manufacturing costs. It was thus possible to maintain competitive wages and salaries and a satisfactory return on our operating investment, while prices were being reduced.

In the postwar years, however, the increase in wages and salaries has made it difficult for improved technology to keep pace. . . .[3]

We are concerned largely with the technology introduced into specific plants, but it is important to keep in mind the beginning of rayon production by the Du Pont Company. Du Pont executives had considered the production of synthetic fibers as early as 1909. In 1919, after the Armistice, all three processes then in use in Europe and the United States—nitrocellulose, cuprammonium, and viscose—were surveyed, but it was concluded after experimentation that the viscose process was preferable. In order to begin production quickly, Du Pont purchased technology from the Comptoir des Textiles Artificiels. (The Comptoir became an affiliate of Du Pont in 1920, and held a joint interest in Du Pont's synthetic-fiber business until 1929 when the French interest was purchased.)

The original rayon process, installed by the American Viscose Corporation at Marcus Hook in 1911, was protected by two key patents: the Courtaulds and S. Napper patent relating to the chemical constituents of the acid bath[4] and the American rights to the Topham spinning box. The Topham patent expired in 1918; nevertheless, Du Pont's first rayon plant, which began operations in May 1921 at Buffalo, employed a *large* (*glass*)-*bobbin* process based on the French technology. Subsequently, technology relating to the *bucket* process was acquired from a Belgian affiliate of Comptoir, and was installed in the early plants constructed at Old Hickory.[5]

Thus, in beginning production of artificial fibers, Du Pont entered an already well-established field. Substantial changes in technique were not developed by the Company until the 1930s; it required several years of research before it was possible to contribute significantly to improvements in product and to reductions in unit costs.[6]

---

[3] *Annual Report*, E. I. du Pont de Nemours and Company, 1958, pp. 10–11.

[4] Br. Pat. 406; 1911.

[5] See *Du Pont Monograph*, Chapter 1.

[6] The entry of Du Pont into the production of artificial fibers and other new products is discussed in detail by Willard F. Mueller, *Du Pont: A Study of Firm Growth*, unpublished Ph.D. dissertation, Vanderbilt University, 1955; and Mueller, "The Origins of the Basic Inventions Underlying Du Pont's Major Product and Process Innovations, 1920 to 1950," in *The Rate and Direction of Inventive Activity: Economic and Social Factors*, National Bureau of Economic Research, Princeton University Press, Princeton, 1962, pp. 323–346.

SOURCES OF "MINOR" TECHNICAL CHANGES (REQUIRING
INVESTMENT) COMMON TO ALL PLANTS

In this section we shall consider the sources of technical changes
common to all the plants. These changes were categorized as "minor" in
Chapter 4, and include increases in the size of the package, increases in
spinning speed and in denier, improvements in the viscose-making
equipment, and the introduction of equipment for the recovery of raw
materials. The use of improved inputs will be discussed in the next section.

*Increased Size of Package:* Throughout the period with which we have
been concerned there has occurred a general trend toward larger buckets
and bobbins. These changes, which permitted increases in the size of the
cake of yarn, required changes in motors, stabilizers, traverse mechanisms,
bobbin structures, bobbin chucks, and other equipment necessary to
yield satisfactory formation of the package. It was also necessary to adjust
the purification process.

Frequently, the larger bobbins and buckets and the related devices were
designed and the precise nature of the requirements defined by the
Engineering Department. The actual development of the equipment was
commonly a cooperative venture between the Engineering Department
and equipment manufacturers. As a rule these developments were not
patentable, since they involved small modifications in existing technology.

In certain instances the necessary devices would be developed by the
Technical Group at the plant itself. Rayon Research personnel were also
responsible for the development projects in some cases.[7]

*Increased Spinning Speed:* Increase in spinning speed depended upon
the attainment of increased bobbin or bucket speed. Further requirements
included modification of the spinning arrangement in the acid bath to
assure an adequate reaction and to decrease the "drag" exerted by the bath,
significant changes in the spinning-bath traverse mechanism to assure
satisfactory cake formation, and adjustments in the process of purification
to accommodate the altered package formation.

To increase the bucket speed or bobbin speed, it might also be necessary
to alter the material used in the construction of the bucket, to increase the

[7] There is no clear "rule" relating to the division which is responsible for the development of the necessary devices. However, where the requirements involved small
changes in existing equipment, the development work might more frequently be
accomplished at the plant itself: this was the case in the development of larger bobbins
and skeins at Spruance Plant I in 1938. (In the case of larger skeins, Rayon Research
personnel were also involved.) Where relatively extensive changes are called for, the
Engineering Department—at times in cooperation with outside suppliers of equipment
—would be responsible.

diameter of the bucket or bobbin, and sometimes to introduce new-type spinning motors.[8]

The requisite equipment was developed, where large changes were called for, by the Engineering Department. Spinning motors, however, were developed cooperatively by the Engineering Department and outside companies, in particular by General Electric and Westinghouse.[9] Equipment manufacturers would usually be responsible for the development of the new materials used in the construction of the bucket or bobbin, although the requirements would be specified by the rayon producer.[10] At times the increased spinning speed could be accomplished at the plant: this was the case, for example, at Spruance I in 1938.

Generally, the development of mechanisms which permitted higher spinning speeds involved alterations in existing technology which were not patentable, although individual features of the improved spinning motors were patented.

In a later section we shall consider in greater detail the introduction of Type 10 spinning machines in 1937, and of tube spinning in 1950 at Old Hickory, and the introduction of high-speed throwing at Spruance I in 1934.

*Increased Denier:* The major changes which were required for an increase in denier include modifications in the spinning arrangement in the acid bath to assure an adequate reaction, small changes in the package formation, and, frequently, increases in the size of the bucket accompanied by alterations in the bucket motor to handle the larger buckets. Most of the necessary equipment was developed internally with the exception of the spinning motors, which were usually developed cooperatively with outside manufacturers.

*Improved Viscose-Making Equipment:* During the 1930s, considerable attention was paid by rayon and equipment manufacturers to the development of continuous processes, automatic-control mechanisms, and large-size units, and to reduction in time cycles in the equipment required during the preparation of the viscose solution.

In the late 1930s, "Size 20 shredders" manufactured by Baker Perkins were installed in Du Pont's rayon plants. The Engineering Department had cooperated in the development of these churns. During the same period

---

[8] In the case of bobbin spinning there exists a restriction on the bobbin speed (which does not exist in bucket spinning), owing to the fact that bath is "thrown off" as the number of revolutions per minute is increased.

[9] As a rule the Du Pont Company called freely upon outside companies in the case of electrical equipment.

[10] Of especial significance is the development of the "Textolite High Speed Spinning Pot" by General Electric; this mechanism made feasible the introduction of larger buckets of improved structure and material.

completely water-jacketed xanthators and "Size 20 vissolvers" developed by Baker Perkins were installed at both Spruance and Old Hickory, where they replaced the original French equipment.

Patent coverage was narrow. Individual features of the improved equipment (such as the blades installed in the new-type shredders) were patented by the equipment manufacturers.[11]

*Recovery of Materials:* Recovery of materials was the most important single cause of the reduction in unit materials costs. Dializers for the recovery of caustic soda were first developed and patented by Cerini in Italy and by Asahi in Japan. The Asahi dializers were installed at Old Hickory and both Asahi and Cerini dializers at the Spruance location.

The recovery of carbon bisulphide was not of great significance at Du Pont plants. Carbon bisulphide is lost largely at the xanthation stage. Du Pont's Engineering Department developed "traps" on lines open to the air during the xanthation stage in order to recover the materials in the case of recovery at Spruance in the late 1930s; local development was responsible for the mechanisms installed at Old Hickory. These devices were not patented. It may also be noted that the use of high-alpha pulps improved productivity in the case of carbon bisulphide.[12]

Both the Spruance and Old Hickory plants installed evaporators developed by the Swenson Evaporator Company of Illinois; these evaporators—part of the equipment required in the recovery of the acid-bath materials—replaced in some cases the evaporators originally developed in France. Crystallizers, however, were developed by the Engineering Department at Du Pont; these mechanisms were not patented.

The replacement of the original excelsior filters by coal filters at Spruance and Old Hickory also depended upon internal research; the coal filters were not patented.

Generally, the internal developments represented adaptations of standard equipment already in commercial use.

*General Comments:* Many of the "minor" technical changes common to all the plants depended on technology deriving from a wide variety of sources, including internal research and development by Du Pont, and research by suppliers of equipment. Internal research and development refers here not so much to the formal activities of Rayon Research, but to the efforts of Technical Groups at the plant sites and those of the Engineering Department.

Responsibility for a project would depend partly on the nature of the technical change: where quite small modifications were called for, the

---

[11] The "Duplex" blades in Baker Perkins' shredders were patented, for example, and used in equipment installed at Old Hickory and Spruance.

[12] The beta and gamma constituents of pulp (wastes) also had to be xanthated.

development work might be accomplished at the plant; in cases of more extensive alterations, the Engineering Department would be required to help. On balance, the most important contribution to the development of minor changes common to all plants was made by Technical Assistance groups. Moreover, the work of the Engineering Department depended less upon its function as a generator of technology based on new formal research and more on its function as a source of consultation and advice for the plants.

In the development of improved electrical equipment, recovery equipment, and viscose-making equipment in particular, outside manufacturers played an important role. Frequently the mechanisms were developed cooperatively by Du Pont's Engineering Department and the equipment manufacturers. It was common, for example, for Du Pont to recognize a particular requirement and refer the problem to an outside company; "solutions" would then be tested at the rayon plants and further improvements suggested. Refinements in the required chemical reactions—such as the alterations in the nature of the spinning bath in the trend to higher spinning speeds—were developed internally.

Most of the improvements represented refinements in existing technology and were not patentable. Isolated instances of patented technology have been referred to, however. Moreover, in the case of acid-bath recovery equipment, some of the more significant developments were patented by outside companies.

### Technological Developments Originating with Materials Suppliers

Reductions in unit materials costs can be attributed in part to improvements originating with the suppliers of raw materials. The nature of the *cellulose* used in the process is of particular importance with respect to both the quality of the product and the efficiency of production. Desirable characteristics of cellulose are its purity (which in part determines the yield), its uniformity of property, and its whiteness; purity and uniformity are of particular relevance in the determination of "productivity." However, the cellulose also influences the productivity of various chemicals and of labor; moreover, the nature of the equipment may be in part determined by the properties of the cellulose. It is therefore difficult to identify particular cost reductions with particular improvements in the cellulosic raw material, but one may safely say that such improvements have played a part in the trend toward lower production costs.

In attempting to estimate the effect of improved *wood pulp* on productivity, a further complication arises as a result of the substitutability in production of pulp and cotton linters in many instances. The efforts of wood-pulp producers were directed toward improvements in the purity and uniformity of property of their product and also toward the development of a wider range of (geographical) sources of supply in order to avoid rising pulp prices. These developments were part of a general effort to displace cotton linters (which already possessed many desirable features) by wood pulp.[13] A wider range of grades of pulp was also made available. But for the improvements in the properties of wood pulp, rayon plants would have been obliged to employ relatively high proportions of cotton linters during the 1930s, when efforts were made to improve the quality of the ultimate product. Although cotton linters were also being improved,[14] the lower and more stable price of wood pulp in conjunction with the improved quality ensured a general trend towards the greater use of wood pulp during the 1930s and 1940s.

An increase in the percentage of wood pulp used at the expense of cotton linters will not, however, be reflected in an increase in the physical productivity of cellulose, for the yield of linters exceeds that of pulp despite the marked improvements in the latter. However, the price of pulp is lower than that of linters, so that there may occur reductions in *unit costs* of production as a result of the switch between inputs made possible by the improved quality of pulp. Our method of correcting recorded costs for changes in input prices deliberately retains the price differentials *between* inputs (and removes only the influence of changing prices over time of each individual input). In fact, we have found that major reductions in unit materials costs were accompanied by sharp increases in the percentage of wood pulp used in total cellulose.

A profound influence has been exerted by the highly purified wood pulps on the quality of the final product. Above all, the development of tire-cord yarn was intimately bound up with the improvements in the cellulosic source.

[13] Prior to the late 1920s northeast spruce was the only wood pulped for rayon. In 1927 the Rainier Pulp and Paper Company built a sulphite plant at Shelton, Washington; research at that plant led to the possibility of using western hemlock, which has a high "alpha-cellulose" content (and is of relatively high purity) and is white in color. In 1939 methods were perfected by Rayonier, Inc. for the use of southern pine in rayon-manufacturing plants and a sulphate plant was constructed at Fernandina, Florida. See "Transmutation of Giant Hemlocks to Rayon Yarn," *Rayon and Synthetic Yarn Journal*, Vol. XIX, May 1933, p. 10, "Observations on Dissolving Wood Pulp," *Rayon Textile Monthly*, Vol. XXII, Jan. 1941, p. 39, and Williams Haynes, *American Chemical Industry* (cited in Chapter 6, note 8), Vol. V, pp. 375–376.

[14] Testing laboratories were established and the uniformity of linters increased, and viscose with satisfactory filtration properties and permitting a whiter end-product was developed. See "Buckeye Cellulose Purification Plant," *Rayon and Synthetic Yarn Journal*, Vol. XIX, Aug. 1933, p. 42; "Technical and Economical Aspects of Rayon," *Rayon Textile Monthly*, Vol. XVIII, July 1936, pp. 33–35.

SOURCES OF TECHNICAL CHANGE AT TEXTILE-YARN
PLANTS: (1) OLD HICKORY[15]

The technology underlying the production of yarn at Old Hickory was largely acquired from the Comptoir des Textiles Artificiels. The plants made use of the so-called "Napper Zinc Bath"; the constituents of the bath were protected by a patent under which Du Pont and other rayon manufacturers were licensed.[16]

We shall discuss the development in subsequent years of roller-bath guides, the cake-to-cone process, the Type 10 machines, tube spinning, beaming of yarn and the various technical changes installed at Old Hickory in the late 1950s. The cake-to-cone process, tube spinning, and the changes introduced in 1958–1959 were instances of "major" technical change.

*1929, Roller-Bath Guides:* Improved stretching mechanisms in the spinning bath were installed at Old Hickory during the late 1920s and early 1930s to increase the tenacity of the yarn and to permit production with fewer breakages. Roller-bath guides were developed internally for this purpose and patented by W. H. Bradshaw of Rayon Research. The improved mechanisms replaced the original French hook guides.

*1932, Cake-to-Cone Process:* The cake-to-cone process was a major technical change and one of the most significant developments in the production of textile yarn.[17] The process originated with research by the Du Pont Company:

> In a recital of major improvements in the rayon process, prominence must be given to the development of the Type 5 (cake-to-cone) process. The statement has been made that this is the biggest job accomplished by the Rayon Department in the viscose process development field. . . . Teamwork between research

[15] The technical changes introduced at Old Hickory—in particular, the cake-to-cone process—were also relevant at Spruance II. Much of the discussion in this section, therefore, will also refer to the technology at Spruance II.

[16] The Napper Zinc Bath contained 1 per cent zinc sulphate, acid, sodium sulphate, and glucose, and was protected under a Courtaulds' patent in the United Kingdom: Br. Pat. 406; 1911. This patent was filed in the United States by Cohn under U.S. Pat. 1,045,731. Industrial Rayon, American Viscose, and Du Pont were licensed under this latter patent.

[17] It will be recalled that the original process at Old Hickory involved several additional stages compared with the wet-reeling process used, for example, by the American Viscose Corporation. The cake-to-cone process was an attempt in large part to reduce the number of steps; as a result labor costs fell directly. Moreover, washing the yarn on the original cake package allowed larger units. There was also less degradation of the yarn because of the reduction of handling, and therefore a larger percentage of first-quality yarn. Uniform dyeing and thorough purification was allowed by the process. Until this time, weaving yarns (which require bleaching, a high degree of dye uniformity, and the avoidance of shrinkage) had presented great problems, which the process was in part designed to overcome.

and production men, with an understanding administrative management, led to a successful industrial development.[18]

In Table 7.1 the details of the process, including the patented features, are outlined. Not all the features were necessarily applied in 1932 when the first weaving yarn by the process was produced; some features represent further improvements in the original process.

*Table 7.1   The Source of the Cake-to-Cone Process*

| Mechanism | Inventor (if Patented) | Year of Patent Application | U.S. Patent Granted |
|---|---|---|---|
| 1. Cloverleaf bucket | S. W. Brainard | 1932 | 1940: 2,218,461<br>       2,218,462 |
| 2. L-bleach process using chlorine water | J. S. Fonda;<br>G. W. Filson | 1933 | 1937: 2,064,300 |
| 3. Improved cone winding | L. S. Sinness | 1938 | 1940: 2,223,923 |
| 4. High-humidity drying | Not Patented | | |
| 5. New types of cake finishes | Not Patented | | |
| 6. Hard-rubber lined steel pipes for soft-water lines | Not Patented | | |
| 7. Corrosion-resistant materials in desulphuring system | Not Patented | | |
| 8. Compensation spinning | Not Patented | | |
| 9. Covering to protect packages in drying (rubber dams)* | J. S. Fonda:<br>G. W. Filson | 1935 | 1937: 2,098,620 |

* This mechanism was used in the case of yarn produced by the cake-to-cone process by means of round buckets rather than "cloverleaf" buckets, and was developed initially for use at Spruance I.

The cake-to-cone process was used in the production of weaving yarn; knitting yarn from the early years of operation had been produced without the intermediate step of skeining. Weaving yarns required a process which would assure uniformity of shrinkage and whiteness and a low degree of "dyeing spread."[19] Shrinkage was controlled in the new process by the cloverleaf buckets, and by high-humidity drying. The color was rendered

[18] *Du Pont Monograph*, Chapter 1, "Viscose Yarns," pp. 131–132.
[19] The production of knitting yarns was generally simpler than that of weaving yarns: the yarn was not bleached, and variable shrinkage and relatively wide dyeing spread was permissible.

uniformly white by the L-bleach process, which used chlorine water. The dyeing spread was reduced by compensation spinning, by the use of cloverleaf buckets, and by high-humidity drying.[20]

The cloverleaf buckets permitted the production of excellent weaving yarn at a bucket speed of 6,000 revolutions per minute. In late 1935 spinning motors operating at 7,700 revolutions per minute were introduced; "flashes" appeared on the yarn, and it was necessary to revert to round buckets in the production of yarn of 150 denier and below. This could be done by making use of rubber dams which slowed the rate of drying on the outside of the cake and also protected the package.

The entire cake-to-cone process was developed by Du Pont Rayon Research personnel. The rubber dams were an integral part of the Type 9 process developed for installation at Spruance Plant I (to be considered presently). A small number of features upon which the cake-to-cone process depended were patented, but the cake-to-cone process *as a whole* was not patented.

An important organizational change, namely "gang doffing," was introduced in conjunction with the cake-to-cone process; the change was perfected at Old Hickory.

*1937, Type 10 Spinning Machines:* The installation of Type 10 spinning machines at Old Hickory in 1937 was described in Chapter 4 as an instance of "minor" indirect technical change. The newly installed equipment permitted a large expansion in volume because of higher bucket speed (and lower twist per inch). The effect on unit costs was very considerable. A new traverse mechanism permitting faster strokes was developed by Du Pont's Engineering Department but was not patented. New-type bucket compartments were designed internally, but were constructed by outside companies. Larger spinning motors were developed by suppliers of electrical equipment; certain features of the new motors were protected by patents.[21]

*1950, Tube Spinning:* The introduction of tube spinning in 1950 at Old

[20] High-humidity drying permitted the avoidance of a shrinkage differential between yarn wound on the inside of the cake compared with that wound on the outside. Compensation spinning refers to a variation in spinning speed during the formation of the cake, with the aim of limiting the shrinkage differential and the dyeing spread.

Technology which has not been referred to in Table 7.1 may also have been relevant but is not mentioned because it was not peculiar to the cake-to-cone process alone. For example, a "constant index system" installed—as we shall see—for the first time at Spruance Plant I was developed and patented by E. R. McKee. The index measures the degree of coagulability of the viscose solution; the dyeing spread of the weaving yarn produced by cake-to-cone process was in part reduced by the constant index system in the viscose-regenerating room.

[21] This development is characteristic of the development of mechanisms permitting higher spinning speed described in the previous section; it was a cooperative effort by Du Pont and equipment suppliers.

Hickory permitted a 40 per cent increase in the spinning speed; the necessary equipment was developed internally and was patented.[22]

*1950, Beams:* In 1950 at Old Hickory (and in 1953 at Spruance II) beams were introduced in place of cones. Converters were able to avoid the stage of beaming from cones which had previously been necessary. Unit costs were not reduced *at the rayon plants,* however, although both investment and the development of new technology were required. This development was not patentable.

*1958, Continuous Steeping and Continuous Shredding:* We have noted in the previous section that considerable effort was exerted during the 1930s, both by equipment manufacturers and rayon producers, to develop continuous processes rather than batch-operated processes. Continuous-shredding equipment, for example, was developed successfully by Baker Perkins in 1938. At the same time, continuous-shredding and continuous-steeping equipment was developed by Du Pont's Rayon Research and Mechanical Assistance (plant) personnel, and installed at the Buffalo location in 1941. The equipment was patented, and was transferred to Old Hickory in 1958 when the Buffalo plants were closed down.

*1958, Dielectric Drying and Mechanized-Drip Purification:* Elements of dielectric drying and mechanized purification were developed by Mechanical Assistance and patented. Dielectric drying allowed significant improvements in the quality of the yarn, and was developed by the research branch of the Engineering Department.

SOURCES OF TECHNICAL CHANGE AT TEXTILE-YARN
PLANTS: (2) SPRUANCE PLANT I

Spruance Plant I was constructed to produce a fine-denier yarn of relatively high strength. The essential elements of the process were the use of a certain proportion of zinc sulphate in the acid bath, and the use of floating rollers in the bath to serve as the means for the application of tension to the newly formed filaments. The first element was part of the bath patented by Courtaulds and S. Napper in England and licensed to Du Pont and other companies.[23] The floating rollers on glass pins were part of a patented process purchased from the Fiberloid Company of Indian Orchard, Massachusetts, the so-called "Essex" Process.[24] Improvements

[22] A patent was granted to Melheiser of Du Pont.
[23] See p. 173.
[24] The use of floating rollers in the spinning bath avoided the mechanism in use hitherto at other Du Pont plants, namely glass hooks for the application of tension; the ultimate uniformity of dyeing was improved by this method and the more effective application of tension was permitted. The technique is important in the progress towards tire-cord yarn.

in the dyeing properties of the yarn were permitted by the introduction for the first time of a "constant index system,"[25] which was patented by E. R. McKee of Du Pont.

We shall now consider certain technical changes referred to in earlier chapters which were peculiar to Spruance Plant I:

*1932–1934, All-Active Spinning:* An alternative-active schedule was followed at the outset at Spruance I, since a number of technical problems remained unsolved at bobbin plants when one nozzle per bobbin was utilized. These problems were overcome by the development at the plant of a wider bath and additional (idle) rollers.[26] The mechanisms were not patented. The introduction of all-active spinning was classified in Chapter 4 as a "minor" indirect technical change, although there were reservations concerning this categorization.

*1933–1934, High-Speed Throwing:* "Minor" improvements in the traverse mechanism and in the composition of the spinning bath (developed at the plant itself) permitted sharp increases in the speed at which the throwing or twisting of the yarn could be accomplished. The required mechanisms were not patented.

*1935, Type 9 (Flat-Wrap) Process:* In 1933, a program was begun by Rayon Research to perfect a process for a bobbin plant which would parallel the cake-to-cone process installed at the Old Hickory bucket plant. The essential feature of the process would be the abolition of the skeining stage. The research work culminated in the development of the Type 9 process which was introduced at Spruance Plant I in 1935. The Type 9 process was an important instance of "major" direct technical change.

The new process—which embodied a number of novel features—was not patented as a whole, and individual elements, in most instances, were not patentable. Three features were, however, protected by patents, namely, a novel method of throwing or twisting ("face-drive" throwing), a covering to protect the cakes during drying (rubber dams), and a device to prepare an unsupported package for purposes of purification.[27] It will be recalled that the rubber dams developed for the Type 9 process were also found suitable for use at Old Hickory in combination with round buckets.

[25] The "index" measures the degree of coagulability of the viscose solution. Usually the index is 4.0; it falls 0.3 in three hours, so that it is spun at an index of 3.7. As a result of the change in the index, the dyeing properties of the ultimate product are altered.

[26] These idle rollers replaced bobbins in certain functions.

[27] Face-drive throwing was patented by E. Z. Lewis, U.S. Pat. 2,232,542 (1936); rubber dams by J. S. Fonda and G. W. Filson, U.S. Pat. 2,098,620 (1937); and the means of preparing an unsupported package of yarn by Harvey *et. al.*, U.S. Pat. 2,736,184.

SOURCES OF TECHNICAL CHANGE AT TIRE-CORD PLANTS:
(1) SPRUANCE PLANT III

We shall consider in this section the inception and the program of development leading to the commercial introduction of tire-cord yarn before turning to particular mechanisms installed at Spruance III.

### *The Inception of Tire-Cord Yarn*

High spinning speed, an important variable in the determination of unit overhead costs (and in the successful washing of the end product), depends upon filaments of sufficient tenacity. In 1926 a research program was established at the Du Pont Company with the aim of developing yarn of higher tenacity. The purchase of the "Essex" process from the Fiberloid Company helped the development program; tension was applied to the newly formed filaments by rollers in the bath and improvements were made to the principle. However, until the late 1920s and early 1930s the research effort was not directed specifically towards the development of tire-cord yarn. Yarns suitable for sewing thread and shirting were considered. As the tension applied to the filaments was increased, it was found that dyeing problems accumulated, so that a product where dyeing was not significant became a desirable outlet.

By the early 1930s, yarn with a dry strength of 2.25 grams per denier was being produced experimentally. At this time the development of tire-cord yarn was made a formal objective.[28] A process for the production of rayon tire cord *capable of competing with cotton* was called for.[29] From the technical viewpoint, uniformity of property was considered a most significant requirement of a tire-cord yarn; efforts were therefore directed at correcting existing textile processes. However, the experimental elimination of certain features of the textile process led to dye resistance, so that not all the mechanisms applicable to tire cord could be applied to textile yarn as well.

The bobbin rather than the bucket was used during the experimental work since it proved more flexible in various respects; in particular, frequent experimental changes were possible, since there are no serious variations in relaxation to limit the size of the bobbin, whereas such restrictions exist in the case of the bucket. The "finishing" time (between spinning and washing) was found to be most satisfactory with the use of the bobbin rather than the bucket. It was determined further that a "long" bath followed by a high-temperature secondary bath for coagulation and regeneration was required, and that the spinning speed would have to be

---

[28] Rubber companies cooperated in the problem of application of rayon to tires.

[29] The following account has been given the writer by W. H. Bradshaw, who in the early 1930s was assigned responsibility for the program.

restricted. Initially, the bobbin was found preferable for the process used commercially, because of the ideal reaction time (given the nature of the bath constituents then available) and because of the larger size of the bobbin compared with the bucket. With later improvements in the bath content, it became technologically feasible to produce tire cord by the bucket process too.[30]

Most of the early developmental work was accomplished by Rayon Research. Later improvements in quality and in efficiency were also perfected for the most part by Rayon Research.

The first tire-cord yarn was produced on a pilot scale in 1935 at Spruance I under the trademark "Cordura." Manufacture of "Cordura" began in 1936 at Spruance III, a plant constructed solely for this purpose. Two rubber companies took all the output, which was of 3 grams per denier tenacity.[31]

### Initial Mechanisms and Materials Used at Spruance III

We shall now consider the relationship between the mechanisms and materials required for the production of tire-cord yarn and its patents. The requirements included high alpha-cellulose pulp, development of mechanisms for applying tension to the spinning thread without sliding friction by means of roller-bath guides, control of the degree and manner of stretching of the nascent yarn through progressive development of spinning tension, long bath travel with higher bath temperature to raise the breaking strength of the gel yarn and thus permit higher spinning tension, improved spinning-bath composition, and the use of viscose free from metallic impurities.[32]

*High Alpha-Cellulose Pulp:* Pulp improvements had profound influence upon the development of tire-cord yarn. Pressure was exerted upon the *pulp manufacturers* to develop a more highly purified source of cellulose. Cotton linters were also of significance since the alpha-cellulose content is very high.[33] Research was also carried out at the Du Pont Company itself on the relationship between high alpha cellulose and tenacity.

*Application of Tension:* The mechanism developed by the Du Pont research organization and installed in Spruance III involved the use of

[30] It was necessary to learn how to keep the elongation of the yarn low.

[31] Rayon tire cord has a relatively high "hot strength" compared with cotton. It was therefore suitable for heavy trucks where the heat of the tire degraded the cotton cord. During the war the problem was rendered all the more urgent by the fact that synthetic rubber was used in place of natural rubber in tires; the former runs hotter. A government program extended the use of the product to aircraft fuel cells and fuel hose, in addition to tires.

[32] *Du Pont Monograph*, Chapter 1, "Viscose Yarns," p. 135.

[33] The significance of high alpha cellulose lies primarily in the fact that a stronger yarn can be produced.

"roller-bath guides." Roller-bath guides were developed in the mid 1920s and installed in the Old Hickory (bucket) plants in 1928 to replace the original French hook mechanism; this development was patented by W. H. Bradshaw. A further redesigning of the mechanism resulted in "vane guides," which were patented by Bradshaw and G. Preston Hoff, and finally a mechanism involving a plurality of wheels upon which the thread was wrapped several times (the wheels rotating at different peripheral speeds), that is, several vane guides, was developed and patented by Bradshaw. It was the latter mechanism that was installed in Spruance III.[34]

An alternative method for the application of tension of relevance for the production of tire-cord yarn called for the use of the double godet mechanism, which was developed and patented by Griffen of the American Viscose Corporation,[35] and installed in certain Avisco plants.

*The Spinning Bath:* The "formula" used in determining the makeup of the spinning bath is crucial for the successful production in tire cord. In the original Spruance Plant III a "high-sulphate bath" was used; this bath was developed at Du Pont but was not patented, since it was closely linked in nature to widely used baths.

*Spinning and Postspinning Equipment:* The novel features of the equipment installed at Spruance III were the large-bobbin machines, centrifugal washing, down-twister equipment and beaming from warpers.

The large bobbins were designed by Rayon Research personnel; the bobbin size itself would not be patentable but certain complementary pieces of equipment were patented.[36] Bobbins had to be rotated on throwing spindles (to twist the yarn) in the case of textile rayon; it would

---

[34] Application for a patent covering the original roller-bath guides was made in October 1929 and a patent was granted in September 1935; the application for the (simple) vane-guide mechanism was made in February 1933 and the patent was granted in June 1937 (U.S. Pat. 2,083,252); and the application for a patent covering the multiple vane-guide principle was made in October 1929 and granted in September 1935 (U.S. Pat. 2,012,984). It will be recalled that the Spruance I (bobbin) plant utilized floating rollers on glass pins, a mechanism purchased from the Fiberloid Company.

[35] The patent covering the double godet was applied for in April 1927 and granted in March 1934 (U.S. Pat. 1,950,922). In this mechanism active use is made of two wheels around which the newly formed thread is wound. (The principle of the double godet was first devised by L. P. Wilson of Courtaulds, Ltd., in 1914 according to R. W. Moncrieff, *Man-Made Fibers*, John Wiley & Sons, Inc., New York, 1957, p. 212; stretch was applied to the filaments between two rotating wheels, revolving at different speeds.) The essential feature of Griffen's mechanism was the prevention of the thread from tracking back on itself as it passed twice around the godet wheels.

[36] The cake at Spruance I was 1.0 pound in weight. The initial weight of the cake at Spruance III in 1936 was 1.4 pounds. Subsequently the cake was increased in size: to 2.1 pounds in 1939, 2.5 pounds in 1943, 3.1 pounds in 1946, 3.9 pounds in 1948–1949, and 4.5 pounds in 1952. The traverse system in the case of larger cakes was patented by E. M. Hicks, U.S. Pat. 2,345,601.

not have been economical to do this with large bobbins. The smaller bobbins were therefore required at textile-yarn plants.

Washing of yarn while it was still in bobbin form derived from research at the Du Pont Company, but required relatively small modifications in techniques already applied quite widely in textile-yarn plants.

The down-twister equipment was part of a combined twister-dryer mechanism introduced into Spruance III. The mechanism permitted the solution of the problem of nonuniform yarns caused by the fact that in the traditional drying processes there occurred differences between the shrinkage of the yarn on the inside compared with the yarn on the outside of the package. A different technique would have been required for the solution of the problem in the case of bucket spinning, and the mechanism was therefore restricted to Spruance III. Essentially the product quality was improved by the technique. The mechanism was in part the result of research at the Du Pont Company itself, and in part due to cooperative development programs between Du Pont and suppliers of equipment to the Company. The drying features of the device were patented.[37]

Further important features of Spruance III were the use of nickel units in the piping system, from the viscose preparation to the mixing stage, to avoid the contamination of the solution which was common when iron piping was used. Operating costs were reduced by the use of such material, since the contact with iron has caused a slow build-up of material on the inside of pipes, requiring frequent cleaning and creating spinning difficulties. The piping was patented and was developed by equipment suppliers.

The equipment installed initially at Spruance III for the transfer of yarn to beams (namely, the spools or pirns, the multiple-end creels, and the beam warpers) was based on technology which was common knowledge in the textile industry at the time.

*Sources of Cost-Reducing Technical Changes Introduced Subsequently at Spruance III*

A number of "major" cost-reducing technical changes were introduced in the late 1930s at Spruance III. In the first place, the plant was redesigned for the production of 1,100-denier yarn; the "direct-slashing" process was introduced as a "direct" cost-reducing technical change, but the increase in denier in any event required the replacement of the original "twister-dryer" apparatus. Second, centrifugal washing was replaced

---

[37] The drying aspect of the device known as "controlled humidity" drying (whereby the moisture content remains relatively high to prevent inside-outside shrinkage differentials, by means of blowing hot air from the inside), was patented under U.S. Pat. 2,130,247, 1938, by H. H. Parker and G. P. Standley, assignors to the Du Pont Company. The twisting aspect—involving the "down-twister" device—was purchased from equipment makers; the down-twister device was standard textile equipment.

by a newly developed pressure-washing system. In the postwar period, the denier was raised further.

*1938, Direct Slashing:* The direct-slashing process—whereby the yarn was stretched and dried during passage from the bobbins to beams without twisting—was developed largely by Rayon Research personnel. The new process was not patented as a whole, but two related features of the process were protected by patents, namely devices for the beaming of zero-twist yarn, and "compensation slashing."[38] The coverage afforded by patents in the case of direct slashing was, however, broader than that afforded by patents to the cake-to-cone process at Old Hickory or to the Type 9 process at Spruance I.

Apart from the new equipment, the change in technique required the development of a new-type "size" in order to assure that the (untwisted) filaments remained together and acted as if they had been already twisted into yarn form. The size was developed by Rayon Research.

*1938, Pressure Washing:* Mechanisms to permit the pressure washing of tire-cord yarn at Spruance III were developed by Rayon Research. Two patents protecting certain pieces of apparatus were taken out; the development as a whole involved minor refinements in already known technology and was therefore not patentable.[39]

*1945, Increased Denier:* Substantial increases in denier during the postwar period depended on new technology developed internally. There were no patents relating directly to the new technology.[40]

### Product Improvements Introduced Subsequently at Spruance III

A number of important changes in the nature of the acid bath designed to improve product quality were introduced in the early 1940s. The plant was redesigned to produce 1,600 denier in the postwar period, and very significant product changes took place during the 1950s.

*1943, Iron Bath:* In 1943, the "high-sulphate bath" was replaced by an "iron bath," and the tenacity of the yarn thereby increased. The constituents of this bath were developed and patented by Du Pont.[41] The bath was in use for a very short period.

*1944–1945, High-Zinc Bath:* A well-known development in the rayon industry was the high-zinc bath which derived from research work at the

---

[38] The beaming of zero-twist yarn was protected by W. H. Bradshaw, U.S. Pat. 2,224,665, and "compensation slashing"—changing the conditions of spinning during the slashing process—by G. M. Karns, U.S. Pat. 2,350,168.

[39] The two patents were Pieratt, U.S. Pat. 2,088,011, and Wilson, U.S. Pat. 2,123,689.

[40] The increase in denier reduced unit costs at the rayon plants and also allowed substantial reductions in unit costs at the converters' plants.

[41] A patent was granted to N. L. Cox, U.S. Pat. 2,364,273.

American Viscose Corporation in the United States and Courtaulds, Ltd., in Great Britain. In the British development heat was applied to the yarn between the godets and a high proportion of metallic salts was used in the bath (at least 2.5 per cent zinc sulphate); as a result the dry strength increased to 3.5 grams per denier since greater stretch could be applied.[42] The high-zinc bath as described by the Givens patent was supplemented by further research at the American Viscose Corporation, the results of which were patented too.[43] When zinc sulphate is used in relatively large proportions, it is necessary to stretch the yarn at high temperatures (hot stretching). The American Viscose Corporation developed a hot-stretch process which was patented by Berman.

The iron bath possessed certain advantages over the original high-sulphate bath and allowed an increase in the tenacity of the yarn, but the high-zinc bath displaced the iron bath in turn because it permitted substantial increases in the strength of tire cord and greater fatigue resistance. (Reductions in unit acid-bath costs were also permitted since glucose could be entirely dispensed with.)

Du Pont was licensed to use the high-zinc bath which, as we have seen, was protected by the Givens patent. Type 146 yarn, introduced in 1945, made use of the high-zinc bath.

*1952–1956, Further Increases in Tenacity:* In the postwar period research was continued at Du Pont on the development of stronger yarns. In 1952, Type 156 "Cordura"—characterized by low-solids viscose and high-zinc bath—displaced Type 146 (high-zinc) yarn which had been produced at Spruance III since 1945. In 1954, Type 156-B "Cordura"—characterized by a lower-solids viscose than Type 156 "Cordura"—was produced at Spruance III. Finally, "Super-Cordura"—yarn of a significantly higher tenacity than that produced hitherto by Du Pont—was introduced at the plant. The technology indispensable to the production of "Super-Cordura"

[42] This bath was protected by U.S. Pat. 2,192,074, granted in 1940. The patentees were J. H. Givens *et al.*, assignors to Courtaulds, Ltd., England. A British patent No. 467,500 was granted in 1935. It may be added here that as early as 1926 a patent was taken out by Lilienfeld of Austria for the spinning of a high-tenacity yarn by extruding a "young" viscose made of cotton into a cold sulphuric-acid bath, and stretching in water (while maintaining tension). A dry tenacity, at the limit, of 6 to 6.5 grams per denier was permitted by the method. Commercial production began incorporating the technique at Courtaulds in England and Glansztoff in Germany, but no use was seen for the end product by the textile industry and production almost ceased. (Br. Pat. 274,521; 1926.) The American Viscose Corporation continued the perfection of Lilienfeld yarn but it proved too brittle, so that the process was abandoned and replaced by the high-zinc method. See H. J. Hegan, "The Historical Development of and the Outlook for Viscose Fibers," *Journal of the Textile Institute*, Proceedings, Vol. 42, 1951, pp. 395–410.

[43] A patent was granted to I. P. Davis of the American Viscose Corporation: U.S. Pat. 2,312,152; 1943.

tire cord was protected by a patent granted to N. L. Cox.[41] The Central Research Department was largely responsible for this development.

Unit costs of production were substantially increased as a result of the more costly processes required by the improved product.

SOURCES OF TECHNICAL CHANGE AT TIRE-CORD PLANTS: (2) SPRUANCE PLANT II-A

Considerable developmental effort was required to permit the production of tire cord in a plant originally designed for textile yarn. The conversion work at Spruance II-A was completed in 1944. Initially the process still retained many of the features characteristic of the original product: after spinning, doffing, and cake wrapping, the yarn was drip washed, desulphured, finished, and dried while in cake form, and then wound to cones. Finally, however, the yarn was stretched during the passage to beams; this stage was absent at the original section of the plant.

The high-zinc bath—developed and patented by Courtaulds—was used from the outset at Spruance II-A.

A process of slashing to beams, not protected by patents, had been worked out with reference to Spruance III, and applied at that plant in 1936; however, considerable developmental work remained before slashing to beams could be introduced at a bucket plant. A novel stretching method was developed at Du Pont, and patented, for tire cord produced by the bucket process. The relevant mechanisms were patented, and installed at the plant in 1943–1944.[45]

A number of cost-reducing technical changes occurred during the 1940s, as we have seen in earlier chapters.[46]

*1946, Desulphuring Stage Avoided:* Experimentation at the plant itself showed that it was possible to produce a satisfactory product without desulphuring the yarn. The removal of the desulphuring stage was an instance of "minor" direct technical change; it was not protected by patents.

*1948, Direct Slashing; Mechanical Handling of Packages; Large Cakes; and Automatic (or Centrifugal) Washing:* A number of "major" technical changes were introduced in the late 1940s. The changes were, strictly, part of a single extensive alteration in process.

[44] U.S. Pat. 2,536,014; 1950.

[45] The technique involved two godet wheels in one single unit and a guide mechanism. The relevant patents were H. W. Swank, U.S. Pat. 2,440,226, and J. Bellezza, U.S. Pat. 2,410,419.

[46] As at Spruance III substantial product improvements were introduced during the 1950s. In particular, the plant was converted for the production of "Super-Cordura" in 1953–1954.

Direct (or wet) slashing (whereby cakes of yarn were transferred to beams without the intermediate stages of coning and drying) was similar to the technique developed earlier by Rayon Research for installation at Spruance III in 1938; it will be recalled that certain mechanisms relating to direct slashing were patented.

Mechanical (or centrifugal) purification replaced the hand wrapping of cakes and subsequent drip washing inherited from the process in use when textile yarn was produced at Spruance II-A. The new method of washing permitted substantial reductions in labor costs, but the technology could not have been applied at textile-yarn plants. Mechanical purification of tire-cord yarn produced in bucket plants was well protected by a number of patents.[47] The mechanical-purification procedure was developed cooperatively by Rayon Research and by the technical organization at Spruance.

The remaining features of the technical change—large-size buckets (4.5 pounds in weight) and the mechanical handling of cakes—were developed internally but were not patented.

*1948, Alternative-Active Spinning:* The transfer from the use of every third nozzle position to alternative-active spinning in the late 1940s was, we have noted, a further instance of "minor" indirect technical change. The development was relatively simple and accomplished at the plant; there were no patents.

SUMMARY

In establishing its first rayon plants during the 1920s the Du Pont Company entered into an already well-established industry. The original technology relating to the bucket spinning of rayon yarn and introduced at Old Hickory was obtained from the Comptoir des Textiles Artificiels; this technology was supplemented by the acquisition (by license) of acid-bath technology. The initial process used at Spruance I, the bobbin plant, was also dependent in large part upon technology developed elsewhere.

In Chapter 4 we noted striking reductions in unit costs over time resulting from technical change. In the present chapter the source of the

---

[47] The most important patent covering mechanical-purification was that of Jackson, U.S. Pat. 2,300,254. A patent covering a shower for the preconditioning of the cakes prior to purification was granted to O'Brien *et al.*, U.S. Pat. 2,647,040, and a further device—known as a cake inserter—was patented by Davis *et al.*, 2,642,655. (Centrifugal purification required the insertion into the cake of yarn of a "core"; yarn spun by the bobbin process is naturally produced on a core.)

Whereas the O'Brien and Davis patents related to particular devices, the Jackson patent was relatively broad.

underlying technology has been considered in detail. It was seen that "minor" technical changes—technical changes based on technology which has been judged "relatively simple" to develop—common to all plants, such as increased size of package, increased spinning speed and (in some cases) denier, improved equipment, and input recovery, were characterized by dependence upon technology which was developed internally but with some important contributions by suppliers of equipment.[48] Frequently, the development projects were undertaken by personnel at the plant itself, attached, for example, to the Technical Assistance to Production groups; these teams were intimately concerned with current operations as well as with improvements therein. Du Pont's Engineering Department played a central role as well. The precise distribution of responsibilities between the plants themselves and the Engineering Department, sometimes aided by outside companies, would depend on the magnitude of the project. Minor technical changes, specific to particular plants, were also developed for the most part by Technical Assistance personnel on the location or by the Engineering Department.

On balance, however, although the Engineering Department played a very significant role, the most important contribution to the development of "minor" technical changes was that by the Technical Assistance groups. Moreover, the greater part of the contribution by the Engineering Department derived from its function as a "consultation agency" for the plants.

It was also seen that the requisite technology was not protected strongly by patents. Indeed, many of the developments represented refinements in existing technology and were not patentable.

The "major" technical changes—in many cases entire changes in process—were largely developed by Du Pont's formal research groups, in particular Rayon Research.[49] However, even in the case of the major

---

[48] We have been largely concerned with the sources of technology introduced at Du Pont plants. We have seen that Du Pont used not only its own research results but also benefited from developments occurring outside its own research and development facilities. At the same time, however, efforts were made by Du Pont research to solve problems of relevance to nonrayon producers. For example, in the production of tires, the adhesion of rubber to rayon proved weaker than that of rubber to cotton. One solution was obtained by the Rayon Research section and patents were granted to Charch and Maney. Alternative methods were developed by other rayon producers and by the rubber companies. References may be found to alternative "strong bond" methods in "Patents and Data on Rayon Cord Tires," *Rayon Textile Monthly*, Vol. XIX, March 1938, p. 84.

[49] The Engineering Department did not play an important role, for the most part. To the extent that it contributed it served in its consultative function. One exception, however, is the development of dielectric drying introduced at Old Hickory in the late 1950s; this project was developed by the research section of the Department. From time to time the Textile Fibers Pioneering Research group also contributed to the major changes.

changes, personnel concerned with current operations—Technical Assistance members—played an important role. Generally, the processes as a whole were not protected by patents, although usually some individual features were patented.

Major cost-reducing technical changes introduced at the tire-cord plants, although not usually protected entirely, were covered somewhat more broadly than the major changes at the textile-yarn plants.[50]

The early years of tire-cord development at Du Pont will be recalled. Formal research work by Rayon Research and the construction of pilot plants and the like were ultimately required. A program was introduced initially to seek solutions for the problems encountered at plants producing regular textile yarn, in particular the weakness of yarns and unsatisfactory launderability. Researchers were led to new applications of the product which had originally not been thought of. The technical requirements for the production of "Cordura" tire cord—the result of the research effort—introduced commercially in 1936, were, however, not well protected. Substantial developmental work was required to permit the production of tire cord at a converted textile-yarn plant; the basic technology underlying the conversion was also not well protected.

Quality improvements at tire-cord plants were developed internally by Rayon Research for the most part and were patented. In some cases technology was acquired by license. Technology underlying the most important product change, "Super-Cordura," introduced during the 1950s, was well protected by patents.[51] "Super-Cordura" was largely the responsibility of Du Pont's Central Research Department.

It may be noted that there is usually a number of alternative routes which can be followed to obtain a particular end. Somewhat different devices and materials may permit the accomplishment of quite similar results. For example, alternative devices for stretching yarn, alternative bath formulas and the like, were developed and installed in other United States plants constructed for the production of tire-cord yarn.[52] The American Viscose Corporation had by 1940 replaced all its original equipment for the production of textile yarn by a skein-reeling technique

[50] It has been hypothesized by one official of the Du Pont Company that because textile yarn was not initially developed by the Company the opportunities for patent protection were smaller than in the case of tire-cord yarn, which was conceived internally.

[51] It has been pointed out by an official of the Company that while "Super-Cordura" was well protected with narrow patents which gave the Company freedom to operate, these patents did not prevent other firms from making similar products.

[52] Although different companies used different bath constituents, a different viscose mix, and different spinning indexes, and although some heated the viscose and others did not, the range of choice between alternative "methods" narrowed as tenacity was increased.

with mechanisms constituting its own version of the cake-to-cone process.[53]

The fact that there are numerous ways of attaining similar objectives may help to throw light on the fact that new processes were frequently not patented as a whole. To protect a process in its entirety entails precise specification of detail which may well suggest to outsiders alternative methods of attaining a similar result. In such cases the rationale of patent protection is defeated, and greater protection is afforded by not claiming broad coverage.

[53] Replacement of original equipment occurred at American Viscose plants at Marcus Hook (Pennsylvania), Roanoke (Virginia), Lewiston (Maryland), and Parkersburg (West Virginia) during the late 1930s. At Front Royal (Virginia), construction had actually begun (1940) for the production of yarn by the original method, but the technique was altered before output was forthcoming from the plant.

# Chapter Eight

# Summary and Conclusions

Recent macroeconomic studies attempting to account for the secular increase in output per head in the United States arrive at the conclusion that the contribution of "technical change" is of far greater importance than is that of the growth of resources per head. The macroeconomists tend to draw strong policy conclusions from their analyses. In particular, it is suggested that those seeking rapid economic growth should direct their attention toward the processes whereby technical change is generated. In contrast with more traditional views it is implied that net investment, or the simple expansion of the capital stock, plays a small role as a determinant of economic growth.

In Chapter 1 we considered the characteristics of a model wherein technical change is measured by the extent to which a linear homogeneous production function applied to United States data has shifted over time. We then evaluated the measurement of the contribution of technical change by a method familiarized by the National Bureau of Economic Research which involves the estimation of an index of "total factor productivity." A number of refinements in the latter approach were also considered.

The strength of the conclusions and policy implications of the macroeconomic studies, it was pointed out, is somewhat vitiated by the all-inclusive character of "technical change." All influences acting upon productivity other than the increase in resources in use are included in the term. Economies of scale of all kinds, improvements in the quality of inputs, improved resource allocation, and the like, are encompassed by the catchall term "technical change."

We discussed in the introductory chapter some attempts in the literature to separate the contribution of economies of scale from that of technical change, and more generally to account for interindustry and intertemporal movements in productivity, by means of statistical correlation analysis. The opinion of W. E. G. Salter that a separation of the effect of scale from that of technical change should not be sought was noted: "It is much more plausible to think of technical progress and economies of scale as complementary to each other."

The question is therefore raised in the introductory chapter whether a detailed microeconomic study might not permit a judgment of the relative importance of alternative causes of increased efficiency. Specifically, it might be possible by close examination of the projects installed at particular plants, and with the use of technological information provided by those intimately connected with the operations undertaken at the plants, to reach some conclusions respecting the relative importance of technical change, and the various constituents thereof.

Moreover, a closely documented microeconomic study might be able to state whether or not investment in plant and equipment was a necessary prerequisite for the application of various technological improvements and whether replacement investments were or were not of greater importance than outlays constituting additions to the existing capital stock.

A third group of questions upon which a microeconomic study might throw some light relates to the source of various technical changes introduced at particular plants: specifically, were the relevant technologies developed by the company in question as part of its formal research activities or were they acquired elsewhere? Were the technologies protected by patents or not?

In Chapter 2 the term "technical change" was defined as referring to changes in the technique of production of given commodities by specific plants, designed to reduce unit production costs. These changes in technique may be of a "technological" nature, and may, but need not necessarily, involve the introduction of different inputs from those hitherto used at the plant (such as, for example, new-type capital equipment or improved raw materials), or they may be "managerial" and consist in improved organization, "Taylorization," and the like.

Our usage of the concept was contrasted with that of other writers. In particular, the definition includes the introduction of new techniques—with regard to the plant in question—regardless of the originality of the underlying technology. Furthermore, the term is divorced from any conceptual association with formal research activities by the company.

By the term "plant-expansion effect" as we have used it in this study, we mean instances of reduction in unit costs resulting from the spreading over a larger volume of output (resulting from plant expansion) of items in total costs which do not increase proportionately with output. Although it is quite common in the literature to consider as "economies of scale" the effects of more efficient equipment and methods introduced at large-scale operations, it was decided to include such changes within the designation "technical change," albeit technical change resulting from the scale of operation.

Annual cost and investment data relating to the production of viscose rayon at a number of plants operated by E. I. du Pont de Nemours and Company were made available for this study. In Chapter 3 we discussed in detail the variables which should be taken into account in attempting to explain the behavior of unit costs over time in the case of rayon production. The necessary technical background was also developed in that chapter.

The problems presented by the analysis of multiproduct plants were avoided by consideration of each plant at the Spruance location (Richmond, Virginia) in isolation. Data relating to the Old Hickory (Tennessee) location referred to three plants together, but the nature of the product and the techniques installed did not vary between them to any considerable extent.

The indexes of "efficiency" used in this study are the unit production costs corrected for changes in input prices. The prices used for correction purposes were provided by the Company. The average wage rate was used for the correction of all labor items and each materials item was corrected individually. Improvements in the quality of product were not treated rigorously as part of the index of "efficiency," because of the difficulty of obtaining statistical measures of quality improvements; however, some attention has been paid to quality changes.

In the case of direct-factory items, standard estimates of unit costs were used in place of actual costs to avoid consideration of series which tend to fluctuate relatively erratically as a result of random events. The standard calculations reflect estimates of the "ideal" performance of which the plant, under given technological conditions, is considered capable. The estimates are altered upon changes in technique designed to reduce unit costs. Standard calculations are not prepared for "overhead" cost items.[1] All labor items and most materials items are included in the study, which is therefore an analysis of changes over time in the productivity of labor and materials. Depreciation and related cost items are not considered in this study because of the problems of economic interpretation.[2]

---

[1] "Overheads" refer to labor and materials costs relating to certain maintenance items, superintendence, the powerhouse, the plant laboratory, and certain other items of "plant burden."

[2] Excluded from consideration are costs allocated to the plant, at least in part, from outside, such as charges deriving from the central administrative offices, taxes of various kinds, research of all kinds and on all products in the Company's laboratories, as well as depreciation. General burden costs at no time amounted to more than 20 per cent of all costs.

THE CONTRIBUTION TO INCREASED EFFICIENCY BY
TECHNICAL CHANGE AND BY PLANT EXPANSION[3]

It was found that a large number of variables influencing unit costs of
production were in operation at any one time. Moreover, in any period
more than one technical change might be introduced. It was possible for
the most part to distinguish the effect on costs of particular variables by
reliance on the judgment of officers of the Company as to the relative
importance of the changes, and by the use of informed assumptions
relating to the theoretical effects of the particular changes *ceteris paribus*:
these assumptions depended, for example, upon knowledge of the proportion of total labor costs which remains constant upon variations in
scale of plant, denier, spinning speed, and other determinants of unit cost
in rayon manufacture. The unit-cost series were presented for *individual*
inputs as well as for *total* unit cost, so that the accuracy of the estimates
of the effect of various technical changes is substantially enhanced. It
should be borne in mind, however, that a considerable degree of sub-
jective—though informed—judgment has been relied upon in the estimation of the contribution of various cost-determining forces.

The reductions in unit factory costs at the plants under consideration
was in most instances quite striking. At Old Hickory, unit costs declined
from 53.51 to 17.55 cents during the 22-year period 1929–1951, or by
4.9 per cent annually on average. At Spruance I unit costs declined during
the 18-year period 1932–1950 from 61.24 to 26.77 cents, or by 4.5 per cent
annually. At Spruance III the unit-cost reduction over the 14-year period
1938–1952 from 23.57 to 11.67 cents amounted to 4.9 per cent annually.
The reduction in unit costs from 27.18 to 19.67 cents during the 14-year
period 1937–1951 at Spruance II amounted to 2.3 per cent annually, and
that from 16.46 to 12.64 cents during the 7-year period 1945–1952 at
Spruance II-A to 3.7 per cent annually.

*The Contribution of Technical Change:* The contribution of "technical
change" has been of overwhelming importance. Of the total net reduction
in unit factory costs, technical change accounted for 100 per cent at
Spruance II-A, 97 per cent at Spruance I, 95 per cent at Spruance III,
and 85 per cent at Old Hickory. At Spruance II, however, the proportion
was only 35 per cent. It was pointed out that Spruance Plant II was not a
"representative" plant, for at its construction it embodied many cost-
reducing technical changes which had been introduced earlier at Old
Hickory. The effect of cost-reducing technical change at Spruance II is

---

[3] The reader should refer to Table 4.29 for a summary of many of the results to be
discussed in this chapter.

therefore not recorded but that of plant expansion remains: the plant was doubled soon after its establishment.

"Technical change" includes the use of improved inputs and improvements in organization. The materials presented in Chapter 4 permitted a more precise breakdown of the contribution of technical change. However, it must be stressed that no complete estimate could be made of the effect of secular increases in input quality over time. It was possible to obtain a minimum estimate of the contribution of improved organization and improved inputs by focusing attention upon particular years when important changes are known to have occurred. The most important single material used in rayon production is cellulose; the effects on unit cost of improvements in wood pulp were recognized relatively simply.

We have found that in the case of textile-yarn plants approximately 2 per cent of the unit-cost reduction attributed to technical change resulted from the use of improved wood pulps;[4] in the case of tire-cord plants the proportion was between 10 and 15 per cent.[5] These estimates relate to the proximate effect of the improved pulps. Indirect effects are not included.[6]

Our estimate for the contribution of improved labor and better organization varied between plants, but in all cases it accounted for less than 10 per cent of the entire net reduction in unit costs resulting from technical change.[7]

The total contribution of both improved pulp and labor and better organization amounted to 7.9 per cent at Spruance I and 10.7 per cent at Old Hickory, the textile-yarn plants, and to 12.7 per cent at Spruance III and 18.1 per cent at Spruance II-A, the tire-cord plants.[8]

*The Contribution of Plant Expansion:* The contribution of plant expansion was relatively small compared with that of technical change, amounting to 11 per cent at Old Hickory and 4 per cent at Spruance III; plant expansion played no part in accounting for the unit-cost reductions at

[4] It will be recalled that improvements in pulp permitted the substitution of pulp for the more expensive linters and thus permitted unit-cost reduction.

[5] More precisely, improved cellulose accounted for 2.1 per cent at Spruance I, 1.3 per cent at Old Hickory, 9.4 per cent at Spruance III, and 13.3 per cent at Spruance II-A. The contribution at Spruance II was as high as 21 per cent, but it has been noted earlier that Spruance II cannot be considered a "representative" plant. See p. 151.

[6] The nature of the cellulose has broad effects throughout the process. In part the kind of capital equipment which can be installed in the viscose-regenerating room ultimately depends upon the cellulose. These indirect effects are excluded from our estimates.

[7] Specifically the contribution of improved organization and improved quality of the labor input has been calculated as 3.4 per cent at Spruance III, 4.7 per cent at Spruance II-A, 5.8 per cent at Spruance I, 7.7 per cent at Spruance II, and 9.4 per cent at Old Hickory.

[8] The contribution at Spruance II amounted to 28.7 per cent.

Spruance I and at Spruance II-A. However, as much as 65 per cent of the unit-cost reductions at Spruance II was explained thereby.

It will be recalled that these estimates refer to each plant considered in isolation. Upon the establishment of Plant III and Plant II at the Spruance location, the total overhead costs allocated to Plant I were reduced and unit overhead costs declined considerably. If this reduction in unit costs at Spruance I is taken into account, then the contribution of plant expansion—namely the construction of two additional plants at the same location—accounted for approximately 10 per cent of the total unit-cost reduction at Spruance Plant I.

A clearer picture of the contribution of the "plant-expansion effect" can be seen by summing all the reductions in unit costs at the four Spruance plants, and calculating the ratio of all reductions due to plant expansion (wherever they occur) to this sum. We find that the contribution of plant expansion amounted to 15 per cent.[9] The contribution at Old Hickory was 11 per cent, so we can say that plant expansion accounted for between 10 and 15 per cent of the unit-cost reductions at the *locations* under consideration.

It is possible that if the cost series available had extended back into the early 1920s, plant expansion might have played a more important role. Furthermore, it will be recalled that the effect of improved equipment installed at larger volume is attributed to "technical change" rather than to plant expansion in our analysis. This procedure is followed partly because of the difficulty of isolating changes in technique which become profitable only at large-scale production. Furthermore, it is not plant expansion *per se*—the expansion of all inputs including the capital structure of the plant—which is relevant, but the expansion of output by *any* means, and the expansion of output itself may result from technical change. Finally, improved equipment installed at high volume requires development and research, as does equipment profitable at any scale of operation. However, it is not believed that technical changes of these kinds played a very important role at the plants under consideration, which were at the outset of considerable size.[10]

*Direct and Indirect Technical Change:* The distinction was drawn in Chapter 4 between "direct" technical changes, which permit the production of given output levels at lower total costs and thereby reduce unit

[9] The entire unit-cost reduction at all plants amounted to 61.73 cents including the reduction in unit overheads at Spruance I owing to expansion elsewhere at the location (4.03 cents). Of this reduction, 9.46 cents was due to plant expansion (4.03 cents at Spruance I, 4.89 cents at Spruance II, and .54 cent at Spruance III.)

[10] Recovery mechanisms, certain high-speed spinning equipment, and continuous equipment in the preparation of the viscose solution are instances of mechanisms which would not have been profitable in small-scale plants.

costs, and "indirect" changes, which permit the production of higher output levels from substantially unchanged plant facilities and complementary inputs.

Indirect technical changes played a considerable part in explaining the net reductions in unit costs at the plants under observation, and were of particular importance in the production of tire cord. For example, one way to reduce unit costs and make tire cord competitive with cotton in the industrial market was to raise the denier and spread overhead costs over a larger volume. The proportion of the net reduction in unit costs due to technical change which can be explained by *indirect* technical change amounted to 75 per cent at Spruance III and to 67 per cent at Spruance II-A. But even in the production of textile yarn indirect technical change played an important role, accounting for 49 per cent of the net reduction in unit costs owing to technical change of all kinds at Spruance I, and 32 per cent at Old Hickory. Thus, not only is it true that certain technical changes are only profitable at high levels of output but it is also true that considerable effort is exerted to permit higher volume by means of technical change.

## THE SOURCES OF TECHNICAL CHANGE

The macroeconomic studies considered in Chapter 1 tended to direct attention away from net investment as a determinant of growth and toward the development of new technologies and the like. In the present study we have considered in some detail the nature of the source of the technical changes occurring at the Du Pont plants.

In Chapter 4 a distinction was drawn between "major" and "minor" technical change and an estimate was made of the contribution to increased efficiency of each category. In Chapter 7 several further questions were considered: in particular, were the technical changes enumerated in Chapter 4 developed by Du Pont itself and were the technologies patented?

*Major and Minor Technical Change:* A technical change was considered "major" if its development was considered "difficult" to accomplish by men skilled in the pertinent arts before the development program; a technical change was considered "minor" if its development was judged a relatively simple process. The distinction was dependent upon the judgment of individuals after the event, recalling their own experience or that of others at some prior date. It may be noted again that the terms "major" and "minor" are in no way related to the size of the ultimate unit-cost reduction or of the investment outlays, if any, required for implementing the technical change. Usually a "minor" technical change involved an "evolutionary" alteration in the existing techniques, and for this reason the change was "relatively simple" to accomplish, whereas a "major" change involved a "significant" departure from existing methods and was therefore "relatively difficult" to accomplish.

Continuous effort was exerted to reduce unit costs by means of minor technical changes at the plants investigated. The cumulative effect of the minor technical changes was in fact greater than that of major changes. Of the net reduction in unit costs due to technical change of both kinds, minor technical change accounted for 83 per cent at Spruance II-A, 80 per cent at Spruance I, 79 per cent at Old Hickory, and 46 per cent at Spruance III. Minor changes accounted for the entire net reduction at Spruance II.

It was argued that the figure for Spruance I may overstate the true contribution of minor technical change in that a highly effective technical change classified as minor was in fact a borderline case. Reclassification would still attribute about one-half of the net reduction to minor technical change.

*Internal Research and Patented Technology:* The basic technology underlying the production of textile yarn was acquired from the Comptoir des Textiles Artificiels in the case of the bucket process. Purchased technology also played a large part in the first bobbin plant. The purchased technology was heavily patented.

In the case of "minor" technical changes we have seen in Chapter 7 that patented technology played a very small role. Certain features of improved equipment and the like might be patented, but for the most part the projects represented small improvements in existing technology and were not patentable. Technology relevant to the minor changes was sometimes developed cooperatively by Du Pont and equipment manufacturers; the rayon plants might call upon outside companies to help in the solution of particular problems and then test and improve upon the devices. Pulp manufacturers also contributed. The *bulk* of these cost-reducing improvements were developed at the plants themselves or by the Engineering Department (sometimes cooperatively with equipment suppliers).

On balance, plant personnel attached to Technical Assistance to Production groups played the most important role in the development of minor technical changes. These groups were intimately linked with current operations, and their function in large part was to keep existing processes "out of trouble." The contribution of the Engineering Department entailed in large part the provision of consultation services for the plants; the Service and Design section of the Department was also closely related to current operations at the plants.

The "major" technical changes were for the most part dependent upon internal research conducted formally by Rayon Research, although Technical Assistance personnel also contributed substantially.[11] Generally, the major process changes were not patented as a whole, although individual features were patented. This was particularly true at textile-yarn plants; at tire-cord plants the patent coverage was somewhat broader, but instances of protection of entire processes were uncommon.

Major effort was required in the development of tire cord itself. This was accomplished internally by Rayon Research. Analysis of the various requisite elements has shown that very few were patented. Quality improvements, and product changes particularly important at tire-cord plants, were developed largely by Rayon Research and were patented. Some technology was licensed from other companies. The technology, developed by Du Pont's Central Research Department, relevant to the production during the 1950s of "Super-Cordura" or very-high-tenacity rayon yarn, was well protected. Certain important chemical features of tire cord were patented, in particular the "iron bath" by Du Pont and the "high-zinc bath" by Courtaulds.[12]

Two further characteristics of the developments recorded in earlier chapters may be referred to at this point. First, it will be recalled from Chapter 7 that there is commonly no "unique" method of accomplishing a particular end. It is often possible to obtain very similar results by means of somewhat different devices and materials. Different companies arrived at similar processes and products.

Second, the early development of tire cord by Du Pont will be recalled. A program of research was introduced to seek solutions for the problems met with in plants producing regular textile rayon. Improvements led to the possibility of producing yarn for other than textile purposes.

## TECHNICAL CHANGE AND INVESTMENT

We have seen that one result of the macroeconomic studies of the causes of the secular increase in output per head has been to attribute to net investment only a small portion of the increased productivity. By "net investment," however, was meant added investment in plant and equipment identical to that already in existence. The writers, in fact, state their belief that investment in new-type capital equipment and, above all, replacement investment may well have played an important role. A recent analysis by R. M. Solow in which all technical change is

[11] The Engineering Department did not contribute significantly to the major changes with the exception of dielectric drying at Old Hickory, which was developed by the Research section.

[12] It will be recalled that although "Super-Cordura" was well protected by narrow patents that gave Du Pont "freedom to operate," the patents did not prevent other companies from producing similar products.

assumed embodied in new-type capital equipment leads to a renewed emphasis on both net and gross investment. The empirical question is raised therefore as to the actual significance to technical change of investment in plant and equipment.

In Chapter 6 we considered the investment outlays required by the technical changes introduced at the rayon plants. The investment figures were corrected for changes in an index of construction costs provided by the Du Pont Company. The Company itself undertakes much of the construction and installations required.

Most of the technical changes recorded in Chapter 4 required for their introduction investment in plant and equipment. The exceptions were the use of improved inputs and improvements in organization. At the textile-yarn plants, approximately 90 per cent of the net reductions in unit costs (resulting from technical change of all kinds) were caused by technical changes dependent upon investment; at the tire-cord plants the proportion amounted to 80–90 per cent. It may be noted, however, that improvements in raw materials may have depended upon investment expenditures by materials suppliers.

It was also seen that "significant" reductions in unit costs required in most cases "significant" investment outlays, whereas small unit-cost reductions could often be accomplished with small investment outlays.[13] There was, however, no simple relationship between the magnitude of investment and that of the unit-cost reduction for, in the first place, the benefits expected from a particular project were in many cases not limited to the reduction in unit costs, and, moreover, many indirect technical changes permitted extensive reductions in unit overhead costs with less investment than a reduction of the same magnitude brought about by direct technical change would have required.

It was further noted that "major" technical changes required "significant" outlays and usually "significant" benefits resulted. Individual "minor" changes—with the important exception of certain instances of *indirect* technical change—usually required small investment and resulted in small cost reductions.

Replacement investment was seen to be more important than investment which added to the existing capital stock. In Chapter 4 a distinction was drawn between "capital-using" technical changes and technical changes which permitted net reductions in unit costs (which were not outweighed by the necessity of expanding the capital stock). A qualitative survey in Chapter 4 of the technical changes introduced at the plants suggested

---

[13] "Significant" investment outlays were outlays exceeding $250,000 (in 1939 dollars). "Significant" unit-cost reductions were all reductions of at least one-half cent in tire-cord production and at least one cent in textile-yarn production (in 1939 dollars).

that for the most part capital-using technical change was not of importance, with the exception of the introduction of mechanisms for the
recovery of raw materials. In these cases reductions in unit materials costs
were only possible because of the "substitution" of equipment for
materials. The statistical data of Chapter 6 indicated that the proportion
of replacement investment to all investment outlays required for the
implementation of technical change amounted to 90 per cent at Spruance
III, 90 per cent at Old Hickory, 75 per cent at Spruance II-A, 72 per cent
at Spruance II, and 58 per cent at Spruance I.[14]

In many instances replacement investment to implement "minor" technical change was exceptionally profitable, because even in the absence
of technical change the existing mechanisms required relatively frequent
replacements.

The potential efficacy of replacement outlays was illustrated in Chapter
6 by a comparison of expenditures at old and new plants. It was shown that
with relatively small outlays incorporating *modifications to existing plants*
it was sometimes possible to reduce unit costs almost to the same level as
that at newly constructed plants. Similarly, modifications to a plant
designed for one product to permit the production of a new product
were possible by relatively small outlays compared with those required
for the construction of an entirely new plant.

An analysis of interplant cost differentials in Chapter 5 suggested
indirect evidence of the importance of investment. Nearly all cases of
"delay" in the application of existing technology could be explained by
the fact that such application would require investment outlays and that
these outlays could not be justified at the time.

### PRODUCT INNOVATION AND QUALITY IMPROVEMENT

Our attention has been focused throughout the study on changes in unit
costs as a measure of efficiency. It is important to remember, however,

---

[14] By additions to investment we refer specifically to added equipment resulting from
the technical change *directly*. It is possible that a technical change reduces unit costs,
and that following a price reduction, for example, output is expanded by the addition
of spinning machines or an entire plant which embodies the new technology. These
"additions," however, are not the *immediate* effect of the technical change and are not
included.

If all investments including those embodying technical change in an expansion
program are taken into account, then clearly "replacement" investment must be
accorded a relatively smaller role.

Even in this case replacement investment remains highly significant and accounts for
75 per cent of all investment embodying technical change at Spruance II-A, 72 per cent
at Spruance II, 69 per cent at Spruance III, 54 per cent at Old Hickory, and 58 per cent
at Spruance I.

It may be added that Spruance II was constructed to embody the technology introduced into the existing plants at Old Hickory.

that improvements in the quality of the product were occurring and that new products were introduced during the period.

*Quality Improvements and Unit-Cost Reductions:* Many of the technical changes considered in Chapter 4 were designed not only to permit reductions in unit costs but also to produce improvements in quality. Indeed in a number of cases the reduction in unit costs was made possible only by altering the nature of the product. This was particularly true in the case of high-denier tire-cord yarn.

In other cases increased quality could only be accomplished at higher unit costs. This was above all the case during the 1950s at tire-cord plants when very-high-tenacity yarn ("Super-Cordura") was introduced.

Many instances of technical change designed to reduce unit costs had the secondary effect of permitting improvements in quality which in turn would permit further unit-cost reductions. The most striking instances are the major technical changes which allowed radical simplifications of process and less handling of the semifinished product by operators.

*The Sources of Quality Improvement:* It is probable that a detailed analysis of product changes would reveal similar characteristics relating to the sources of the underlying technology that were seen to exist in the case of technical change designed to reduce unit costs.

The development of tire cord, described in Chapter 7, required "major" effort although the technology was not broadly protected by patents. On the other hand, as we have already noted, the development in the postwar period of "Super-Cordura"—also requiring "major" effort— was well protected.

*Quality Improvements and Investment:* In many instances improvement in quality required investment in plant and equipment. Spruance III was constructed especially for the production of a new product, tire cord, and some investment outlays (though relatively small in amount) were required for the conversion of Spruance II-A to tire cord. The quality improvements which result from technical change designed primarily for the reduction of unit costs are also, of course, taken into account in determining the profitability of the required investment outlays.

### SOME IMPLICATIONS OF THE ANALYSIS

It has been possible, in this microeconomic study of individual plants, to break down the catchall "technical change," to analyze some of the characteristics of the underlying technology, and to arrive at an estimate of the importance of investment for the introduction of technical change. In this final section we shall briefly consider some implications of the results. We shall discuss in particular the relationship between investment and technical change, the relative importance of "minor" technical change, and the small role played by patent protection.

### Investment and Technical Change

We have seen that over 80 per cent of the cost reductions resulting from technical change at each plant depended upon investment. Replacement investment was of particular importance: usually at least two-thirds, and in some cases as much as 90 per cent, of the investment outlays required to implement technical change represented replacement of, or alterations to, existing equipment. Qualitative evidence suggests that the capital-labor ratio did not rise over time at the plants, and that the capital-output ratio declined.

Although it is true that the various changes in technique we have encountered often required "significant" investment outlays—outlays considered as such by management—it is clear that it is possible to incorporate within a given structure sufficiently productive technology to permit an older plant to produce almost as efficiently as a newly built plant. Moreover, in terms of a comparison with the outlays required to establish the new plant, the sum total of the outlays needed to accomplish the alterations at the older plant is relatively small.

The Company undertakes its own engineering, and the Engineering Department directs construction outlays at the plants. The close integration of research, design, construction, and manufacturing tends to result, it has been claimed, in the rapid accomplishment of increased productivity at a relatively small expenditure.

The recognition of the phenomenon of highly productive though *relatively* modest replacement expenditures lends support to the view expressed by some macroeconomists concerned with economic growth that considerable attention should be devoted to the rate at which the existing stock of capital is altered to introduce technical change, rather than simply to the variables which determine the rate of expansion of the capital stock.

The recognition of the efficacy of replacement investment incorporating technical change is important both in accounting for certain anomalous features of past experience and for throwing light on current policy issues relating to economic growth. A most singular feature of the pattern of productivity change during the interwar period, for example, is the fact that despite a vast disparity between the volume of net investment occurring during the 1920s compared with that of the 1930s, the rates of increase in productivity during the two decades were not dissimilar. Thus between 1920 and 1929 output per man-hour increased by 26.6 per cent and between 1930 and 1939 by 22.2 per cent. Yet in the first period the sum of the annual net changes in the stock of "Producers' Durables and Construction" amounted to $59.16 billion compared with only $7.54 billion during the entire decade of the 1930s. Accordingly the rate of increase in the capital-labor ratio was considerably greater in the 1920s than in the 1930s, when almost no change occurred.[15] Thus despite a great difference between the net investments of the two periods, the productivity performances were not unlike. Whatever the productivity increase was due to in the 1930s it can scarcely have been closely related to net investment. Moreover, whereas the absence of net investment need not preclude continued increases in productivity, its presence does not necessarily assure it; the record of the 1920s is scarcely better than that of the 1930s. To some extent this can be explained simply by the fact that in a period of "demand pull," such as the 1920s, when profits are high, the "need" for cost reductions is small, whereas in the 1930s, when profits were low or negative, the "need" was urgent.

There is a growing body of evidence, at the microeconomic level, that even without new investment it is possible to raise the efficiency of existing plants. Thus, for example, the Horndal works in Sweden had no new investment for a period of fifteen years and yet output per man-hour increased by 2 per cent annually.[16] Our own study does not relate to the causes of the historical pattern of productivity increase at the macroeconomic level, but it illustrates the great potential of replacement investments constituting alterations to existing plants. Gross investment incorporating technical change into existing plants may well explain part of the experience of the 1930s.

A recent study comparing the rates of growth and investment in several European countries and the United States within the last decade presents data which show that no country achieved a very rapid growth rate without a high rate of investment, although a number of countries which did invest heavily failed to achieve a high growth rate.[17] The author attempts to account for this phenomenon by distinguishing between investment in *structures* and in *machinery and equipment*. He argues that the impact on growth of a given volume of investment in the latter form is greater than that in the former: with respect to gross investment, he

[15] For productivity data see John W. Kendrick, *Productivity Trends in the United States* (cited in Ch. 1, note 19), Table A-XXII, pp. 334–335. For investment data see Simon Kuznets, *Capital in the American Economy*, NBER, Princeton University Press, Princeton, 1961, p. 492. Data on the capital-labor ratio are examined in Kendrick, *op. cit.*, p. 85.

[16] This case is referred to in Kenneth J. Arrow, "The Economic Implications of Learning by Doing" (cited in Ch. 1, note 18), p. 156.

[17] T. P. Hill, "Growth and Investment According to International Comparisons," *Economic Journal*, Vol. LXXIV, June 1964, pp. 287–304.

writes, "replacement investment is much more likely to act as a vehicle for technical progress when it consists mainly of machinery and equipment than when it is mostly construction. The basic reason is simply that the functions served by buildings and works are not capable of being transformed in the way that the operations performed by machines can be completely revolutionized." Our study, which has illustrated the effectiveness of alterations within a given structure which itself is almost unchanged, tends to support this view.

It should be recognized that there is probably a limit to the potential effectiveness of alterations to existing facilities. Ultimately the opportunities may be exhausted without some intervening major outlay. Moreover, new plants may well be required in an expanding economy. Nevertheless, the potential of the kind of investment programs which we have found so effective should not be minimized. Furthermore, although the construction of entirely new plants may be required in an expanding economy, we have found that it is often possible to expand the volume of output markedly without large additions to plant capacity. Of the reduction in unit costs resulting from technical change, over two-thirds in the case of tire-cord production and between one-third and one-half in that of textile-yarn production was caused by mechanisms and processes which permitted expansion of volume *without* the necessity of expanding the physical plant, or, in our terminology by "indirect" technical change. Thus an intimate relation between technical change and volume was confirmed.

The importance of this relationship suggests that a growing market may be required *to stimulate an important portion of improved technology*. The rate of growth of productivity may well be faster in a growing market if potential indirect technical changes are discovered and introduced. Incidentally, the large part played by indirect technical change may make the use of correlation analysis to distinguish the effect on productivity of increased volume from those of technical change totally misleading.

### The Importance of "Minor" Technical Change and the Low Degree of Patent Protection

Policies designed to stimulate the development of improved techniques may be disappointing unless more is known about the precise nature of the underlying technology. For example, is large-scale, formal technological effort on the part of the company required? Does patent protection play an important role? Our study has thrown some light on these problems.

In the first place, we have seen that "minor" technical changes—based on technology judged relatively "simple" to develop prior to the actual development, and usually representing "evolutionary" advances rather than significant departures from existing methods—accounted for over two-thirds of the unit-cost reductions attributable to technical change at most of the plants considered. Moreover, in some instances even individual "minor" technical changes have had substantial effects on costs.

Needless to say, further studies will be required before the relative importance of minor changes in technology can be established, although some authors have suspected the generality of the phenomenon. Thus, for example, Machlup distinguishes between big steps forward in the arts and small improvements in the following terms:

> A technological invention is a big step forward in the useful arts. Small steps forward are not given this designation; they are just "minor improvements" in technology. But a succession of many minor improvements add up to a big advance in technology. It is natural that we hail the big, single step forward, while leaving the many small steps all but unnoticed. It is understandable, therefore, that we eulogize the great inventor, while overlooking the small improvers. Looking backward, however, it is by no means certain that the increase in productivity over a longer period of time is chiefly due to the great inventors and their inventions. It may well be true that the sum total of all minor improvements, each too small to be called an invention, has contributed to the increase in productivity more than the great inventions have.[18]

In addition, some evidence has been accumulated in recent years to suggest that the large industrial corporations may well be a more important source of "improvement" inventions than of major inventions.[19] Partly because it has usually been taken for granted that the major corporation would be responsible for major inventions, little is known about the sources of minor technical changes at large companies.

The minor technical changes encountered in our study were in most cases developed internally by Du Pont. Some important contributions were made by equipment manufacturers (although much of the work in these cases involved cooperative ventures), and by suppliers of raw materials. The larger part of the minor changes were developed at the plants themselves by personnel intimately concerned with current operations, whose function was often to keep existing operations trouble-free, rather than by Rayon Research and other formal research groups. The Engineering Department also made significant contributions to the development of the minor changes. However, it was in its function as a consultation agency to the plants that it made its most important contribution, and in this

---

[18] Fritz Machlup, *The Production and Distribution of Knowledge in the United States*, Princeton University Press, Princeton, 1962, p. 164.

[19] The evidence to support the argument that "improvement inventions" are the "principal product of the research laboratories of the large industrial corporation" is examined in D. Hamberg, "Invention in the Industrial Research Laboratory," *Journal of Political Economy*, Vol. LXXI, April 1963, pp. 95–115.

capacity the Department was also very closely linked to current operations. Even the development of "major" technical changes, largely dependent upon internal research conducted formally by Rayon Research,[20] involved considerable contact with operating personnel.

As far as the source of minor technical change is concerned, and to some extent this also applies to certain major changes, students of economic growth should place less emphasis upon formal large-scale research work, and correspondingly pay more attention to the manner in which attempts are made by groups attached to the manufacturing plants themselves, supported by Engineering personnel, to develop improvements to existing operations. Much new technology appears to be generated as a by-product of current production; our study tends to support the view to some extent that a considerable portion of technical change "can be ascribed to experience, that is to the very activity of production which gives rise to problems for which favorable responses are selected over time."[21]

Attention should therefore be paid to the various methods adopted by corporations designed to exploit "minor" technical changes and the relative efficacy of these methods.[22] For it may well be that part of the difference between productivity rates in different countries lies in the attitude of management to continual changes and modifications to existing plants. Even where two similar economies exist with respect to the adoption of major changes, an unwillingness to seek out methods for the stimulation of the minor changes would lead to a considerable difference between productivity rates.

It is important, however, to qualify our stress on the efficacy of "minor" technical changes. There seems to exist what may be called a "saturation effect"[23] whereby without some preceding major change the potential stream of minor changes will be exhausted. In the plants under investigation,

---

[20] There were also isolated contributions by Pioneering Research, the Central Research Department, and Engineering Research. The Central Research Department was responsible for "Super-Cordura."

[21] This view is incorporated into the model analyzed by Arrow, *op. cit.*, p. 156. The analysis is, however, limited to technical change in the capital-goods industry alone. Once constructed, the capital good cannot be altered or improved. Thus a considerable portion of the technical change which we have encountered would be excluded; in our case study, "learning" also appears to have taken place in plants *using* the capital goods. We have seen that even the development of tire cord had its origins in problems encountered in the production of textile yarn.

[22] Very few studies exist in the economic literature on the subject of the source of minor technical change. An important analysis of various types of schemes introduced at a number of French plants to stimulate the flow of minor innovation or "improvement" innovation and of the savings in cost resulting therefrom, is to be found in Jan Dessau, "Définition et Rémunération de la Petite Innovation," *Economie Appliquée*, Vol. XV, No. 3, July–Sept. 1962, pp. 405–444.

[23] The term "effet de saturation" is used to describe the dependence of "minor innovations" on preceding "major innovations" by Dessau, *op. cit.*, p. 427.

the most striking stream of minor technical changes were introduced during the *first* 10 to 15 years after the construction of a new-type plant. Moreover, at plants which, though newly constructed, embodied many of the minor changes introduced elsewhere, the productivity increase due to further minor changes was less striking than at the initial plants. This suggests that the minor changes are related to and dependent upon the occurrence of some major change, which would usually derive from large-scale formal research work. Nevertheless, granted that there is a limit, small alterations in technique can be expected for a considerable time after the initial introduction of a major change.

We have recognized that close cooperation between Du Pont's suppliers of materials and equipment apparently helped speed up the rate of productivity. On the other hand, close relationships with customers of the plants are obviously also a feature of importance. For a significant part of the cost reductions were only possible upon some degree of alteration in the nature of the plants' end product; customers had to be prepared to accept such changes.

It may also be noted that the use of such indexes as research and development outlays as indirect measures of research effort directed at increased efficiency, would have been unsatisfactory, in part because of the contribution of outside companies but largely because of the fact that much effort exerted by such groups as Technical Assistance to Production would not have been recorded among the formal research activities of the Company.

We turn to recall the observation that a substantial part of the technology underlying the recorded increase in productivity was not protected by patents. This was particularly true at textile-yarn plants. Cost-reducing technical changes introduced at tire-cord plants were better protected, although here too processes were generally not patented as a whole; individual features of new processes were frequenctly protected. An important product change—the introduction of "Super-Cordura"—was well protected, although other firms were not prevented from producing similar products. The technology underlying the original development of "Cordura" itself, however, was not well covered.

An important part of the explanation for the small degree of patent protection is the fact that such a considerable amount of the productivity increase was based on "minor" technical changes; the relatively small modifications to existing practice are not patentable. However, we have noted that even the "major" technical changes, involving entire processes, were in many cases not well covered by patents. In the case of the cake-to-cone process, for example, a small number of individual features were patented, but the process as a whole was not covered.

To protect an entire process requires very detailed and narrow specifications. Because there are usually a variety of ways by which a particular end can be achieved, such detailed information may well suggest to other companies alternative ways of accomplishing the desired end. Paradoxically, greater protection may be afforded, therefore, by not claiming patent coverage; this may help account for the fact that certain "major" changes were not broadly protected.

A possible explanation, suggested by an officer of the Company, for the difference in patent protection between tire-cord plants and textile-yarn plants relates to the fact that tire-cord was developed within the Company so that opportunities to develop patentable technologies were greater than in the case of textile yarn, where the initial technology was acquired from outside the Company.

Whatever the reason for the small extent of patent protection at the plants investigated, it is clear that to use the number of patents obtained as an indirect measure of technological change would have been quite misleading. One cannot conclude from the above remarks that patents are generally unnecessary for the assurance of economic progress. But one implication appears to be that a sharp distinction should be drawn between technological effort the outcome of which is almost assured and technological effort involving substantial expense and considerable risk as to workability or reception.[24] Without the possibility of patent protection management might be inclined to devote attention mainly to the former developments. Without the periodic "injections" of important breakthroughs, however, there is probably a limit on the number of projects which can be accomplished with little risk.

---

[24] Even the cake-to-cone method—the most important of our "major" technical changes at textile-yarn plants—should not be defined as "major" with respect to riskiness, although it was a difficult project to develop.

# The Correction of
# Unit-Cost Data

In this appendix we consider the manner in which the unit-cost data presented in Chapter 4 were corrected for changes in input prices.

## OPERATING LABOR AND LABOR ITEMS IN "DIRECT MAINTENANCE" AND "OVERHEADS"

In the case of operating labor, and the labor element in the direct-maintenance and the overhead categories, unit costs were corrected by use of annual series of the "average hourly wage rate" paid at the Spruance location and at Old Hickory; there were slight differences between the two series. Approximately two-thirds of the *direct-maintenance* category represented labor and the remainder materials. The two elements were recorded separately on the annual cost sheets. *Overheads* include superintendence, laboratory and assistance, maintenance of structures and other plant installations, power costs, and a category referred to as "all other plant burden." Each of these constituents was recorded separately. It was assumed that the entire "superintendence" category represented a "labor" expense, and that 90 per cent of the "laboratory" and "all other plant burden" costs represented "labor" and the remainder materials. These estimates were obtained from officers at the locations. The power item was divided between labor, coal, and materials on the basis of spot checks taken each year for the month of December. The maintenance item was divided between labor and materials in the same proportion as the direct-maintenance item.

In correcting the labor items, the unit costs in a particular year were simply divided by the ratio of the average wage rate paid in that year to the average wage rate paid in 1939, our base year.

One disadvantage of this procedure lies in the fact that if substitutions between inputs, as a result of changes in relative input prices, occur, then the corrected unit costs are stated at too high a level; the combination of inputs actually used will not be the optimum one for the relative input prices existing in 1939. It is not believed, however, that simple input substitution as a result of relative price change played an important role *in the absence of technical change*, so that the procedure can be justified. Moreover, an alternative procedure—treating the average wage rate as a variable in a multiple correlation analysis of changes in uncorrected unit costs—would be even less satisfactory because of the very large number of other explanatory variables which exist in the present case.[1]

For the correction of *actual* labor costs—such as those falling within the "overhead" category—it is possible that the use of a series of average annual *earnings* would have been preferable since such a series reflects the number of hours actually worked more accurately than a series of average *wage rates*.[2] However, standard rather than actual costs are used in the case of operating labor and labor in direct maintenance; in these instances the average wage rate is preferable since standard costs represent what should be accomplished under *near-perfect* (rather than actual) conditions where overtime and the like would be irrelevant.

## MATERIALS ITEMS IN "DIRECT MAINTENANCE" AND "OVERHEADS"

For the correction of the materials constituent of direct maintenance and overheads, the wholesale price index of construction materials published by the Bureau of Labor Statistics was used. An index of this nature is believed to cover most accurately the more important items of "materials" in direct maintenance and overheads. The costs of coal in "power" were corrected by using the actual prices paid by the plant.

## VISCOSE-SOLUTION AND ACID-BATH MATERIALS

*Each* chemical in the viscose-solution and acid-bath grouping of major materials was corrected by using the actual prices paid by the plant for that particular chemical.

A number of serious difficulties were faced in the case of cellulose. It is common, as we have noted, for rayon plants to use in any single period a

---

[1] These alternative methods of correction are discussed in Joel Dean, "The Relation of Cost to Output for a Leather Belt Shop," N.B.E.R., *Technical Paper* 2, Chicago, 1941, p. 15.

[2] For example, assuming that ten men work an eight-hour day and a five-day week, or 400 hours per week, at the straight rate of one dollar per hour, and a further 100 hours of overtime at $1.50 per hour then their total earnings will be $550 per week. Dividing by the average wage rate ($1.00) the number of hours worked is estimated at 550; if the average earnings, $1.10, are used for correction purposes, the number of hours estimated is 500, which is the correct amount.

variety of pulps and linters. It was assumed that any price differential between the brands used reflected the relative efficiencies (and other benefits) *to the plant* of these brands. In general, that is to say, the more expensive pulps and linters were assumed to be of greater advantage to the plant.[3] Ideally, each brand should therefore be treated as a *separate input*, and should be corrected for changing prices by use of its own price series. To treat each wood-pulp and cotton-linters brand used separately requires knowledge of the prices paid for each brand in the base year, 1939. In 1932, for example, one wood-pulp and one linters brand was used at Spruance Plant 1; the prices paid per pound for each were recorded on the cost sheets and the 1939 prices for these brands were known since each was also purchased in 1939. The following calculation was made to derive the corrected unit costs for 1932:

| Year | Cellulose Source | Price per Pound Purchased (in cents) | Unit Cost (in cents) | Price Relative* | Unit Cost Corrected (in cents) | Total Unit Cost Corrected (in cents) |
|------|------------------|------|------|------|------|------|
| (1) | (2) | (3) | (4) | (5) | (6) | (7) |
| 1932 | Wood Pulp: | | | | | |
| | "Rayonier" | 3.62 | 2.48 | 102.3 | 2.42 | 4.51 |
| | Cotton Linters: | | | | | |
| | "Hercules" | 6.30 | 2.56 | 122.6 | 2.09 | |

* Rayonier, 1939, known to cost 3.54 cents per pound and Hercules 5.14 cents.

However, it is quite common for a particular brand of pulp or of linters to appear in certain years but not in the base year. In such cases it was sometimes possible to obtain some notion of the base-year price from the pulp manufacturer; in other cases, however, an estimate was made of what the pulp price *would have been in* 1939.[4] These estimates have been confirmed by officers at Du Pont and Rayonier, Inc., which over time has been the most important single supplier of pulp to the rayon plants. However, it must be borne in mind that an element of uncertainty remains in those cases where the 1939 price is not known with certainty.[5] It should also be recognized that any given brand of pulp or linters changes in quality over time.

A second disadvantage of this method of correction lies in the fact that the

[3] This need not be the case invariably. The plant may be forced to purchase a pulp, for example, at a high price because the supply of lower-priced pulp has been exhausted. The assumption we have made is believed to be reasonably accurate, however.

[4] This was done by ascertaining the relative price relationship between the pulp, and another pulp appearing both in that year *and* in 1939 and assuming that the same proportion would hold good in 1939 if both appeared. If the assumption that the relative price relation is unchanged does not hold good, there may be considerable error.

[5] This is particularly true for pulps appearing for the first time *after* 1939. In some cases the pulp did not exist commercially in the base year.

ultimate (corrected) unit costs of cellulose are not, strictly speaking, comparable between plants: unless each plant uses the same brands of wood pulp and cotton linters in the same proportion, the input mix differs so that in effect *different* inputs are being considered. This fact must be borne in mind in attempting interplant comparisons.

An alternative method avoids the first problem: here an average cost (to the plant) of cellulose is estimated, and a price series is drawn up based on the average cost to the plant of cellulose each year. The following steps would be taken: first, one would estimate the average "price" paid at the plant each year for all the brands purchased, $\left( \sum_{i=1}^{n} p_i q_i \right) \Big/ \left( \sum_{i=1}^{n} q_i \right)$, where $i$ represents a particular brand of cellulose of which there are $n$, $p_i$ represents its price, and $q_i$ the quantity used. In this way a series of annual price relatives can be constructed based on the 1939 average "price" taken as 100. Then, one would calculate the *total* unit cost each year (that is the cost per unit of output $x$), $\left( \sum_{i=1}^{n} p_i q_i \right) \Big/ x$, and, finally, divide the total unit cost each year by the price relative for that year.

The principal disadvantage of the second method lies in its treatment of dissimilar grades as if they were identical. Moreover, the average "price" each year is in fact not a price at all, but simply the average cost to the plant of a unit of some heterogeneous "input"; the resultant corrected cost series would be highly ambiguous. For these reasons the first method described, in which each grade is corrected separately, has been used.

Similar problems arose in the treatment of caustic soda and glucose where both solid and liquid grades were used. In these instances similar procedures to that described in the correction of the unit cellulose costs were followed.

## MATERIALS ITEMS EXCLUDED FROM THE ANALYSIS

A number of materials items appeared on the cost sheets but were not considered explicitly within unit factory costs in the tables of Chapter 4. These items include "packing cases and supplies" and "miscellaneous materials." Correction of "miscellaneous materials" requires the use of the wholesale price index of chemicals published by the Bureau of Labor Statistics. Correction of "packing cases and supplies" was attempted by the use of a rule-of-thumb calculation suggested by an official of the Du Pont Company, namely that prices increased at one per cent annually until 1939 and at one and one-half per cent thereafter. Since these items represent a very small percentage of total materials, and since the procedures for correction are less satisfactory than in the case of other items, it was decided not to include these two categories.

# The Characteristics and Relative Advantages of Alternative Sources of Cellulose

The cellulose used in the manufacture of rayon derives from wood pulp and cotton linters. Moreover, there are numerous different grades of each material available at any time. The manufacturer will choose the different materials on the basis of relative prices, price expectations, yield and advantages in processing, and the desired properties of the end product.

Cotton linters are typically higher in price than wood pulp, and their prices are more volatile. These two characteristics mitigate against the use of linters. On the other hand, cotton linters are more productive than wood pulp. (Productivity or yield depends in part upon the purity of the input in terms of its alpha-cellulose content.) Moreover (at least during the 1920s and 1930s), linters could be processed more satisfactorily. Finally, cotton linters provide a stronger (but coarser) filament.

During the 1920s it was common to use wood pulp extensively because of its relative cheapness and stability of price. The quality of pulp, however, was low both in terms of yield and ease of processing. As a result the quality of the end product suffered.

The requirements of the market for rayon became more severe during the early 1930s, and it was necessary to make use of linters instead of wood pulp despite the higher and more volatile price. During the 1930s and 1940s considerable effort was exerted by pulp suppliers to increase the yield and improve upon those characteristics of pulp which would permit more satisfactory processing. The trend after the late 1930s and early 1940s has been toward the greater use of wood pulp; although the yield of linters remained higher, the differential was outweighed by the relatively low price of pulp.[1]

---

[1] See for example C. L. Moore, "Progress in Rayon Pulp Manufacture," *Rayon Textile Monthly*, Vol. XVIII, Sept. 1937, pp. 72–74, and C. L. Moore, "Can Cotton

The percentage of wood pulp at Old Hickory and at Spruance I and II—the textile-yarn plants—is typical of the pattern in the rayon industry as a whole. At Spruance I, wood pulp alone was used in 1930; the proportion declined to 50 per cent during the three-year period 1931–1933, and remained at that level until a further decline to 41 per cent in 1938, and to 30 per cent in 1942. Thereafter, there occurred a steady increase in the proportion of pulp, to 48 per cent in 1943, 77 per cent in 1946, and 100 per cent in 1947. At Old Hickory, the proportion of wood pulp in 1928 was 97 per cent; the proportion declined to 56 per cent during the three-year period 1929–1931 and remained at that percentage until 1936; thereafter, the proportion increased and in 1939 cotton linters had been completely displaced. The proportion of wood pulp used at Spruance II (established in 1935) amounted to 56 per cent until 1938, but increased thereafter until linters were completely displaced in 1941.

Cotton linters have a particularly important advantage in the production of tire-cord yarn (where tenacity is a prime requirement), and have held their own in the case of this product to a greater extent than in the production of textile yarn. At Spruance III during the period 1936–1946 wood pulp was not used at all. Thereafter, wood pulp was introduced as its quality improved; the percentage of wood pulp fluctuated year to year but remained at approximately one-third, although during the 1950s the proportion increased to one-half. At Spruance II-A wood pulp was not used until 1946; thereafter the proportion increased to approximately 50 per cent. In 1954, upon the introduction of "Super-Cordura," wood pulp was (temporarily) displaced.

---

Entirely Replace Wood Pulp in the Rayon Industry?" *ibid.*, pp. 75–76. See also R. B. Evans, *Survey of the Development and Use of Rayon and Other Synthetic Fibers*, Southern Regional Research Laboratory, United States Department of Agriculture, New Orleans, Louisiana, Oct. 1954; and G. J. Esselen and W. M. Scott, "Cellulose as a Chemical Raw Material," *Chemical Industries*, Vol. 43, July 1938, pp. 14–19.

*Appendix C*

# Statistical Data

*Table C.1  Old Hickory: Output, Denier, and Percentage of Capacity Operated*

| Year | Pounds Production (000) | Average Denier | Percentage Capacity Operated (Nozzle Basis) |
|------|------------------------|----------------|---------------------------------------------|
| 1929 | 15,695 | 157.0 | 100.0 |
| 1930 | 11,810 | 160.0 | 73.8 |
| 1931 | 14,527 | 164.0 | 88.6 |
| 1932 | 13,149 | 155.2 | 84.6 |
| 1933 | 17,744 | 154.6 | na* |
| 1934 | 22,198 | 155.7 | na |
| 1935 | 24,792 | 163.3 | na |
| 1936 | 25,464 | 155.4 | na |
| 1937 | 30,617 | 158.9 | 82.3 |
| 1938 | 24,504 | 151.0 | 69.3 |
| 1939 | 31,216 | 147.9 | 90.1 |
| 1940 | 32,379 | 148.3 | 93.2 |
| 1941 | 34,977 | 160.0 | 93.3 |
| 1942 | 31,728 | 138.2 | 98.0 |
| 1943 | 34,837 | 149.4 | 99.7 |
| 1944 | 37,385 | 159.6 | 98.8 |
| 1945 | 39,326 | 167.8 | 98.8 |
| 1946 | 37,877 | 168.2 | 99.3 |
| 1947 | 40,789 | 170.0 | 98.0 |
| 1948 | 46,056 | 185.0 | 99.3 |
| 1949 | 44,027 | 176.6 | 98.0 |
| 1950 | 49,610 | 191.3 | 98.0 |
| 1951 | 52,022 | 204.1 | 98.4 |
| 1952 | 47,860 | 248.8 | 77.8 |
| 1953 | 45,987 | 232.6 | 80.3 |
| 1954 | 41,781 | 237.0 | 73.6 |
| 1955 | 46,715 | 240.6 | 85.4 |
| 1956 | 33,822 | 223.3 | 69.4 |
| 1957 | 28,706 | 202.4 | na |
| 1958 | 24,346 | 216.2 | na |
| 1959 | 25,932 | 239.0 | na |
| 1960 | 19,962 | 221.1 | na |

* *na:* not available.

*Table C.2   Spruance Plant I: Output, Denier, and Percentage of Capacity Operated*

| Year | Pounds Production (000) | Average Denier | Percentage Capacity Operated (Nozzle Basis) |
|------|------|------|------|
| 1929 | 1,038 | 116.7 | 47.0 |
| 1930 | 2,494 | 111.5 | 56.7 |
| 1931 | 3,983 | 97.3 | 81.7 |
| 1932 | 3,315 | 94.8 | 67.7 |
| 1933 | 5,628 | 100.6 | 87.5 |
| 1934 | 6,286 | 104.9 | 97.0 |
| 1935 | 6,476 | 111.3 | 99.3 |
| 1936 | 6,608 | 106.8 | 99.0 |
| 1937 | 6,822 | 101.5 | 92.9 |
| 1938 | 5,884 | 115.9 | 73.0 |
| 1939 | 7,475 | 105.9 | 92.0 |
| 1940 | 7,994 | 98.8 | 99.5 |
| 1941 | 9,449 | 112.8 | 100.0 |
| 1942 | 9,449 | 111.2 | 99.7 |
| 1943 | 9,925 | 113.8 | 100.0 |
| 1944 | 10,505 | 118.5 | 99.6 |
| 1945 | 10,031 | 113.9 | 99.0 |
| 1946 | 8,736 | 100.9 | 97.0 |
| 1947 | 8,252 | 89.0 | 99.7 |
| 1948 | 9,262 | 98.6 | 97.7 |
| 1949 | 7,379 | 98.6 | 77.2 |
| 1950 | 9,518 | 97.8 | 99.9 |
| 1951 | 9,454 | 110.1 | 87.0 |
| 1952 | 6,615 | 186.8 | 38.1 |

*Table C.3    Spruance Plant II: Output, Denier, and Percentage of Capacity Operated*

| Year | Pounds Production (000) | Average Denier | Percentage Capacity Operated (Nozzle Basis) |
|------|------|------|------|
| 1935 | 3,089 | 144.4 | 99.2 |
| 1936 | 7,808 | 149.7 | 99.9 |
| 1937 | 8,103 | 150.0 | 96.5 |
| 1938 | 6,042 | 130.9 | 55.0 |
| 1939 | 13,678 | 132.5 | 91.0 |
| 1940 | 14,990 | 131.9 | 99.8 |
| 1941 | 15,492 | 136.1 | 100.0 |
| 1942 | 16,551 | 139.9 | 99.8 |
| 1943 | 17,834 | 141.4 | 100.0 |
| 1944 | 9,085 | 134.2 | 99.6 |
| 1945 | 7,809 | 132.4 | 93.5 |
| 1946 | 8,132 | 131.5 | 97.9 |
| 1947 | 8,624 | 138.1 | 99.5 |
| 1948 | 9,019 | 137.3 | 99.0 |
| 1949 | 9,067 | 135.0 | 99.0 |
| 1950 | 9,782 | 151.2 | 100.0 |
| 1951 | 10,127 | 159.3 | 99.4 |
| 1952 | 7,584 | 158.3 | 74.6 |
| 1953 | 8,973 | 212.5 | 71.1 |

Table C.4  *Spruance Plant III: Output, Denier, and Percentage of Capacity Operated*

| Year | Pounds Production (000) | Average Denier | Percentage Capacity Operated (Nozzle Basis) |
|------|------|------|------|
| 1936 | 217 | 250.5 | 81.2 |
| 1937 | 1,487 | 260.3 | 86.1 |
| 1938 | 2,832 | 264.3 | 88.0 |
| 1939 | 4,409 | 301.7 | 86.0 |
| 1940 | 6,538 | 447.2 | 97.7 |
| 1941 | 10,506 | 630.4 | 100.0 |
| 1942 | 13,979 | 968.6 | 99.3 |
| 1943 | 16,563 | 1,100.0 | 99.2 |
| 1944 | 18,910 | 1,100.0 | 98.8 |
| 1945 | 22,174 | 1,100.9 | 99.5 |
| 1946 | 22,554 | 1,206.2 | 94.2 |
| 1947 | 25,096 | 1,307.1 | 96.7 |
| 1948 | 29,312 | 1,518.1 | 97.4 |
| 1949 | 32,520 | 1,644.9 | 99.1 |
| 1950 | 33,587 | 1,650.0 | 100.0 |
| 1951 | 35,398 | 1,691.4 | 100.0 |
| 1952 | 36,164 | 1,725.5 | 99.9 |
| 1953 | 32,957 | 1,650.0 | 95.9 |
| 1954 | 16,835 | 1,744.1 | 51.6 |
| 1955 | 25,161 | 1,737.3 | 97.0 |

Table C.5  *Spruance Plant II-A: Output, Denier, and Percentage of Capacity Operated*

| Year | Pounds Production (000) | Average Denier | Percentage Capacity Operated (Nozzle Basis) |
|------|------|------|------|
| 1944 | 15,881 | 1,100.0 | 74.1 |
| 1945 | 22,081 | 1,104.9 | 94.0 |
| 1946 | 24,286 | 1,251.0 | 88.9 |
| 1947 | 28,106 | 1,332.2 | 95.8 |
| 1948 | 31,918 | 1,525.1 | 96.2 |
| 1949 | 38,154 | 1,632.8 | 97.7 |
| 1950 | 40,800 | 1,609.3 | 99.1 |
| 1951 | 43,554 | 1,625.8 | 99.9 |
| 1952 | 44,977 | 1,635.5 | 99.8 |
| 1953 | 41,682 | 1,648.4 | 85.8 |
| 1954 | 51,341 | 1,655.1 | 98.1 |
| 1955 | 56,105 | 1,661.6 | 100.0 |

*Table C.6   Indexes of Average Hourly Wage Rates and of Construction Costs*

| Year | Average Hourly Wage Rates: Spruance (in dollars) | Index 1939 = 100 | Average Hourly Wage Rates: Old Hickory (in dollars) | Index 1939 = 100 | Index of Construction Costs: Du Pont 1939 = 100 |
|------|------|------|------|------|------|
| 1929 | .377 | 51.9 | .414 | 58.5 | 88 |
| 1930 | .440 | 60.5 | .438 | 61.9 | 86 |
| 1931 | .428 | 58.9 | .431 | 60.9 | 77 |
| 1932 | .381 | 52.4 | .384 | 54.2 | 67 |
| 1933 | .389 | 53.5 | .395 | 55.8 | 72 |
| 1934 | .521 | 71.7 | .488 | 68.9 | 84 |
| 1935 | .530 | 72.9 | .515 | 72.7 | 83 |
| 1936 | .586 | 80.6 | .561 | 79.2 | 88 |
| 1937 | .704 | 96.8 | .668 | 94.4 | 100 |
| 1938 | .730 | 100.4 | .696 | 98.3 | 100 |
| 1939 | .727 | 100.0 | .708 | 100.0 | 100 |
| 1940 | .785 | 108.0 | .768 | 108.5 | 103 |
| 1941 | .859 | 118.2 | .856 | 120.9 | 112 |
| 1942 | .964 | 132.6 | .959 | 135.5 | 124 |
| 1943 | .992 | 136.5 | .962 | 135.9 | 134 |
| 1944 | 1.006 | 138.4 | .956 | 135.0 | 145 |
| 1945 | 1.044 | 143.6 | 1.020 | 144.1 | 155 |
| 1946 | 1.139 | 156.7 | 1.103 | 155.8 | 178 |
| 1947 | 1.375 | 189.1 | 1.285 | 181.5 | 208 |
| 1948 | 1.427 | 196.3 | 1.386 | 195.8 | 227 |
| 1949 | 1.473 | 202.6 | 1.438 | 203.1 | 215 |
| 1950 | 1.527 | 210.0 | 1.508 | 213.0 | 225 |
| 1951 | 1.675 | 230.3 | 1.657 | 234.0 | 236 |
| 1952 | 1.747 | 240.3 | 1.737 | 245.3 | 248 |
| 1953 | 1.879 | 258.4 | 1.832 | 258.8 | 264 |
| 1954 | 2.003 | 275.5 | 1.946 | 274.9 | 267 |
| 1955 | 2.120 | 291.6 | 2.105 | 297.3 | 280 |
| 1956 | 2.240 | 308.1 | 2.184 | 308.5 | 294 |
| 1957 | | | 2.352 | 332.2 | 307 |
| 1958 | | | 2.450 | 346.0 | 322 |
| 1959 | | | 2.549 | 360.0 | 338 |
| 1960 | | | 2.687 | 380.0 | 350 |

# Bibliography

A. GENERAL

*Books*

Denison, Edward F., *The Sources of Economic Growth in the United States and the Alternatives Before Us*, Supplementary Paper No. 13, Committee for Economic Development, New York, 1962.

Goldsmith, Raymond W., *A Study of Saving in the United States*, Princeton University Press, Princeton, 1956.

Kendrick, John W., *Productivity Trends in the United States*, National Bureau of Economic Research, Princeton University Press, Princeton, 1961.

Klein, Lawrence R., *An Introduction to Econometrics*, Prentice-Hall, Inc., Englewood Cliffs, N.J., 1962.

Kuznets, Simon, *Capital in the American Economy*, National Bureau of Economic Research, Princeton University Press, Princeton, 1961.

Machlup, Fritz, *The Economics of Sellers' Competition*, The Johns Hopkins Press, Baltimore, 1952.

――――, *The Production and Distribution of Knowledge in the United States*, Princeton University Press, Princeton, 1962.

National Bureau of Economic Research, *Cost Behavior and Price Policy*, New York, 1943.

Salter, W. E. G., *Productivity and Technical Change*, Cambridge University Press, Cambridge, 1960.

Schumpeter, Joseph A., *Business Cycles*, McGraw-Hill Book Co., Inc., New York, 1939.

Terborgh, George, *Dynamic Equipment Policy*, McGraw-Hill Book Co., Inc., New York, 1949.

Terleckyj, Nestor E., *Sources of Productivity Growth. A Pilot Study Based on the Experience of American Manufacturing Industries, 1899–1953*, Unpublished Ph.D. dissertation, Columbia University, 1959.

Wicksell, Knut, *Lectures on Political Economy*, The Macmillan Company, London, 1935.

221

*Articles*

Abramovitz, Moses, "Resource and Output Trends in the United States Since 1870," *The American Economic Review*, Proceedings, Vol. XLVI, May 1956, pp. 5–23.

———, "Economic Growth in the United States," *The American Economic Review*, Vol. LII, Sept. 1962, pp. 762–782.

Arrow, Kenneth J., "The Economic Implications of Learning by Doing," *The Review of Economic Studies*, Vol. XXIX, June 1962, pp. 155–173.

Aukrust, Odd, "Investment and Economic Growth," *Productivity Measurement Review*, No. 16, Feb. 1959, pp. 35–53.

Brown, Murray, and Joel Popkin, "A Measure of Technological Change and Returns to Scale," *The Review of Economics and Statistics*, Vol. XLIV, Nov. 1962, pp. 402–411.

Dean, Joel, "Statistical Determination of Costs With Special Reference to Marginal Costs," *Journal of Business*, Vol. IX, Part 2, Oct. 1936.

———, "The Relation of Cost to Output for a Leather Belt Shop," National Bureau of Economic Research, *Technical Paper 2*, Chicago, 1941.

Dessau, Jan, "Définition et Rémunération de la Petite Innovation," *Economie Appliquée*, Vol. XV, No. 3, July–Sept. 1962, pp. 405–444.

Domar, Evsey D., "On the Measurement of Technological Change," *Economic Journal*, Vol. LXXI, Dec. 1961, pp. 709–729.

———, "On Total Productivity and All That," *Journal of Political Economy*, Vol. LXX, Dec. 1962, pp. 597–608.

———, *et al.*, "Economic Growth and Productivity in the United States, Canada, United Kingdom, Germany and Japan in the Post-War Period," *The Review of Economics and Statistics*, Vol. XLVI, Feb. 1964, pp. 33–40.

Douglas, Paul H., and C. W. Cobb, "A Theory of Production," *The American Economic Review*, Supplement, Vol. XVIII, March 1928, pp. 139–165.

Douglas, Paul H., "Are there Laws of Production?" *The American Economic Review*, Vol. XXXVIII, March 1948, pp. 1–41.

Fabricant, Solomon, "Study of the Size and Efficiency of the American Economy," in *Economic Consequences of the Size of Nations*, ed. E. A. G. Robinson, St. Martin's Press, Inc., New York, 1960.

Fellner, William, "The Influence of Market Structure on Technological Progress," in American Economic Association, *Readings in Industrial Organization and Public Policy*, ed. Heflebower and Stocking, Richard D. Irwin, Inc., Homewood, Ill., 1958, pp. 277–296.

Gilfillan, S. C., "The Root of Patents, or Squaring Patents by Their Roots," *Journal of the Patent Office Society*, Vol. XXXI, Aug. 1949, pp. 611–623.

Griliches, Zvi, "The Sources of Measured Productivity Growth: United States Agriculture, 1940–1960," *Journal of Political Economy*, Vol. LXXI, Aug. 1963, pp. 331–346.

Hamberg, D., "Invention in the Industrial Research Laboratory," *Journal of Political Economy*, Vol. LXXI, April 1963, pp. 95–115.

Hill, T. P., "Growth and Investment According to International Comparisons," *Economic Journal*, Vol. LXXIV, June 1964, pp. 287–304.

Kaldor, Nicholas, "A Model of Economic Growth," *Economic Journal*, Vol. LXVII, Dec. 1957, pp. 591–624.

Kendrick, John W., "Productivity Trends: Capital and Labor," *The Review of Economics and Statistics*, Vol. XXXVIII, Aug. 1956, pp. 248–257.

Massel, Benton F., "Capital Formation and Technological Change in United States Manufacturing," *The Review of Economics and Statistics*, Vol. XLII, May 1960, pp. 182–188.

———, "A Disaggregated View of Technical Change," *Journal of Political Economy*, Vol. LXIX, Dec. 1961, pp. 547–558.

McGraw-Hill, Department of Economics, *Annual Surveys of Business' Plans for New Plants and Equipment.*

Segal, Martin, "Introduction of Technological Change in Industrial Plants," *Explorations in Entrepreneurial History*, Vol. VI, Oct. 1953, pp. 41–61.

Schmookler, Jacob, "The Changing Efficiency of the American Economy, 1869–1938," *The Review of Economics and Statistics*, Vol. XXXIV, Aug. 1952, pp. 214–231.

Solow, Robert M., "Technical Change and the Aggregate Production Function," *The Review of Economics and Statistics*, Vol. XXXIX, Aug. 1957, pp. 312–320.

———, "Investment and Economic Growth: Some Comments," *Productivity Measurement Review*, No. 19, Nov. 1959, pp. 62–68.

———, "Technical Progress, Capital Formation and Economic Growth," *The American Economic Review*, Proceedings, Vol. LII, May 1962, pp. 76–86.

Spiethoff, Arthur, "Business Cycles," in *International Economic Papers*, No. 3, 1953, pp. 75–171. (A shorter version of "Krisen," *Handwörterbuch der Staatswissenschaften*, Jena, 1923.)

Walters, A. A., "A Note on Economies of Scale," *The Review of Economics and Statistics*, Vol. XLV, Nov. 1963, pp. 425–427.

## Public Documents

Temporary National Economic Committee, *Hearings*, Analysis by the United States Steel Corporation Supervised by Theodore Yntema, January 23, 24, and 25, 1940, 76th Cong., 3rd Session, Part 26, pp. 14,032–14,082.

### B. SPECIAL[1]

## Books

Avram, Mois H., *The Rayon Industry*, D. Van Nostrand Company, New York, 1927.

Haynes, Williams, *American Chemical Industry*, Vol. V, *Decade of New Products*, D. Van Nostrand Company, Inc., New York, 1948.

Leeming, Joseph, *Rayon. The First Man-made Fiber*, Chemical Publishing Co., Inc., New York, 1950.

Markham, Jesse W., *Competition in the Rayon Industry*, Harvard University Press, Cambridge, 1952.

Moncrieff, R. W., *Man-made Fibres*, John Wiley & Sons, Inc., New York, Third Edition, 1957.

Mueller, Willard F., *Du Pont: A Study of Firm Growth*, Unpublished Ph.D. dissertation, Vanderbilt University, 1955.

Wheeler, R. E., *The Manufacture of Artificial Silk, with Special Reference to the Viscose Process*, D. Van Nostrand Company, New York, 1931.

---

[1] This section includes books, articles, and public documents relating specifically to rayon or to the Du Pont Company.

*Articles*

Anon., "Transmutation of Giant Hemlocks to Rayon Yarn," *Rayon and Synthetic Yarn Journal,* Vol. XIX, May 1933, p. 10.

Anon., "Buckeye Cellulose Purification Plant," *Rayon and Synthetic Yarn Journal,* Vol. XIX, Aug. 1933, p. 42.

Anon., "Technical and Economical Aspects of Rayon," *Rayon Textile Monthly,* Vol. XVII, July 1936, pp. 33–35.

Anon., "Patents and Data on Rayon Cord Tires," *Rayon Textile Monthly,* Vol. XIX, March 1938, p. 84.

Anon., "Observations on Dissolving Wood Pulp," *Rayon Textile Monthly,* Vol. XXII, Jan. 1941, p. 39.

Anon., "Rayon Labor Productivity," *Rayon Organon,* Vol. XVII, Sept. 1946, pp. 140–148.

Du Pont *Annual Reports,* 1955 and 1958 on organization of research activities.

Du Pont *Monograph,* Chapter 1, "Viscose Yarns."

Esselen, G. J., and W. M. Scott, "Cellulose as a Chemical Raw Material," *Chemical Industries,* Vol. 43, July 1938, pp. 14–19.

Hegan, H, J., "The Historical Development of and the Outlook for Viscose Fibers," *Journal of the Textile Institute,* Proceedings, Vol. 42, 1951, pp. 395–410.

Mauersberger, H. R., "Review of Rayon Machinery Developments," *Rayon and Melliand Textile Monthly,* Vol. XVI, Sept. 1935, pp. 57–68.

――――, "Review of Rayon Machinery Improvements," *Rayon Textile Monthly,* Vol. XX, Sept. 1939, pp. 110–113.

Moore, C. L., "Progress in Rayon Pulp Manufacture," *Rayon Textile Monthly,* Vol. XVIII, Sept. 1937, pp. 72–74.

――――, "Can Cotton Entirely Replace Wood Pulp in the Rayon Industry?" *Rayon Textile Monthly,* Vol. XVIII, Sept. 1937, pp. 75–76.

Mueller, Willard F., "The Origins of the Basic Inventions Underlying Du Pont's Major Product and Process Innovations," in *The Rate and Direction of Inventive Activity: Economic and Social Factors,* National Bureau of Economic Research, Princeton University Press, Princeton, 1962, pp. 323–346.

Russell, Arthur O., "The First American Dializer Unit," *Rayon and Melliand Textile Monthly,* Vol. XVI, Sept. 1935, p. 87.

Schuelke, Eric, "Recent Developments in Rayon Machinery," *Rayon and Synthetic Yarn Journal,* Vol. XIII, July 1932, pp. 12–15.

Vollrath, H. B., "Progress in Machinery for the Chemical Plant," *Rayon Textile Monthly,* Vol. XVII, Sept. 1936, p. 55.

――――, "Progress in Machinery for the Chemical Plant," *Rayon Textile Monthly,* Vol. XVIII, Sept. 1937, p. 68.

――――, "Progress Towards Continuous Processing in Viscose Manufacture," *Rayon Textile Monthly,* Vol. XIX, Sept. 1938, pp. 72–74.

*Public Documents*

United States Bureau of Labor Statistics, Willis C. Quant, "Wages in the Rayon Industry, May 1944," *Monthly Labor Review,* Vol. 59:6, Dec. 1944, pp. 1141–1157.

United States Department of Agriculture, Southern Regional Research Laboratory, R. B. Evans, *Survey of the Development and Use of Rayon and Other Synthetic Fibres,* New Orleans, La., Oct. 1954.

United States Tariff Commission, *The Rayon Industry,* Washington, April, 1944.

# Index